Praise for **MA AND ME**

"Heartfelt and evocative." —Karla J. Strang, *Ms.*

"Familial ties and the scars of war are exquisitely examined in this luminous debut . . . A nuanced meditation on love, identity, and belonging. This story of survival radiates with resilience and hope." —*Publishers Weekly* (starred review)

"*Ma and Me* is an important new entry in the growing body of American refugee and immigrant literature, shining a fearless light on the experiences of queer people whose families have survived the trauma of war. It also stands apart as a work of lyrical beauty, exploring culture, duty, guilt and family with heartbreaking clarity." —Christy Lynch, *BookPage*

"[A] piercing memoir . . . [*Ma and Me* features] well-wrought vignettes of a complicated mother-daughter bond."
—*Kirkus Reviews*

"Reang writes like a flower blooms—beautifully."
—Kitty Kelley, *Washington Independent Review of Books*

"At a time when there are more refugees than ever in history and borders are places of violence and cruelty, two essential stories of our time converge in *Ma and Me*: Americanization's multigenerational costs, and the way this converges with lesbian life." —Sarah Schulman, author of *Let the Record Show*

Kim Oanh Nguyen

Putsata Reang

◻

MA AND ME

Putsata Reang is an author and a journalist whose work has appeared in *The New York Times*, *Politico*, *The Guardian*, *Ms.*, *The San Jose Mercury News*, and *The Seattle Times*, among other publications. Born in Cambodia and raised in rural Oregon, Reang has lived and worked in more than a dozen countries, including Cambodia, Afghanistan, and Thailand. She is an alumna of residencies at Hedgebrook, the Kimmel Harding Nelson Center for the Arts, and Mineral School, and she has received fellowships from the Alicia Patterson Foundation and Jack Straw Cultural Center.

MA AND ME

MA
AND
ME

A MEMOIR

PUTSATA
REANG

MCD ⬭ PICADOR FARRAR, STRAUS AND GIROUX NEW YORK

MCD
Picador
120 Broadway, New York 10271

Originally published in 2022 by MCD / Farrar, Straus and Giroux
First paperback edition, 2023

Title-page and part-title art by Na Kim.

The Library of Congress has cataloged the MCD hardcover edition as follows:
Names: Reang, Putsata, 1974– author
Title: Ma and me : a memoir / Putsata Reang
Description: First edition. | New York : MCD / Farrar, Straus and Giroux, [2022]
Identifiers: LCCN 2021059702 | ISBN 9780374279264 (hardcover)
Subjects: LCSH: Reang, Putsata, 1974– | Lesbians—United States—Biography. |
    Lesbians—Family relationships—United States—Biography. | Cambodian
    American women—Biography. | Cambodian American women—Family
    relationships—Biography. | Parents of gays—United States—Biography. |
    Lesbians—Identity.
Classification: LCC HQ75.4.R43 A3 2022 | DDC 306.76/63092 [B]—dc23/eng/
    20220106
LC record available at https://lccn.loc.gov/2021059702

Paperback ISBN: 978-1-250-86712-4

Designed by Abby Kagan

Our books may be purchased in bulk for promotional, educational, or
business use. Please contact your local bookseller or the Macmillan Corporate
and Premium Sales Department at 1-800-221-7945, extension 5442, or
by email at MacmillanSpecialMarkets@macmillan.com.

Picador® is a U.S. registered trademark and is used by Macmillan Publishing
Group, LLC, under license from Pan Books Limited.

For book club information, please visit facebook.com/picadorbookclub or email
marketing@picadorusa.com.

mcdbooks.com • Follow us on Twitter, Facebook, and Instagram at @mcdbooks
picadorusa.com • Instagram: @picador • Twitter and Facebook: @picadorusa

D   10   9   8   7   6   5   4   3   2

For April

There will be no end to war unless each of us calms the conflicts within ourselves.

—VIỆT THANH NGUYỄN

You can never repay your mother.

—BILLY COLLINS

A NOTE ON PRONUNCIATION

In my mother tongue, "Khmer," pronounced "come-eye," is used to describe a people, a language, and a culture.

The word "Ma," meaning mother, is pronounced "mak." And "Pa," for father, is pronounced "baa."

AUTHOR'S NOTE

In the summer of 2010, when my father had a heart attack, my mother, for the first time, was both willing and eager to tell me about her life. His close call triggered something urgent in her: a need to empty herself of the many stories and secrets she had kept inside, stories about her life that had for so long burdened her. I began to record our conversations in early 2011. She was sixty-six years old.

Ma spoke to me in Khmer, as she does to this day, and I translated and transcribed her words into English. When she wants to make a point, when she wants to ensure that I am not only listening but hearing her, she speaks in English. Only now, as I consider her Khmer jammed up against her second language, what I refer to as her "Khmenglish," does it occur to me that her effort to speak English is her yearning to be heard and seen, a passage between cultures, her own way of stepping across our battlefield to me.

Some names have been changed to respect the privacy of select individuals.

PART I

CAMBODIA

CROCODILE AND TIGER

There is a saying in Khmer, the language that left me in my youth but links me to a land across seas because it plinks off my mother's tongue: "Joh duc, kapeur; laurng loeur, klah." *Go in the water, there's the crocodile. Come up on land, there's the tiger.* Ma was twenty-two years old when she had to decide. The grandmothers in the village scolded her, "You're too old. Your father is a drunk. No one will want to marry you."

Being college-educated and unmarried at age twenty-two made my mother an anomaly twice over in rural Cambodia. Her mother married at fifteen; her older sister at eighteen. Matches made among elders. Her time was coming, she knew, but as she snuck past her teens and entered her twenties, she hoped to be forgotten.

The boys started coming around before she finished college. A simple village girl whose feet clapped across her dusty town in a pair of plastic flip-flops, my mother was raised by a benevolent uncle who deemed her brain too valuable to waste in the rice paddies. He told her, "When you get an education, you can do anything you want." And she believed him.

These boys, the sons of professors and businessmen,

followed her straight to her uncle's door, begging to marry her. She wanted none of them. She wanted, instead, the thing that Khmer girls are not born to have or raised to want— dreams. She dreamed of becoming a businesswoman and traveling the country. Maybe even the world. She dreamed of living free.

But soon after she finished college, a rumor reached her ear. Her father, who had been mostly absent from her life, had arranged her marriage. He came around now that there was a profit to be made, when the dowry for his daughter might sustain more months of gambling and drinking. But Ma's dreams were bigger than his greed. Before the invitations were sent, she fled.

She traveled east on a local bus that took her to Cambodia's capital, Phnom Penh, where she transferred to a regional taxi to Prey Veng province, on the eastern edge of Cambodia, mere miles from Vietnam. Her older brother lived there. He was sensible. He was kind. He would, she hoped, hide her.

But it was 1967, and that strip of earth along the Cambodia-Vietnam border shook and broke open beneath her feet when bombs from American B-52s burst in the paddies. The night sky lit up with machine-gun fire from the jungles, and she ran to the riverbed with her brother and his family, cupping her ears against the whistle of weapons, curling her body against the dirt somersaulting all around her.

A thought sprinted across her mind—I could die here. In the end, a part of her did. Along with an estimated 150,000 Cambodians. Casualties of a Western war imported to Vietnam, then stretched into Cambodia. "Collateral damage" was what the Americans said.

My mother realized she could stay with her brother and die trying to hide. Or, she could go back home and get married.

What do you do when you cannot go in the water or come up on land?

❏

I was two when my mother taught me how to run and hide.

"Mouy, bee, bei . . . rort!" she would say. *One, two, three . . . run!*

Rort! Boern! Run! Hide!

And I would scoot off the sofa and skedaddle for a far corner or a closet or a bedcover and stay perfectly still. *Rort boern.* A game we played. I laughed and laughed when she found me, never successful in tricking her; she always knew where to look.

But then, one year later, another kind of running.

"Get down," Ma said, hastily fastening her seat belt, eyes darting. "Keep quiet."

She had woken us kids from our slumber and rushed us to the car.

"Like this?" I said, my body laid out on the back seat with my sister Chan.

She craned her neck to check the rearview mirror.

"Yes, gohn," she said. "Lower."

I rolled to the floorboard. My brother, Sope, was jumpy in his seat.

"Where are we going?" he asked, peering out the passenger-side window as our mother shoved the car's gear into reverse and we shot, like a rocket, clear out of the driveway and into the lamplit stillness of our street.

"Nov aur sngeam!" she snapped, *stay still*, her voice starched with tension, struggling through her tears to shush her babies.

I felt the ridges of the plastic floorboard, cold and gritty, stamp their pattern into my cheek, and heard my own wheezing. Before she told us to duck, I had caught a glimpse of him, standing in the darkened doorway, hands on his hips, his lips spitting words I could not hear through the closed car window.

Why were we leaving my father?

There was so much I didn't yet know, things about my parents' lives and our family's past that I would eventually come to learn by watching, and later, by asking. I didn't know, for instance, that my mother had run away from her husband, from her family, before. Or that duty was what brought her back every time—because a Khmer wife stays.

I also did not know that when your mother teaches you to run and hide, you will keep doing it until it forms into habit, until it becomes your very best skill.

◻

My mother, Sam-Ou Koh Reang, raised four daughters and two sons—including two of my cousins whom she loved like her own, not counting five other cousins who had passed through our home—on a lunch lady's salary. She called us "gohn," a term of endearment reserved for one's children, and she used it liberally, whether we were hers or not. We called her "Ma" until the first stray grays peeked from her hairnet, and then she became "Yay Thom," or Big Grandma, because she was the eldest of her siblings who had escaped the genocide in Cambodia and immigrated to America. And in our culture, to be the eldest was to be the mother, to have the duty of taking care of everyone. Ma had a heart big enough to hold us all, and we thrived.

We graduated high school and then college and then left

her, one by one, to go on and become the thing she most wanted us to be, the kind of people whose offices she'd once dusted and mopped, who spent their days clacking at a computer keyboard with nameplates on their desks, laser-engraved with perfectly straight and even letters, rather than stitched in serrated cursive above the right breast pocket, the way her own name appeared on her white cafeteria smock.

"Use your brains, not your back," she told us when we were kids. "Don't be like me."

She urged us all toward academic and professional excellence: Sinaro, Sophea, Motthida, Chanira, Piseth, and me. From our crowded ranch house on a corner lot in almost all-white Corvallis, Oregon, we grew up to become experts in finance, communications, business, and academia. One among us, Chan, has a doctoral degree. I am a journalist, the one in the family who wanders, who has always struggled to stay.

That my mother arrived in America without a single dollar or English phrase to help her, that she worked her way up from being a janitor at Oregon State University's student health center to running her own stall at the campus food hall, slinging chicken cashew stir-fry and rice stick noodles in two massive woks; that none of her babies ended up "dead or dealing drugs or under a bridge somewhere," spoke to her striving, to her diligence and fortitude in Khmer mothering.

"I just did what I needed to survive," she'd say to friends and strangers alike, careful to maintain a mother's modesty.

She made sure her family survived, too. A single story, a tale told so many times it has become family legend, proves it. Just one in a rotation of myriad fables and fictions she spun that kept us suspended in a warm cocoon of wonder. Except this one was different.

"This one," she assured me each time, "is true."

☐

There wasn't much to eat on the boat. They gave us rice and sardines but sometimes the rice wasn't fully cooked and sometimes the rice was burnt. Grandpa Sin yelled and screamed. He was hungry. It was so hot, your dad tied a krama to the railing and the big gun to make a cover over our heads.

All we saw was sky and sea, every day. That was it. When we stopped in Thailand, all these Thai people came on board. They were dignitaries and medical people. Do you know Soya's mom? She was part Thai, so I asked her to translate for me. I wanted medicine for my baby.

They gave me a pouch of IV but there was no needle. I said, "What do I do? My baby is so sick." And they said, "Open that and feed her with a spoon."

I fed you day and night, Put. You swallowed a little at a time. Then the next morning, Seng got a cabbage and a banana. The Thai people gave us food but wouldn't let us stay in their country. I took a piece of cabbage leaf and gave it to you to hold and you grasped it. Before then, it's like you were in a coma. Your eyes rolled back in your head. The IV helped you. I thought, Okay, my baby is alive. About two or three days later, you started a small cry. Your lips and face were so dry.

After a while, you didn't move again. I was thinking, What am I going to do if my baby dies? Where am I going to bury my baby?

☐

Cambodian Naval Ship P111 was built for a crew of twenty-eight men, with officers' quarters, a galley canteen, and two heads belowdecks. But on April 20, 1975, the landing craft rode low and slow, weighed down by more than three hundred people and everything they had hoisted on board. One woman dragged a mattress on deck, which she flopped down near our family, and piled her children, husband, and other relatives on top. The family stayed like that, marooned on their own private island in the middle of all of us.

Three days earlier, Cambodia had fallen to the Communist Khmer Rouge regime, and my family hurried to the dock at Ream Naval Base to board one of four Cambodian navy vessels reserved for military personnel and their families.

There were kids and pigs and no space for either to run around. Up on deck, the sun burned so hot, Ma was certain her family would shrivel up and die. My family cordoned off a spot under one of the two fifty-millimeter mounted machine guns at the front of the ship, marking a perimeter with flip-flops and *kramas*.

"Think about it, all of us, for almost a month, in that one spot," Ma said. She was in the living room, her head turned toward the TV, where the local news was on. She spoke to the screen rather than to me. Easier that way, to transmit old pain into the impersonal glow of polarized light than watch her youngest daughter's face break with emotion.

◪

It wasn't easy to sleep, there wasn't room. So we mostly just sat, and then we squeezed in together like a row of grilled catfish on a stick and slept.

I cradled you in my sarong, Put. You didn't move, like you had nothing left in you, no energy, no spirit. You had diarrhea for days. When you pooped, nothing came out except clear sticky liquid. I

stood up and rotated my sarong and sat down again so you would
have a clean place to sleep. I just kept doing this until there were
no more clean sections, then I changed into my silk sampot, the one
my mother made me in her loom, and I washed my sarong with a
bucket of seawater.

The captain was walking around, checking on his passengers.
He wore a uniform that was so white it was gleaming. I don't
know how he kept his uniform so clean. We had been on the boat for
several days already. When he saw me and he saw my baby wasn't
moving, he told me, "Miss, do you see, we are so crowded here. If
your baby dies, you have to throw your baby in the water or else
the corpse will spread disease to everyone else." When he said this,
my spirit left my body.

I explained to the captain that you were just sick. I begged him.
"Let me keep my baby. We are Buddhist. Please let me bury her
when we reach land." I looked him right in the eyes. You don't do
that in Cambodia. It's disrespectful. I was desperate. I didn't know
what to do. The captain agreed to let me keep you. I was so sad,
so I passed you to my stepmother. I went belowdecks to the storage
room where they kept all the bags of rice. I collapsed against them
and cried.

That was so difficult. I don't want to remember anymore, Put.
How many times were you close to dying? Out of all my kids, you
were the weakest. You were the smallest of all. You were the hardest
to take care of.

Over the years, people have asked me, "Do you have any
memories of that time?"

"No memories," I will say, "only feelings. Things my body
knows."

Like hunger. Like leaving. My first feeling was flight. Running away became my enduring lesson in surviving.

And over the years, as my mother retold this story, she smoothed out the corners but kept the core the same. Every now and then, she would abide my curiosity for more details. "Ma, did you think I was dead?"

"I had hope, just a little, you were still alive," she said.

According to my mother, I had survived on drips of water she drew to my lips, and a stubborn, unsinkable hope, the kind that only mothers have, that she whispered into my ears.

In another telling of the story, years later, Ma said that I was heavy. "What do you mean I was heavy?" I asked, feeling a little bit sad and more than a little guilty—I didn't want to think that I had burdened her. How could a malnourished one-year-old baby be *heavy*?

"You were not light," she said. "My arms ached so much from holding you."

So she passed me to my aunt Pech, my cousin Piseth's mom. Who passed me over to my Grandma Thoen, my mother's stepmother, who eventually passed me back to Ma. In this way, the mothers took turns, cycling sorrow between them.

Now that I am older and have seen so many photographs of refugee mothers from Syria, Somalia, Nigeria, gripping their babies like buoys on overcrowded boats in the Mediterranean Sea, I think I know what my mother meant. Heavy, as in *My daughter might not make it on this journey I decided for her.* Heavy, as in *How did I fail?* Heavy is the feel of death.

How many mothers have had to wonder where to bury their babies?

In that moment when my mother fought to keep me, the terms of my life were set: Ma was the savior and I was the saved. After hearing the story so many times, I made a promise to myself: I would do my best to make her happy. I would strive to be worthy of her rescue.

For a long time, I believed I owed Ma my life: whatever she wanted me to be, I would be; whatever she wanted me to do, I would do.

I tried to live an immaculate existence, tucking my flaws behind a façade of perfection. I graduated high school and then college with honors, pressing awards into my mother's hands. I turned the storytelling skills that she passed on to me into a full-time career, scrambling for scoops and front-page stories at newspapers up and down the West Coast. Eventually, I had a home, a high-paying job, money in the bank. I sent my parents on vacations and put several of my cousins through school. I filled my parents' home with treasures from my travels—statues, paintings, rugs.

And Ma had made a myth out of me, spinning so many stories about my travels and adventures that some of her friends did not believe I was real.

"Is this the one?" one of them said as I sat in Ma's kitchen, tucking into a bowl of noodles. I was on leave from a journalism job in Cambodia, always choosing to go home when I had time off, rather than on holiday.

Ma's friend smiled and squeezed my arm as if to confirm I was not a ghost. "Is this your baby girl with the big job and all the money? The one who almost died on the boat?"

Ma smiled and nodded. Her friend turned to me.

"Your mother talks about you all the time," she said, still holding my arm. "She says you are special."

I worked to maintain that reputation, for her. My mother guarded our family's reputation with ironclad diligence. Reputation was the tall shadow that tipped into the room before you entered the door. Reputation let you walk with a straight spine in the world, your armor against all the ways the world judged. Reputation made you marketable for marriage. In my mother's world—the one before now, the one she exported to America—reputation was everything.

"I won't let anyone look down on me," she said, a regular refrain, by which she meant, "Don't do anything stupid," because a mark on any one of us was also a mark on her.

So, I tried harder. I worked toward repaying my debt to Ma by trying to achieve a single vision I had of myself, the image my mother carefully, methodically crafted of me: that of the dutiful Cambodian daughter, devoted to her family. The youngest of the brood, who would fulfill her parents' wishes.

Without knowing it, for a long time unable to detect my mother's sleight of hand in holding and molding me, I would become the keeper of our culture, the vessel for her secrets and sadness, the captive audience for all her stories.

But the image of the good Cambodian daughter was only that, a fiction Ma created to keep her own and our family's status elevated in the eyes of our Khmer community. A story of the finest weave, like the silk her own mother spun to clothe and cover up her family's imperfections when she was young. A myth that unraveled around the truth of who I am.

When I told Ma, in my twenties, that I was gay, she said she still loved me, but she clearly hoped it was just a phase. When I told her, in my thirties, I might never get married, she brushed me off with a wave of her hand. When I told her, at forty-two, I planned to marry my partner—a woman—the scaffolding of our bond collapsed, spewing splinters too deep to tweeze out.

We fought for days.

Which turned into months.

Which have now become years.

Our fighting left us stuck on either side of a broken bridge, my father and siblings ensnared in the battlefield between us. I could choose not to marry my partner and let Ma preserve her reputation and an important piece of her Khmer identity, or I could live free.

One time when we were ribbing each other, not so long ago, Chan asked me with a wry smile: "How do you know Ma *didn't want* to throw you in the water, Put?"

Ma herself had joked along these very same lines. When I made her mad, she would tell me, "I nearly dropped you in the water, gohn." But I never let myself believe it. No child wants to know she was so easily disposable.

How do you know Ma didn't want *to throw you in the water?*

I had no answer, no way to know that in the end, that is what she would do.

◻

By my own math, it comes out close to twenty years that I have been trying to tell this story, or some version of it. It kept getting away from me, shifting and trying to be what it was not. A sort of identity crisis, the same as mine. We don't always know who or what we're meant to be. But if I have learned anything along the way, it is this: a story is going to go its own way, and sometimes you just have to sit back and let it.

We are both storytellers, Ma and I. The difference is

merely in form. She peddles in fables and folktales, wrapping stories in approximations and a gossamer of myth. As a journalist, I deal in hard facts and truth. This story, then, is my attempt to tease the truth out of her fictions. To build a bridge of story that brings us back together.

■ MA

You want to know about my marriage? Why don't you go ask your father and get out of here? I'm busy cooking something for us. How many thousands of dollars are you paying me for this interview, Put? Let's eat something first, then you can ask your questions.

I had no choice. My dad said I had to marry. I could not say no, because everyone was pushing me. If I said no, I would be kicked out of the family. But I couldn't hide, because of the war. I had to run. You could hear bombs. Ping! Ping! Ping! Ping! I was so scared. I thought, Where am I supposed to go?

When I came back from Prey Veng and people knew I was home, everyone came right away and put up the wedding tents. Yay Yeim came. Ta Khann came. The villagers from Preah Thom, that's your dad's side. The day of the wedding, I hadn't even taken a bath. I had no mother to help me. Yay Leour gave me her watch to wear. My cousins brought makeup and put it on me. I never wore makeup before. I never had lipstick or powder.

We had a big wedding. There was seafood soup. There was vermicelli noodle and pork stir-fry. There was pickled mudfish with vegetables. People who came late didn't have anything to eat. Your dad's side ate all the food. Your dad didn't have a single dollar when we got married. Did he even give a dowry? No, I don't think he did. Maybe he gave a water buffalo. That's how much I cost.

□

The summer of 2010, when I was thirty-six years old, still unmarried and unmoored, my mother called me home from Cambodia. I had been living and working in Phnom Penh, fulfilling my dream of being a foreign journalist—a job I wanted but a word I resisted. The word "foreign" cut like a betrayal in the context of Cambodia: I was indeed a foreigner in my own homeland, but then what did that make me in America, where my parents raised me? Where I still felt American even though I knew my brown skin made me different?

I had been born into the lush topography of my ancestors' Cambodia, born into its wishbone of muddy lakes and rivers and broadleaf forests of ebony trees tinseled with vines. As a baby, before my feet ever touched the earth, I was abruptly severed from that land. As an adult, a daughter of Cambodia come home, it was that paradox, of a beautiful landscape set within my country's dark history of genocide, that captivated me and compelled me to stay. That, and the fact that I was gay.

But my father's heart attack and my mother's call drew me home, which, by then, was no longer in Corvallis, where I grew up. The home I would return to as an adult, after years of running away from people and places I loved, was a five-bedroom, two-and-a-half-bath behemoth in the Salem suburb of Keizer, Oregon, in a tony subdivision pretentiously called "The Vineyards," that my parents bought when they retired. My siblings and I called it ostentatious and our mother called it necessary. It was just the two of them, Ma and Pa. There were no more kids. No more genocide survivors trying to make their way over. No reason for such a big house.

"I want a place for my grandkids to stay," she said, and when they finally arrived, ten in all, at one point filling her family room like a day-care center and turning her kitchen into a makeshift school cafeteria, she just sat back satisfied, rocking and grinning in her La-Z-Boy recliner.

I arrived at Ma's kitchen counter clutching black-and-white photographs. Three and a quarter by three and a quarter inches, they felt unfamiliar in my hands, dimensions from another time. Perfect squares, capturing a moment my mother wished to forget.

When I was younger and tried to talk to my parents about Cambodia, they made it clear that the past was another country they had no wish to visit. "I don't remember" was the simple lever they used to uncork themselves quickly from my questions, the dead end to my constant curiosity. I would wait some weeks or months more, and then ask another question about our lives before we fled Cambodia. And again, the familiar dodge: "I don't remember." It was part of their Buddhist upbringing to leave the past alone. Don't look back. Go on.

As a grade schooler, when I asked Ma about her life, she distracted me with folklore and myths. She told me about clever animals who outsmarted predators and village fools who survived on the strength of their resourcefulness. Ma described a world of towering coconut trees and banana leaves the size of kayaks, sunsets the color of a cook fire that seemed to singe the very rice paddies they slid into, and rivers so full of catfish you could walk across on their backs to reach the other shore.

Ma told me stories of her mother, my grandmother Nhim, whose sugar palm cakes with fresh coconut cream steamed in banana leaves thickened the air with a sweet aroma so powerful it could hypnotize villagers. She talked about her family's water buffaloes—those barrel-chested beasts of the countryside that were stubbornly slow but dependable workers, plowing the river-fed fields until the sinking sun drove animal and farmer back home. It was a rich world, so vastly different from the reality of our lives in rural Corvallis, Oregon, full of evergreen forests and food in freezers, that I always begged Ma for more. I knew these stories were folklore, but they reverberated, even now, with profound truths and lessons in living virtuously, honorably, obediently.

The protagonists of Ma's stories were smart, hardworking, clever, and resourceful—qualities that made Ma nod with approval and made me strive to be those things, too. But her stories sometimes left me confused, uncertain of where I stood in her eyes. I alternately felt strong or weak, smart or dumb, hardworking or lazy, depending on which story she spun. Each one came spiked with its own moral code. Delivered in measured doses, designed to teach, cajole, or warn, these stories beat like secrets inside me.

For years, I kept trying to burrow my way into the folds of Ma's memory, into the stories I sensed were stored somewhere beneath her surface. I loved the legends and myths, but I wanted to know about *her*.

Now here I was, holding wedding photos taken in 1967, causing her to remember. It is a cruel thing to do, to make your mother go backward like that. Like so many other sacrifices she made for her children, she did this for me because I asked. Because she was so close to losing my father. Because she knew I would not stop asking.

In one photograph, my mother sits next to my father, her face cast down, drained of joy. A clutch of family members crowds the background, Ma's best friend, Sata, half of my namesake, peering above a dense cluster of shoulders like a line of cursive. Banners and blessings in Mandarin hang along the bare plank walls, likely for the benefit of my paternal grandfather, a Chinese rice farmer known for his prolific garden of bitter melon and morning glory and reliably productive rice paddies. The photo was taken in my maternal grandfather's stilt home in Takeo provincial town, just south of Cambodia's capital, Phnom Penh, where the Mekong River scatters into skeins of water used by fishermen and traders to ply their wares.

A sense of levity and restrained jubilation are etched in the faces of the guests. How could any of them know that within a decade, nearly everyone there in the background at my parents' wedding would perish in Communist leader Pol Pot's "Killing Fields"? My paternal grandfather, my mother's best friend, my father's groomsmen, cousins, aunts, and uncles, captured in the lingering light of the photographer's frame. All of them gone.

My mother's expression that day is different from the guests'; it holds a deeper sadness of living. She wore a simple *av pak* and a silk *sampot*, a traditional wedding outfit of blouse and long skirt, made from a bolt of fabric my grandfather purchased at the morning market just days before her wedding and set down, unceremoniously, at his daughter's feet. The silk Grandpa selected was flimsy and coarse, not the smooth, structured silk her mother wove in the ancient loom beneath her family's home when she was growing up. She missed Nhim. A daughter needs her mother on her wedding day.

Before the wedding procession, a rush of cousins applied a line of rouge to her lips. Someone pressed a single orchid behind her left ear, turning her into the bride she never wanted to be. Her aunt hastily unfastened her wristwatch and joggled it over my mother's delicate wrist. "There," she said, annoyed that the girl lacked basic jewelry to adorn herself. "Now you're not so bare."

But to this day, even with that watch, my mother can't tell you what time her marriage became official, when the red strings were tied to her and my father's wrists and final blessings were made for a prosperous, happy life together.

"Let me see," Ma says, squeezing into the counter stool next to me and reaching for the photo. She hadn't seen these pictures since the time they were taken.

"Why aren't you smiling?" I ask, as Ma angles the photo closer to her face, her reading glasses abandoned somewhere upstairs. "Aren't weddings supposed to be happy?"

"Don't be foolish, Put," she says, shooting me a look I know well, one that says, *You should know better.* "That's Cambodia. Weddings are serious. You're not supposed to smile.

"My father was so angry when I returned from Prey Veng," Ma said. I had known she had fled before the wedding date was set, but I had yet to hear this part of the story. "He grabbed the metal rod holding up the mosquito net on his bed and hit me. I rolled on the floor to avoid his strikes. He just hit me until he got tired and threw the rod to the floor."

She shook her head, as if the mere mention of that moment wounded her all over again.

In the photo, no one can see she is in pain as she prostrates herself before the *achar*, the ceremonial adviser, her body compressed into a question mark. Nobody knew about the blood on one of her legs dissolving into her skirt—or the scars that would form later—from the angry lashes of the rod that had rained down, blow after blow. Punishment for the humiliation she caused her father by running away.

I had questions, but years of interviewing people taught me to wait, that bombshells sometimes fall at the end of pregnant pauses.

"I knew if I married, I would lose my freedom forever," she said finally, her eyes locked on the picture. "You should know. You're a journalist. I wanted to go here and there, like you."

Her admission struck a blow, piercing my heart. She had been the adventurous one in our family, always eager to check out new places. Whenever I moved to a new city for a newspaper job, she followed me. To check things out, to see how her baby girl was living, her curiosity about the world rivaling my own.

My mother was thirty years old when she crossed the Pacific Ocean, carrying me in her arms. I was thirty years old when I crossed back the other way, carrying a pad of paper and pen—our lives, hers and mine, becoming a series of perilous crossings. I had been far away from Ma for nearly seven years by then, hopscotching the globe for work. I had found a studio apartment in the heart of Phnom Penh, which I would use as a base from which to boomerang to other locales. At one point, I had considered never returning to America.

But there in the stubborn warmth of Ma's kitchen, which feels like a bunker for the end of time, counters and cabinets lined with jars of pickled garlic, limes, duck eggs, and mustard greens, and three freezers full of discount meat, it is only Ma and me, and all the space between now and then, back when those wedding photos were taken.

My mother peers into one of the pictures as if to find

something particular there, something only she can see. I don't know what memory she is trying to get back. For a moment, I think she is done talking. But then she speaks again, and her words hit like stones, landing hard on my heart.

"That was the saddest day of my life."

◻ SOMETHING TO HIDE

I wasn't the obvious choice of helper for Ma to recruit after my father's surgery. When my phone rang, so late at night in Phnom Penh, I hesitated. Each of my sisters and my brother lived out of state, two of them halfway across the country. I had them beat by an ocean, hunkered in my studio halfway across the world. Of her children, I was the farthest from Ma—both in terms of miles and expectations. My life was the most unconventional. To Ma's mind, my being gay was an unacceptable stain on our family's reputation, so I stayed away, letting Cambodia hold me and hide me.

But when Ma called, her voice throttled by sobs, I couldn't find it in me to ignore her. I was the one she always called when she was sad or scared. I went home because it was my duty as a good Cambodian daughter to be there, but also because I could not quell the impulse to take care of her.

Something happened to both Ma and Pa after their brush with my father's death. The curtain that had been drawn against my parents' past opened up, and I came home just in time to slip into that space, to explore the glades of my parents' history, the pain and loss, and their helpless surrender to it all.

In the same way Pa's heart attack sparked in Ma a need to unburden herself of stories, so, too, did it amplify my need to capture what she had to say while they were both still alive to tell me.

Over the next two years, I would spend hundreds of hours at my parents' home in the Vineyards, eating my mother's food, escorting my parents through the snarled and suppressed strands of their history. When it was too much, when Ma had lightened a little more of her load and my heart overflowed with the weight of her tragedies, I headed to my own home in Portland, a newly built, too-big house that I'd bought in early 2010, sight unseen, from Cambodia. An impulse investment, claiming American roots from abroad, and a decoy for my mother, drawing her attention away from the fact that I was still not married. Acquiring a home, it turns out, is much easier than acquiring a husband. Portland became my retreat, a place to heal from the kind of trauma that sloughed off from those stories.

In Keizer I would learn the extent of my mother's scar tissue—how the many stories she had told over the years were scrubbed of the darkest facts about my parents. I grew up without hearing the story of my mother's attempt to flee her own wedding, hearing hardly any stories at all about her or my father's lives, until I was deep into adulthood. But I understood, even at a young age, that theirs was not a happy union. Their constant quarreling, my mother's repeated threats to run away, my father's rage—I grew up incubated in chaos and conflict. I see now what was so difficult for me to understand when I was a child, when I'd see my friends' parents laughing and dancing and wondered why mine were never like that: that kind of levity is a luxury when you are simply trying to survive.

My parents' stories were spellbinding, surprising, and disquieting, doled out over the years spent in their kitchen like poker hands, the deck reshuffled at the start of every visit, and when we were done, I would realize the truth of the connection between my mother and me, which began with a country and the wars we were born into. I would realize that the day a Khmer girl is born is the day she comes into debt, purely by the fact of her existence. That she owes her parents for bringing her into the world, for raising her, and that the only way she can settle the score, or *sang khun,* is by getting married, when the authority over her is transferred from her parents to her husband.

I would learn about secrets long scuttled away, but take a stick and tap my family tree and all sorts of stories tumble out. Stories that would help me understand how easy it is for daughters and mothers to misinterpret, misunderstand, and disappoint each other. How years of silence and broken hope and gathered grief would leave Ma and me shipwrecked on our separate shores of hurt.

The business of interviewing your mother is treacherous, like slow, gut-twisting steps through a minefield. We were new to this. A daughter raised to swallow her emotions and discouraged from questioning the inner dimensions of her parents' lives, much less her own, was now gently probing.

I brought a digital recorder and placed it at the far corner of whatever room we were in. We were almost always in the kitchen. She cooked. I questioned. Both of us doing the thing we were good at. I took fast notes, but I was afraid to miss something. I wanted all of what she had to tell me before it was too late. A part of me worried whether her days, like my father's, were numbered. Whether it would be her next in the operating chamber, her heart exposed and someone with a laser light peering in. I wanted to be the first to look. I pushed Record.

◙

The elders used to tell us, "First came the locusts, then came the Japanese." The locusts landed in the rice fields and it was the village children's job to run and chase them away. They flew up in big swarms and filled the sky, blocking the sun, so many it turned the day completely dark. Those little insects ruined the rice crop that year. Everyone was hungry. And then the Japanese came. The soldiers came into our village and asked my grandparents for shelter from the monsoons and food from their rice pot. My grandparents couldn't say no. They all had big guns on their shoulders. I don't know who they were fighting. I guess the Americans, because the Americans were bombing the Japanese. The more I think about it, Cambodia has always been under attack by someone or something. There has always been a war.

◙

It was 1945. Cambodia was at the center of a tug-of-war between French colonialists, who had by then ruled Cambodia for more than eighty years, and Japanese forces who hoped to gain dominance over Southeast Asia and access to the region's natural resources. American allies entered the fray, bombing Japanese bases across Cambodia before eventually returning Cambodia back to the French. Into that tumult, my mother, Sam-Ou, was born, the third of nine children.

Aside from the Japanese soldiers who sought respite beneath their stilt homes, the battle over Cambodia didn't impact my ancestors greatly. They seemed to live oblivious to the extent of the tragedies unfolding in their country, already inured to the hardships of fleeing. According to family lore, my great-great-grandparents had fled famine and peasant revolts against monarchy rule in what was then Indochina. They traveled for months by foot, rice balls and boiled eggs softening in their pockets, finally arriving at a strip of land where the sediment-rich Tonle Sap River provided the perfect conditions to grow rice and raise babies.

My great-grandfather headed the district's transportation department in Takeo. Saing San was a handsome man, unusually tall, who favored natty suits and two-tone shoes with bows and pointed tips. He carried a cane, though no one seems to know whether he needed to.

Everyone called him "the Corporal." When his daughter, Nhim, my mother's mother, gave birth to my mother, he bequeathed to Nhim an abundant share of the family's rice paddies, which stretched from the highway to the hills "beyond the tip of seeing," my mother told me. Nhim inherited the family home, too, which, when Ma lived in it as a toddler, buzzed with activity from a retinue of servants my great-grandparents employed.

It was an era of elephants, which you rode if you were wealthy. The Corporal owned four, left to stable in a neighboring village where there was more room. During holidays, the Corporal would round up the elephants and transport his family to the pagoda. The lumbering hulks heaved their way down narrow lanes, past rows of tamarind trees and bleeding hearts slung along bamboo fences. They kicked up so much dust you could hardly see through the plumes, but the village kids ran and laughed alongside them anyway. "The Corporal's coming!" villagers would say, then plunge out of the way, because with money and a uniform came power.

"Mai came from a very rich family," Ma told me, as we sat in her family room. Willamette Valley fog hung low outside the window, like spirits begging to enter, my mother rocking slowly in her recliner as I sat nearby. Whenever she talked about her mother, she used the reverential term "mai."

"Then she married my father. They got land and my grand-mother's gold jewelry, her bracelets, necklaces, earrings. We had plenty of money until my father played cards and lost it all."

No one can say how Grandpa Sin got so lucky as to marry the Corporal's daughter. He hailed from a simple farming family nearby. Maybe it was all the rice paddies his family claimed or just a deal struck between friends, but young Sin was hastened out of the monkhood just in time to marry Nhim before the Corporal had a chance to change his mind. The Corporal and his wife had been seduced by the idea of Sin. How bad could a man dedicated to the monastic order be?

Grandpa Sin had barely slipped out of his saffron robe, sun glinting off his shaved monk's head, when a priest blessed the young couple and flicked holy water on their heads. Nhim's parents had probably consulted a fortune-teller, because no marriage in Cambodia proceeded without discussion of birth dates and stars and zodiac signs, but the match was not auspi-cious, and the promise of happiness began and ended on that single prayer.

Though Sin and Nhim began their new lives with abun-dance, the young couple began to lose their fortunes, slowly at first and then all at once as my grandfather, along with his schoolteacher's salary, disappeared into gambling halls. On weekends, he pedaled his bicycle home, swerving herky-jerky down the dirt road, a bottle of liquor inside a plastic bag swinging like a pendant from one handlebar.

"By the time he got home, he was usually drunk," Ma said, a tinge of embarrassment hardening her words as she recalled spying her father sloppily make his way home.

Still, Nhim was prepared. She boiled a chicken, whacked it in half, and set aside the best pieces for her husband. But in a drunken stupor, Grandpa Sin chucked the chicken in an open field, and when Sam-Ou's younger sister, Samnang, hungry and brazen, went to retrieve the food, he snapped a switch from the tamarind tree and whipped red stripes into her legs.

"He was drunk, so he just lashed out at anyone, and Samnang was in his way," Ma told me. "All of his children were hungry, but he didn't care."

He left no money for Nhim to raise their babies. So Nhim bred silkworms and wove stylish silk shirts, skirts, and kramas, sparing her children the misfortune of wearing rudimentary clothes made of fiber from a kapok tree—a pitiful sign of poverty—and sparing herself the judgment of others. My mother learned, early in her youth, that there were ways to conceal a shameful situation. A lesson Ma would pass on to me.

Nhim's life became a relentless hustle to ensure her children's survival. Such was the duty of a Khmer wife and mother. She picked fruit and scavenged shoots from the jungle, preserving every scrap of leftovers—mangoes, watermelon rinds, young bamboo—into pickles. And when the rice supply ran low, she boiled maize and stirred it into her rice pot, food fit for pigs, inhaled by her hungry children. They lived this way, braced by their mother's determination, through droughts, floods, and famines.

But there were too many mouths to feed, so Nhim did

what other Khmer families do, given the circumstances: she gave a couple of her kids away.

When my mother was five, and her younger sister, Sam-nang, was three, they went to live with Nhim's younger brother in Takeo provincial town. The girls did not protest, they did as they were told. Having only two boys, Nhim had none to spare, needing the strength of her sons to work the fields. Two girls would also benefit my bachelor great-uncle. Nhim promised her brother the girls would cook and clean, the way good Cambodian daughters do.

But Uncle San had a radical way of thinking, far different from Cambodian men in the 1950s who expected girls to grow up and into servants, existing purely to serve their husbands. Girls, Uncle San believed, had the same potential as boys to learn.

He saw no reason to waste a pair of perfectly good brains, so he bent his long body into a small wooden chair and sewed school uniforms by candlelight after work, his knees constantly bumping against the legs of the treadle sewing machine table. In the morning, he pressed books into his nieces' palms and shooed them off to school.

After school, my mother and aunt did their chores. At night, it was my mother who took to her studies with vigor.

"She would recite the alphabets out loud, the whole house echoed with your mother's voice," Aunt Samnang told me recently. "She was always busy studying."

As she got older and looked around, surrounded by the sons and daughters of business tycoons and politicians, all the girls wearing the latest imported fashions while she wore her uncle's handmade clothes, she knew she didn't quite belong.

But Uncle San kept encouraging her.

"Gohn," he called out to his nieces one night as they studied in the far corner of his home. "Study hard. Grow your brain. When you have an education, you can do anything."

A mantra he repeated often, and when I met him on my first trip to Cambodia, one he would also say to me.

Sam-Ou and Samnang flourished under their uncle's care. Uncle San rubbed Tiger Balm into their temples and fed them rice soup when they caught a cold. He drove them to the coast, picking up Nhim along the way and cruising with the windows down in his silver four-door Simca, cackling as his passengers' bodies jumped and jangled, the sedan dipping into and out of potholes by the dozen. In the entire fifteen years Ma lived under his roof, not once did Uncle San lay a hand on her, unusual for the simple fact that men in Cambodian society were granted social permission to hit their wives and children. She never wanted to leave. "He was like a mother and a father together," Ma said.

Year after year, as his nieces kept growing, my great-uncle sat at his sewing machine piecing together simple white shirts and blue skirts, giving the girls a single riel in the mornings to buy their breakfast at the market. With the rest of his salary as a driver for Takeo's governor, he bought books and, later, bikes, which the girls rode from their uncle's house in Takeo provincial town back home to their village at least twice each year, when Uncle San cajoled his nieces to go help their mother.

When my mother was eight years old, Nhim put her in charge of the silkworms, spreading the fat white caterpillars onto mulberry leaves, wide as a baseball mitt, to let them eat their fill.

During fallow months, my mother helped her mother

process the silk, carefully extracting raw fiber from the silk-worms' cocoons by slowly stirring them in boiling water and gathering long wisps of silk, like dental floss, that Nhim would hand-pull three times through a spinning spool until the thread emerged smooth and glossy. My mother, lacking the skills to operate the loom, was content just to watch her mother's measured movements.

"My mother could do anything," Ma told me. "She was always doing something. She couldn't sit still."

During harvest season, Ma and her siblings rose at dawn and went off to the fields to help their mother plant a new crop of rice. Barefoot and back-bent, methodically pressing nubile rice stalks into holes they made in the mud with their thumbs, Ma learned to move quickly lest the leeches latch on to her legs. But the work rarely felt too onerous, surrounded as she was by her siblings. They kept each other going.

Afternoons, to cool off and shake the day from their shoulders, my mother and her siblings raced each other to the pond between the village and the red dirt road that connected them to Takeo provincial town, where they lived and studied during the school year, and farther beyond to Phnom Penh. Ma splashed in the murky, mocha-colored water, fully dressed in a sarong and shirt to maintain her modesty. The children plunged and laughed and played, lured back to land by the sweet perfume of palm sugar caramel bubbling in an enormous vat atop this or that auntie's cook fire.

Evenings, my mother followed her older brother, Yain, to the rice paddies with long bamboo poles, a lantern, and a net. At twelve years old, Yain proved an expert at stalking frogs, tiptoeing through the paddies as my mother followed, her eyes scanning the tops of the banyan trees and her heart thumping with fear of the spirits said to sit upon the branches. When Yain felt satisfied by a location where the croaking was loudest, he smacked his long pole once, twice, three times, quick and contained as a fly fisherman, sending a spray of slumbering frogs vaulting as my mother raced to pluck them from the air. She laughed with joy as she and her brother leapt like the critters they caught, tacking so fast across their mother's paddies that they tripped and tipped their basket enough for a few frogs to leap back out into the inky dark.

At home, she knew what was coming, grilled frogs tenderized in her mother's lemongrass marinade. All the days of her youth were like this, free and salty-sweet, fortified by her mother's food and encased in the safety of her siblings in the village, and her uncle in Takeo provincial town.

"We had fun growing up," Ma told me, as the streetlamps outside blinked on. "There were times it wasn't easy, but there were a lot of kids in my family. We helped our mother and we helped each other."

My grandfather, meanwhile, traveled to nearby provinces to teach math before spending a stint in Phnom Penh, where he continued to indulge in cards and cognac. Finding himself alone in Cambodia's bustling capital, he sought comfort in the arms of other women. When Nhim learned of his affairs, she piled all of her husband's clothes and his hammock in the dirt courtyard in front of their stilt home, added kindling, and torched the mound with a flaming tip borrowed from her cook fire.

When Grandpa Sin returned home to find his belongings turned to ash, the uproar echoed through the village and quickly drew a crowd. Grandpa shoved Nhim to the ground, knocking her head with his knuckle and cursing her in front of everyone. He lunged for the largest branch from a stack

Nhim used for her cook fire and began hammering her on the head, like a carpenter pounding an errant nail back into place.

"She even bowed her head to make it easy for him to hit her, and she screamed at him, 'Go ahead and hit me! Hit me until I'm dead!'" Ma said.

My mother and her siblings scattered, near enough to watch but beyond their father's reach.

"I climbed up into the mango tree. My father couldn't reach me there because he was fat and he couldn't climb the tree," Ma told me. "I watched everything and just cried. What could I do? We were all afraid of him."

My grandmother surrendered to her husband, quietly took what she knew she had coming.

In the morning, her face swollen from crying and her head tender from bruises, she served Grandpa his breakfast noodles and coffee. And by the following year, she was pregnant with their ninth child, my aunt Vuthy.

To my mother, looking back on it now, Nhim paid a terrible price for being such a dutiful wife. When my mother was sixteen years old, her father summoned her home. Nhim had fallen suddenly ill, her belly bursting with pain.

The village *kru*, the shaman, surmised a baby was rotting in Nhim's womb. How else to explain her grossly swollen belly? The village elders gossiped their own theories, this and that about the spirit catching my grandmother.

When a full day passed and Nhim's condition worsened, my grandfather took her to the hospital in Phnom Penh. But no one there could pinpoint a cause or a cure for her suffering. So, my grandmother just lay in her hospital bed, day after day, until a full month had passed. Uncle Yain came one day toting rice soup and salted fish, even though Nhim's appetite had vanished. When he arrived, my grandmother's bed was empty, the slightest impression left in the spot where her body had been. Nothing left to see but rice soup and salted fish splattered across the tile floor.

My grandmother died during the Khmer New Year, in April. A time of celebration, of children charmed by firecrackers and men and women dancing *rorm woerng* by moonlight at the pagoda, their hands fluttering at their sides like little wings.

"Everyone was having a good time except us," Ma said. "We were all mourning."

Grandma Nhim was barely forty years old, leaving my mother suddenly motherless at age sixteen. Ma took note of Nhim's life, full of sacrifice and choices that were not hers to make. She promised herself, as she watched her older siblings bathe and dress their mother's corpse for cremation, that she would never end up in a trap like that. Sam-Ou would make a better life. She would graduate college, get a job. She could do anything with an education, her uncle had said. And she would not, under any circumstance, allow herself to be at the mercy of a man.

But a good Cambodian daughter has duties she cannot escape. It was my mother's duty to get married, have children, extend her family line. It was her duty to honor and respect her parents, to sang khun. No matter how much she resisted, she could not be cleaved from her culture.

◘ BROKEN HOPE

The earliest photograph I have of my mother is on her student identification card from College Santhor Mok. Cropped at her chest, the image shows her hair teased above the bangs, in the fashionable bouffant of the time. The school year is 1964–1965. She is twenty years old, four years after her mother died.

In the photo, her mouth is slightly ajar, her lips frozen between a smile and a frown. It is as though a part of her already knows what is to come, her uncle's high hopes for his nieces destined to unravel at the seams.

◘

My life at college was normal. I wasn't a good student or a bad student, just okay. I was good at math. When it was time to sit for our exams to get our college degree, I went with my friends Sata and Sokhon to Kampot. Sata came from a wealthy family. We stayed with her relations in Kampot. They had a real toilet in their house. I had never seen a real toilet. They made vegetable stir-fry and they put a pat of butter on top before they served it that made the vegetables glisten. Whoever heard of using butter in stir-fry? I thought, This must be how wealthy Khmer people eat.

After my exam, I came back to Takeo to live with my father. He had remarried a widow with one young daughter and he had a house across town from Uncle San, near the police headquarters. It had a huge pomegranate tree. Oh, those tasted so good! I decided to take a certification exam to become a teacher. I thought I could teach math like my brother Yain, and my father. But I didn't pass. Then I tried to make my own business. I bought piglets and raised them. When they got big and plump, I sold them at the market. Whenever I got a little money, I used it to make small loans to women in town and then I went later to collect interest. I thought about selling silk. I knew how to select silk because of my mother. I wanted to travel to the provinces and sell sampots. After college, I just did what I wanted to do. Do you know, Put, for one year, I was completely free?

▣ HAPPIEST DAY

In the summer of 2012, I was running. Half marathons, marathons, ultramarathons. I couldn't stay still, my body long habituated to motion. Moving for jobs, never for people. For the previous two years, Ma had been nagging at me.

"You have a brand-new house, Put," she said. "Why don't you stay?"

I had told myself and Ma that the minute Pa recovered from heart surgery, I would be gone. But now that I was back in Oregon, reunited with old friends and closer to my nieces and nephews, I thought maybe I could try to stay awhile. Running relieved the itchiness in my legs to keep going, this unremitting impulse I had to flee.

I had convinced Chan to run a race with me, a half marathon on a bluebird August day in Eugene, Oregon, where we used to live as college students. It would be Chan's first half marathon, and I smiled with pride. She had been juggling being a mother and a wife, a full-time job, and taking classes at the University of Washington to see if she wanted to pursue a doctoral program. That she arrived at the start line was itself a minor miracle. That she crossed the finish line was an even bigger triumph.

After the race, Chan called Ma.

"I just finished!" Chan said. "Thirteen miles."

I sat in the back seat between my niece and nephew, elated for my sister, listening to Ma on speakerphone as my brother-in-law, Todd, steered the car north on Highway 99 toward Keizer, where we would spend the weekend with Ma and Pa.

"Oh, that's a lot of miles," Ma said. "Did you win?"

Chan jerked the phone away from her face, as if she had been slapped.

"No, I didn't *win*. I crossed the finish line," Chan said. "That's a win in my book."

"Well, why did you go do the race if you weren't going to get first place?" Ma said. "I raised my children to be winners."

Chan turned and looked at me, exasperated. We rolled our eyes in unison.

"She doesn't understand," I said to Chan after she hung up, feeling anguished for my sister and hoping she wasn't hurt by our mother's comments. She wasn't. Chan let Ma's words roll right off her.

"It doesn't matter what Ma thinks," Chan said.

But Ma's words, every last one of them, mattered to me. I took them as gospel. My siblings, as children of refugees, as refugees themselves, had the same obligation as I did to show gratitude to our parents for their quiet sacrifice. But how do you repay the woman who gave you life and then *saved your life*? A deeper sense of duty was the divide that separated me from them. I was weighted down by debt, by the story.

That summer, when Chan and her family returned home to Seattle, I stayed in Keizer with my notebook and recorder. If the story of the baby on the boat was my burden, if narratives have the power to frame, contain, and drown us, I needed to uncover more of my mother's story to understand what had made her run away, before she was even married and then afterward, and what ultimately made her stay.

"Why do you always have so many questions, Put?" Ma asked. "There's no end to them."

"Because there's a lot I want to know," I said. "There's a lot you never told me or anyone. Don't you want your grandkids to know about your life?"

There were things she had wanted to communicate to her grandchildren, stories she had wanted to tell. But language divides them, even now—my nieces and nephews only speak English, and Ma is most comfortable speaking Khmer. She had tried once or twice to tell her grandkids fables, with one of my sisters or my brother nearby to translate. But the grand-kids looked up quizzically at their grandmother, a story's rhythm, nuance, and power lost in the fitful interludes of translation.

"All these stories I told you and your sisters and brother," she said, "I don't know if anyone is going to pass them on to their kids. When I'm gone, the story ends."

I understood then that her talking to me was as much a kindness as it was an act of self-preservation.

"What do you want to know?" Ma said.

□

In the beginning, after I got married, I was scared. I didn't know if my husband was going to give me food to eat or what I would have to do. My role was to make sure he had clean clothes and make sure there was food when he got home. In Cambodia, you took good care of your husband. Not like here in America. In Cambodia, you worship your husband. You bow down to him and do everything you can for him. You would cut up a banana and put it in a dish for him. When you made food, you would cover it to keep the flies out. No one taught me how to be a wife. I learned on my own. It wasn't easy being married. I was used to doing things on my own. You can't do whatever you want when you're married. You follow what your husband says.

□

They rented a small stilt hut at Chroy Changva Naval Base, where my father worked as an inventory clerk, on the banks of the Tonle Sap River across from Phnom Penh. A cool breeze kicked up into open windows in the afternoons when my mother took a break from cleaning and cooking.

When my father's parents, Ta Khann and Yay Yeim, arrived one day for a visit, they helped Ma plant a garden of lemongrass, morning glory, and ridge gourd. To stretch Pa's paltry pay, Ma bought the cheapest fish she could pluck from the bins of Cham fishermen who anchored their boats in the marsh, mud gulping the heels of her feet as she marched across. On weekends, after earning extra money taking night patrol shifts on the base, my father put his bride on the back of his bicycle and pedaled over the Chroy Changva Bridge into town, where they indulged in Khmer crepes filled with minced pork and bean sprouts.

A year after they married, in 1968, my father climbed a coconut tree outside his parents' home in Smong village and hacked down a heaving branch of fruit—a gift to the *devadas*, the angel spirits, for giving him a healthy baby girl. They named her KhanSinaro, in honor of both Ta Khann and Grandpa Sin and despite the agony it caused Ma to name her firstborn after her own father. My father lit incense and set the coconuts on the family altar, giving thanks for such good fortune.

It was the happiest day of my mother's life.

"Before, I just lived with him, I didn't love him," Ma told me. We were sitting at her kitchen island, where Ma snipped stems off of mustard greens, preparing them for the wok. My father was upstairs, working his way through a stack of pirated Khmer DVDs, gifted by friends following his heart surgery. "Then I had his child. I saw him take care of me and his baby. I learned to love him."

Good fortune seemed to follow my father at every turn. Just before Baby Sin's birth, my father was promoted to an administrative position at the navy's regional base in Ream, on the southern coast of Cambodia. He loaded into a taxi his wife and daughter, an assembly of pots and pans, and a mattress, the trio traveling nearly a full day through endless miles of rice paddies and palm plantations before the taxi driver deposited them in front of the navy barracks in Ream.

In the morning, my father carried Baby Sin to his office, to the shoreline, to the market, parading her around town like a prize—the type of ceremony expected when a son is born. But Sin was my parents' firstborn, and her birth left them exultant. Pa held his baby aloft so long, my mother worried she might never learn to walk. While father and daughter were away, Ma filled the barracks with the fragrance of her banana tapioca pudding, coconut rice with black-eyed peas, and steamed kombucha squash with palm sugar.

But bitterness has a way of following sweetness. When Sin was one year old, my father was recruited to serve as his boss's attaché for a trip to nearby Kampong Som. Ma could not help but be suspicious, having heard the rumors on the base about my father's supervisor. Ma worried my father would be unduly influenced by his boss, known around town as a ladies man. What could my mother do? It was his right and his prerogative as a Khmer man and husband to do whatever he wanted, and it was my mother's job and duty as a wife to stay home, to take care of their baby, and to obey him.

When my father returned, the evidence of his transgression was on full display: a smear of lipstick on the collar of his military dress whites where a woman might have bent her head into his shoulder.

"Your dad was sleeping with a prostitute, so everything he bought, I gathered it up, his bike, his lantern, his clothes. I threw it all away. He was so mean to me," Ma said.

The very next day, she packed a small suitcase and left.

My mother fled to Takeo, taking Baby Sin with her, hiding out for a couple of weeks at her father's house. But when word reached the village of my father's intention to take another wife if he was left alone for much longer, my mother hoisted herself and her baby onto a horse-drawn cart and returned to Ream, unable to bear the shame of divorce.

Brawling was in her blood, so when she got home, she took an ax and banged the walls of the barracks with it, screaming at my father, "Come on! Come out here!"

"Your dad ran so fast," Ma told me, giggling. "All the people on the base were watching. I used an ax as a warning, so he would learn his lesson. He thought I was so easy."

And she thought, at least for that moment, that it was possible for a Khmer wife to have the upper hand.

A second promotion, and a second baby, arrived in 1970. My parents lit incense and made an offering again to the spirit angels, expressing their gratitude for so many good things. Another girl, my sister Khun Malyn.

"She had white skin that was so beautiful, it glowed," Ma

told me. "She was perfect. Everybody said she would have an auspicious future."

Ma was on her haunches sweeping the floor of their studio while Sin played with rocks on the landing the day Khun Malyn started crying and wouldn't stop. When Pa came home for lunch, he cradled and crooned to his newborn. But the baby was inconsolable. She kept crying in piercing screams, until her breathing slowed, her voice quivered. Her body turned blue and perfectly still.

"She lived one month and fifteen days," Ma told me. "That's what I remember."

Ma dressed Khun Malyn in a white smock she had sewn with a single button at the nape of the neck and positioned her baby on top of a little pillow. Pa wrapped her in a krama before rolling her in a straw mat, double-knotting each end with rope. He took his bundle to the jungle behind the barracks and chose a spot where a light sea breeze blew in and cooled the earth. He buried her beneath a young palm tree, to better mark the tiny grave.

That same year, Cambodia's top military leader, General Lon Nol, staged a coup against Prince Norodom Sihanouk—a move supported by U.S. military officials, who believed Sihanouk was allied with the Vietnamese Communists. Pa was elated. He believed Cambodia had a chance to regain some stability and fend off the spread of communism that threatened the country. My father distrusted the prince, who outwardly advocated neutrality between the United States and Vietnam but then secretly allowed Viet Cong soldiers to move men and munitions along Cambodia's borders. My father believed this kind of double-crossing would surely propel his country toward doom.

He didn't know then that his country's own Communist

revolt was forming in the jungles of northeastern Cambodia. The downfall of the ruling monarchy and the chaos created with a new regime prompted the rise of the Cambodian Communists. In 1970, the Khmer Rouge launched their revolution.

Looking back, I can see that my sister's death was a portent of things to come for Cambodia and for our family. It marked the beginning of the end of America's interference in Cambodia. Khun Malyn's sudden and mysterious death also put the first notch of trauma into my parents' lives. More loss would come, as if the universe was testing both my parents' marriage and my mother's ability to stay despite so much accumulating grief.

My father was still asleep upstairs when I left my parents' house that evening. As I drove north on Interstate 5, toward Portland and my own house, I couldn't help but think of all those times when I was a child and I flinched as my father burst into a wild rage when I or one of my siblings cried. He had no patience for tears, a shadow darkening his face when he heard so much as a whimper or glimpsed someone's watery eyes. If we dared cry when he punished us, he hit us harder—with a shoe, a chopstick, or my mother's wooden ladle, which ultimately cracked in half against my brother's calf when Sope got caught stealing a toy from the drugstore.

To Pa's mind, crying was catastrophe.

And so I learned to gulp against emotions surging up from my belly and flooding my throat. I learned to snuff out my sadness before it had a chance to spread. I learned that silence was the safest way to hide.

I thought of my father's best friend in Cambodia, whom I met when I moved there in 2005. He told me that my father was "the greatest man." That he loved to dance and tell jokes that made the whole village laugh; that he would help anyone who asked. And I wondered if we were talking about the same man.

I thought about how trauma has a before and an after. That we cannot be the same as who we were at the start, before trauma burned its brand into our lives. How it ricochets from one generation into the next. And how some of us are bedeviled from the start, burdened with the bad luck to carry more of it than others.

▣ SOME KIND OF HELL

I order chocolate croissants, pear tarts, and a baguette from their favorite French bakery in my Northeast Portland neighborhood. Things I know they will like. My mother's voice plays on a loop in my head, a saying she has told me many times and that I follow without question. "Let your elders eat while their throat is still upright," she'd said when I was growing up. "Do you know what that means, gohn?

"It means when your elders are still healthy, when they can still walk and talk and they are able to swallow, bring them good things to eat," Ma had said. "There will come a time when they are too old and too sick, when their throat is lying down, that means they're dead. Then it's too late to give them something to enjoy."

I know that when I visit my elders, I am to never arrive empty-handed, that I must take care to bring sweets each time. I know that the definition of "elders" is broad, encompassing my older siblings all the way to my grandparents. I know that ever since I could drive, I took bags of oranges and apples and boxes of dates and chocolates to Grandpa Sin, even though he had diabetes. Ma told me to bring him sweets anyway. "He won't live long," she'd said as I entered my twenties. I let him eat while his throat was still upright. I do the same for my parents, making my best effort to be dutiful.

As Ma cuts into a croissant and pours herself coffee, I pull out my notebook and pens. When I ask her to describe her life in the months leading up to our escape from Cambodia in 1975, Ma is sanguine, her voice specked with longing.

"We lived a good life before we fled," Ma says. "I raised pigs and chickens and ducks. We had enough money to help our relatives buy motorbikes and build homes. We had good things to eat. If there was no war, we had no reason to leave."

A sequence of good news followed Khun Malyn's death. In 1971, my parents' sorrow switched to jubilation when my brother Sophea was born, and the very next year, Pa got promoted yet again. With three stripes on his epaulette, he was building up both his military rank and our family's fortunes, serving as an accountant for his regional base. He rode slowly and steadily home from work, the equilibrium of his brand-new Mobylette motorbike thrown off by the weight of so much fish—barracuda, pomfret, mackerel, snapper—swinging from bags on both handlebars.

The fish came from seamen who bribed my father for the correct permits to enter Cambodia's waterways. In addition to gifts of fish, these men slipped riels, Cambodian dollars, under the table, too, which he collected for his boss. His boss kicked some back down to Pa.

As we sit in Ma's kitchen, pinching at crumbs in the pastry box, I listen to Pa tell me about his work in Ream. He has fully recovered from his surgery and he seems eager to share at least a little bit about his life. He speaks of the system of kickbacks that enriched our family as being perfectly normal.

"Wasn't that corruption?" I ask him.

"It wasn't corruption," Pa says, matter-of-fact. "It was our culture. That's how things were done."

In Ream, when my father returned home each evening, he kissed the soles of my siblings' feet as they slept and proudly presented a bag of money to my mother. She sat on the floor of their stilt home with her sister-in-law, my aunt Pech, and counted out the money overflowing from her rice basket, cinching stacks of bills into neat bricks of cash held together with thin rubber bands.

"There was so much money," Ma said. "Our eyes got glassy counting it all. Sometimes we got tired and fell asleep surrounded by all the money."

Pa not only had enough money to build a home for our family, he built Grandpa Sin one, too. Grandpa moved his second wife and stepdaughter to Ream in 1973 when fighting between the Khmer Rouge and Lon Nol's soldiers reached Takeo province.

When I asked Ma why so many relatives sought help from them, and why she was so willing to help, she was nonplussed.

"That's our culture, gohn," she told me. "Family members and relatives always go look for whoever is the most successful and stay close by that person, so maybe they can become successful, too. That's how we survive."

The lesson was an important one, describing a way of being that is old as stone: in our Khmer culture, there is no such thing as the individual; the success of any single one of us depends on the success of all of us.

As my family thrived in Cambodia, my parents made sure they pulled as many others along with them as they could. Ma flew from the small airport near Ream to Phnom Penh, where she deposited a suitcase full of cash at the Banque Nationale du Cambodge, and checked in on family members in the capital.

She used those trips to also oversee construction of yet another home she and Pa were building near one of the major markets in town. Pa was convinced that with help from the Americans, Cambodia would be restored to peace. My parents planned to move to Phnom Penh once the war was over.

A rotation of visitors came and went, my mother dutifully adding more scoops of rice to the pot to feed everyone. She took care of everyone, mostly without complaint, knowing she and my father had plenty to share. Yay Yeim made regular trips to siphon some of her son's salary so that she and Ta Khann could build a stone house in the village. Uncle Yain arrived to borrow money for a new motorbike. And Uncle Sovann, Ma's younger brother, turned up in Ream after going AWOL following a horror he couldn't erase from his mind: his best friend's head blown "clear off" by a mortar round as they fought the Communists in a distant province.

More relatives came, in tides of two and three, aunts and cousins, nephews and nieces. At one point, my parents sheltered thirteen people in their home in Ream. Most returned home, a few remained with my family, and two moved out to start their own families after my parents helped marry them off.

In July of 1973, my parents financed and organized the marriage of Aunt Vuthy, and three months later, they repeated the effort for Aunt Pech, both of my aunts marrying military men after having relocated to Ream as part of an exodus of Khmers seeking safety from the fighting between Khmer Rouge guerrillas and Cambodian government forces that had spread inland.

"Your father's parents were poor," Ma said. "They were living off your dad's salary. And Grandpa Sin, he had no money, either. We were the only ones who had money to pay for a wedding, so we did. It was the right thing to do."

For both weddings, my parents rented the biggest tents they could find and ordered the best seafood they could afford, family and friends drinking and dancing by moonlight until the hired band played its last set and the revelers dispersed home, the roosters already crowing their sunrise song. At each wedding, my father was the first to appear on the dance floor and the last to leave it, my mother content to watch from the sidelines, cradling her latest newborn, my sister Chanira, born in November 1972. As far as my parents knew, the war was happening in other parts of the country, not on the coast, not in their idyllic beachfront hamlet where sea salt and sugarcane brined the air.

But across Cambodia, General Lon Nol's U.S.-backed army was being decimated to the tune of more than one thousand soldiers per week. In 1973, as the fighting reached a fever pitch, a call was issued for more men to dispatch to the front lines.

My father was not trained in combat. He was skilled in spreadsheets and logbooks and had only ever held a pen. But that did not matter. His boss pressed a pistol into his hand and ordered him onto a truck bound for the neighboring province, Kampot, where Khmer Rouge soldiers were quickly gaining ground.

My father left Ma to tend to the family's chickens and pigs and my siblings. She gathered her three kids and her courage and went to watch him leave. She told him, "Be careful. Come home. Don't make me raise our children alone."

For weeks the women of the base kept each other company, consulted one another with any news from Kampot. One day, someone heard a truck was returning from the front. The women, jittery with joy, dashed to see their husbands again. But when the truck chugged onto the base and stopped in front of the main administration building, excitement twisted into full-blown horror as corpses were lifted from the truck bed and laid side by side on the ground for the women to come look, to come claim their men.

"My god," Ma said, a glint of horror flicking past her eyes even now, forty years later, as she unspooled the story for me in her family room, the ceiling fan on slow rotation above us. "There were so many dead. So much screaming, I nearly went deaf."

Ma walked toward the bodies slowly, curiosity and fear alternately tugging her forward and pulling her back. Was my father among the dead? The only way to know was to look straight on. To peer into all the faces.

Relief washed over Ma when my father was not among the bodies. But this was only the beginning. The very next week, another truckload of bodies arrived. Ma went again to check the faces, struggling each time to force herself to look.

It was then that the war became real for her. War made widows out of wives. Once you see a broken and bloodied body, all life drained from the face, you never forget. Trauma, once suffered, clings stubbornly to the archways of memory, rivets itself permanently in the brain.

My father was nearby in the living room as Ma and I talked in the kitchen, my mother's stories sparking more questions in me. He was close enough to hear us, so I asked a question, pitched like a hand grenade, skittering to a stop at his feet: "Did you kill anyone?"

He hesitated, staring blankly at the TV screen, and in that hesitation, all of what I thought and felt about him hung suspended between us.

"No," he finally said, after a silence that seemed to stretch too long. "It was me who almost died."

It was my father's fortunate fate to have contracted malaria fighting in the jungles of Kampot. When he staggered home, gaunt and grimy, Ma took him for an old man coming to beg for food. As soon as she realized it was him, she leapt from the shade and sprinted toward her husband.

"He barely opened his eyes," Ma told me. "It was like he was already dead."

I tell this story because in telling our story, mine and Ma's, I have tried to imagine what the war was like. But I cannot fathom what war does to a man, to his family, to the wife who must wait.

I tell this story because, according to Ma, something was taken from my father when he returned from the front lines, as if he'd been hollowed out. Those parts of him that had been tender and buoyant were now gone. Something also got altered inside of Ma when she stared death in the eyes, when she was made to look at the toll of war. And those things, that darkness, followed my parents to America, where they passed their traumas down to me and my siblings, a constant shadow cast across our lives.

It was in the way they obsessed about saving food and money. It was in the way they buried their emotions, unwilling to acknowledge feelings good or bad, and in the way they expected my siblings and me to do the same. It was in the way Ma fled from danger or pain, an impulse she planted in me. It was even in the way Ma would become so desperate for her kids to marry someone Khmer, giving her assurance that the customs and traditions she and my father brought to America would not be lost as my siblings and I assimilated. In my mother's mind, every decision and action was rooted in survival: of family, clan, and culture.

Mostly, the trauma was made manifest in my parents' steely determination to never have to pry open the rusted hinge of their past, and instead to cast their gaze in one direction only: forward.

It's hard to sit here and say why Ma told me some stories and not others. But I believe Ma chose to tell me this particular one, about how she and Pa were directly confronted with the havoc of war, because it has been too heavy for her to bear alone, and she was ready to release some of the burden. I was there that summer of 2012 to help hold some of her sorrow for her. I was an adult but still her baby, still the vessel she chose to empty her sadness into.

My father went through some kind of hell only he knows, out on the front lines of a civil war precipitated by an American-made war in Vietnam. He won't talk about it, and I have stopped asking. Some stories are not worth the pain of remembering.

I sat for a while in Ma's kitchen, stunned silent. Afraid to ask any more questions. Afraid to know more. My mother rocked in her recliner as she talked, her gaze cast somewhere far away. If my mother was tired or triggered from telling so many stories, from being asked to keep chiseling at her past, she never said. But once in a while, she would get up, go to her room, and close the door. As she would do tonight.

Before she ended this interview, she had one last thing to say.

"Your father was so sick with malaria when he came home," Ma said. "I fed him babar and put cold compresses on his body to keep his fever down. I took care of him, carefully, until he got better. He was lucky to be alive."

You could say that that made me lucky, too. The very next year, I was born.

◫ SIZE OF A MANGO

Something was different this time, deep in my mother's belly. No soccer kicks against the walls of her womb as when each of her previous children were growing inside of her. No gliding or flipping. No, this baby was different.

"You didn't move," Ma said. "I worried I would have trouble giving birth to you. I worried I would die and that you would die if I gave birth at home. That was my situation."

There we were, Ma and I, our lives interwoven from the start.

My mother followed the same Khmer protocol as she did with her prior pregnancies: eating copious amounts of ginger (the heat helped drain toxins from the body) and avoiding lifting heavy objects (too much strain, and the baby might suffer). She and my father lit incense and prayed. But Ma had been unwell while she was pregnant with me, suffering a stubborn bout of hemorrhoids. It was the medicine she took, she believes, that left me drunk and debilitated in her womb.

She consulted my father, who agreed she should travel the twenty miles to the hospital in Kampong Som, where trained doctors would deliver me. The first and only one of her babies who would be born in the sterile setting of a hospital, rather than at home like my sisters and brother. Ma's best friend volunteered to go with her so that Pa could stay home and take care of Sin, Sope, and Chan, plus the pigs, chickens, and ducks.

In the spring of 1974, something was also different at Ream Naval Base. A strange silence had enveloped the land and the air was charged with an anxious energy. If anyone believed the country was falling to the Communists, no one spoke those worries out loud, not even my mother, not even when the daily alert rang from the naval base speaker signaling for citizens to take cover in the bomb shelters dug in the dirt in front of their homes, the straw mat Ma laid against the bunker wall no match against the groundwater that soaked her and her children. No one admitted the Communists were advancing on Ream. To utter such concerns might stoke them to life.

Across Cambodia, the Khmer Rouge had captured one province after the next and had begun instituting new rules and policies meant to keep the population in check—a precursor to the concentration camps that would follow later. When my mother and her best friend hailed a taxi from Ream to Kampong Som, all major roads were cut off, patrolled now by military checkpoints.

By the time they arrived, an hour later, they entered a ghost town. The nation's elite and the foreign tourists who once populated beachside shacks cradling fresh coconuts in their laps and eating barracuda grilled in banana leaves, now gone. A sinking feeling twisted in my mother's gut: something was about to fail.

Three days after she arrived at Monorom Hospital, I came out, too soon, "the size of a mango," Ma said. Barely weighing four and a half pounds, not a plump, robust baby like Sin, Sope, and Chan were, I had a big head and twiggy arms and legs, like a small, winged thing. I slipped out easily into the hands of a waiting doctor. My mother was satisfied only after the doctor held me upside down and smacked me once on the butt. When I cried out, she exhaled with relief.

When Ma took me back to the village, the other mothers weren't sure my mother was carrying anything at all.

"They just saw a rolled-up towel and nothing in it," Ma said. "But you were there, when they peeled back the layers."

I was born in the Year of the Tiger, on April 27, 1974, into so much money it overflowed from my mother's rice basket, into a country being shredded by war. "Putsata" is the name she gave me, "Put" meaning Wednesday, the day I was born; and "Sata" for her best friend, whom she would never see again, one of the many missing and presumed dead in the war.

A month before my birth, people spoke of hope. U.S. ambassador John Gunther Dean had arrived in Phnom Penh in March 1974 to negotiate a peace deal between the Khmer Rouge Communists and the U.S.-backed Lon Nol government. But by then, the Khmer Rouge had control over more than half of Cambodia's provinces. There would be no peace, for my country or for me.

You have to understand,
no one puts their children in a boat
unless the water is safer than the land.

—WARSAN SHIRE

▣ THE WEIGHT OF THINGS

Counted in pounds, my family didn't carry all that much the day we left our home. Pa carried his black briefcase. Inside, he kept neatly arrayed military papers and identification cards, his children's birth papers and my parents' marriage registration, a pair of black sunglasses, a set of wedding photographs, a government-issued pistol.

In his other arm, he carried a child. He and a neighbor girl alternately carried Chan, who was two years old, and my cousin Piseth, who was two months old. Piseth's mother didn't want to leave. She begged and begged my father to let her wait for her husband, a marine who was on patrol on Rabbit Island, which would become the last stand between government forces and the Communists. He was coming home soon, she said. She would wait.

"But your dad," Aunt Pech told me as we talked one day over lunch in downtown Portland, a break from interviewing my parents, "he wouldn't let me wait."

My father, being the older brother, outright rejected his sister's pleas to stay back. He was there at the office when an urgent message crackled over the radio. "If you can get out, go. Good luck and goodbye," the voice from central command in Phnom Penh said. Then the radio went dead. It was April 17, 1975. The Communists had captured Cambodia.

Aunt Pech carried a small bag with kramas to wrap baby Piseth, a few shirts and pants for her husband in case he caught up with them, her favorite heels, his boots. He would find them, she told herself. He would catch up. And he would need his boots. The stories we tell ourselves, pulling hope out of thin air, when the truth is too painful to bear.

Sin was seven years old, and Sope was four. My cousin Seng, my mother's nephew whom my parents were raising, was eight years old. They were too little to carry much, so they scampered alongside our family's cart, our pigs jinking between them, as everyone darted to the dock where military personnel and their families frantically loaded onto four evacuation ships.

Uncle Sovann pushed the cart, because he had nothing or no one to carry. He tried to keep it steady, but the cart's contents jumped with every bump in the dirt and gravel road. There were a few plates and spoons and two pots—one with rice, still steaming when you lifted the lid; another with fish soup Uncle Sovann had just made for dinner. There were two suitcases, one full of cash and the other with my father's military uniforms, his name and rank carefully removed; Ma's silk sampots; my siblings' clothes. And there was not much else, because what do you pack when you don't know where you're going or for how long?

Ma carried the family's collection of twenty-four-karat gold tied tightly inside a white cloth and tucked snugly in a red-checked krama cinched around her waist. There were bracelets, necklaces, rings, things passed down from my mother's mother and a few pieces she purchased with my father's salary.

Ma also carried me, the youngest of her four children. "You barely weighed anything," she said. "You were so small, almost a year old, and still so small." And Ma carried the slightest hint in her round belly of a brother I would never know, that none of us would, that would become my parents' first loss in America. But that is another story, one that belongs only to them.

I was too little to be of any use; at nearly one year old, my feet had not yet touched the earth. Ultimately, I would come to carry all the hopes and fears my mother whispered into my ear.

My father pinballed between the evacuation ship and rows of stilt homes on his motorbike, collecting more family members. Grandpa Sin was another one who refused to leave. He wanted to wait for Aunt Vuthy, a nurse at a hospital in Kampong Som. Again, my father would not take no for an answer, the men nearly coming to blows before my father hoisted Grandpa onto the back of his motorbike while Grandpa clutched an armful of Aunt Vuthy's clothes and a collection of her cutlery.

Just as the ship was about to embark, as a petty officer prepared to pull the gangplank from the pier, Pa and Grandpa leapt on, the very last passengers to board.

It didn't add up to much, what my family packed in the final minutes before leaving home. But how do you count loss and regret and sorrow? How do you measure the things you carried inside and that you will continue to carry for all of your life? How do you weigh the guilt of leaving and living?

As the ships pulled from shore, my father kept his gaze locked on the land as his country grew smaller and smaller; Ma focused on her four children, her fears growing larger and larger.

What do you do when you can neither stay on the land nor go in the water?

"If we had stayed, we would have been killed," Ma said, not knowing how accurate her prediction would be. Military officials would be rounded up and slaughtered by the hundreds back in our village within days after my family fled. Word eventually filtered to our relatives in Takeo that when Khmer Rouge soldiers entered Ream, they asked for my father by name.

The sea was our best exit. But leaving home was dangerous, too. And where were we leaving to? Nobody knew, the determination having been made by men of higher rank than my father that the water was safer than the land.

If we had stayed, we would have been killed.

A conviction that would come to anchor in me.

For three weeks, the ship drifted directionless at sea, stopping in Thailand, Indonesia, and Malaysia—countries unwilling to grant us asylum. In the distance, whales breached, and in the dawn, waves rocked the ship, crashing over the bow and worrying the elders on board that both whales and waves might tip and sink us.

And for the last thirteen days, my mother prayed.

"Please let my baby live," she cried to the devadas, rocking back and forth as I slept motionless in her sarong.

For thirteen days, she tried to stay under the radar of the ship's captain, unsure if she would succeed a second time in winning the battle to keep me on board.

For thirteen days, my mother held on to hope. Which is to say, she clung to me.

On the twenty-first day at sea, the ships reached the American naval base at Subic Bay in the Philippines, dropping anchor some sixty miles from the entrance to the base as the ships' captains awaited permission to enter U.S. territorial waters. Before the Americans allowed our ship to enter port, an American flag was thrust into the hands of the Cambodian crew. My father watched as the Cambodian flag came down and the Stars and Stripes rose up, high above his head, a small moment that happened in haste and that would come to signify everything.

It was May 10, 1975, and everyone was alive.

My mother barely waited for the long lip of the ship's deck door to drop open before she jumped out and thrust her baby toward the arms of the first American soldier she saw. He pointed her to a building with a red cross on the front.

"I didn't know how to speak English to tell the doctors you were sick," Ma said, as I sat on the sofa in her living room, listening. "I just passed you to them."

My mother recalled the whiteness of the room where a nurse needled an IV into my arm. The whiteness of the people. Of their clothes, of the walls, and of the floor. The cool, clean tiled floor was the thing she would never forget: the way she could spread out, as if she had all the space in the world, and lie perfectly flat, with the incredible lightness of empty arms, the sweet release into sleep.

"Do you have the pictures of when we did our passport?" Ma asked me. "That was in the Philippines. You just see my arm. My arm, carrying you."

PART II

AMERICA

◨ THE RABBIT AND THE SNAIL

Who wants to hear a story? Then come sit close, over here by me. Someone turn down the TV. It's so loud. You kids watch too much TV. I have a story to tell. Be quiet and keep still. Listen to me. The elders in the village used to tell us this story. It is an ancient story, so I will tell it to you.

This is the story of the Rabbit and the Snail. One day the Rabbit and the Snail met each other at the pond. The Rabbit accused the Snail of being in its territory, drinking from its pond. The Snail insisted that this was his pond. So, the Rabbit issued a challenge to settle the dispute once and for all: they would enter a race together, and whoever won the race would have rights to the pond.

Do you know who won the race? Wait and listen. I will tell you.

On the day of the race, the Rabbit was so sure he would win, he called out to the Snail, "Hey, Mr. Snail, why don't you go and take a head start? Just call out and tell me where you are along the way."

The Rabbit, feeling very sure of his abilities, lounged in the shade of a tree, knowing he had plenty of time to catch up because rabbits are very fast.

But the Rabbit was unaware that the Snail had come up with a strategy. The Snail called all his brethren, who looked exactly like him, to position themselves at different points along the race route, and in that way, the Snail appeared to always be out in front.

When the Rabbit finally decided to get up and try catching the Snail, he became breathless. How could it be that the Snail was somehow still ahead, every so often calling out, "I'm over here now, Mr. Rabbit!"

When the Snail reached the finish line and won the race, the Rabbit was perplexed but deferred to the Snail, allowing the Snail to claim the drinking pond as his.

This is just a story the elders would tell for teaching lessons. The Snail was small and slow, but he was smart and capable. This is why we shouldn't underestimate the smallest things.

▣ FAILURE TO THRIVE

In my mind, it is always just the two of us, my mother and I, even when we are what is missing. In the single photograph taken of my family at Subic Bay Naval Base, where we stayed for one month while being processed to go to America, the image is incomplete. My father, skinny in a butterfly-collar shirt and bell-bottoms, holds Chan, all cherubic and short-haired. Sope stands on a picnic bench, a little boy squinting into the glare of tropical island light. In front of Sope, Sin stands, hands to her sides, obedient and oldest. We are six as a family unit, but in this photo, there are only the four of them, against a backdrop of the Grande Island Beach shack where, in other times, U.S. military personnel and their families stationed at Subic Bay would come to picnic, to laugh and swim and play volleyball on the shore. A place for recreation and for my family and thousands of Vietnamese and Cambodian refugees, a place for re-creating. For fresh starts, and new dreams. The photo of my father and siblings captures that first point of transfer from one world into the next.

"How come there's no me, and there's no you?" I ask Ma. It is spring 2013, and this will be among the last interviews

I will have with her before packing my house in Portland and putting it up for rent, having accepted a new journalism job in Thailand. For three years living in Portland, I have almost perfected the downward dog and the warrior's pose and drunk more tea than coffee and sat in the evenings on a meditation pillow, trying. Trying to reengineer my brain and body for stillness, for staying. But I'm not meant for this. Not meant to be tied to a place for too long. The feeling of flight tucked into my tendons. And so I go. I keep moving because that is what I know.

In Keizer, the smell of fresh-cut grass mixes with the heady pine-resin aroma of hops in the fields around the bend from the Vineyards. Ma has come in from tending rows of chayote hanging like bats in the quiet cave of the trellis my father made and watering garden beds brimming with bird's-eye chilis, tomatoes, and mustard greens, when I show her the faded photo of my father and siblings in the Philippines.

"At that time, I was still in the hospital watching over you," Ma said. "I stayed with you so long, I didn't get to have my picture taken along with everyone else."

She wants to exist, to count and be counted. I, due to my frailties, have caused this first split in our family, have created this absence in the photo. Another rupture to come, forty years later, and more family photos that will be incomplete. But for now, in that moment when my family is divided four and two, at least I am not alone. At least we are two. At least I still have my mother.

Early medical records make my situation clear. Scrawled across a single sheet of a doctor's green notepad, three words float on the page: "Failure to thrive." Those words now feel less like diagnosis than indictment. This is not the story I wish to have. Labels are harder to escape than countries.

There is a time in America when I cannot convince my mother that I will live. At Dr. Berry's office in Corvallis, Oregon, my mother speaks with hand and body gestures. There are no other Khmers in Corvallis, hence no translator to help her and Dr. Berry comprehend each other. A solution comes in the form of a high school student, the daughter of one of the members of the local church. She speaks French, as do my parents—a legacy of Cambodia's French colonization. And in this three-way translation, in Dr. Berry's examination room, the adults and the teenager piece together what the matter is with me.

"She is very malnourished," Dr. Berry explains to Ma. He will be my doctor for the next seventeen years, with kind eyes and bushy brows that make me laugh when he waggles them. Dr. Berry gets the gist of the details about our escape from Cambodia and of the twenty-three days at sea when I ate nothing. He shakes his head. "A miracle."

I am fifteen months old, and weigh fifteen pounds on Dr. Berry's scale.

Dr. Berry will check my ears, nose, and throat and then order a litany of tests to examine my blood and look at my lung function. Ma will watch a nurse draw a long syringe and push the needle into my back. I will writhe, the spinal tap causing me to screech in pain. My mother, wrecked by the sight of her suffering child, will cry, too.

"We were not used to this, all these people poking and probing my baby," Ma said.

I also have asthma, it turns out, so severe that Ma will be afraid to put me down in my crib at night, worried I might struggle to breathe and then stop breathing altogether. Khun Malyn died after running out of tears. Now here is a baby threatening to run out of breath. Ma decides to hold me upright in her arm at night, my head lolling on her shoulder as I fall asleep. She will learn to sleep like that, too, upright on a chair with her baby girl. In the morning, she will spoon-feed me the medicine Dr. Berry prescribed.

"One night you labored so hard to breathe," Ma told me recently, "I whispered in your ear, 'If it's too difficult to live, gohn, you can go.'"

Her words carry so much weight. I think for a moment, How could she have fought so hard for me on the boat, only to let go of me so easily, so early in America? I wonder, How many ways can a child make her mother suffer?

There are times when my mother tells me too much story. When I ask for one detail, she gives me a dozen. And within those dozens, I am left feeling inadequate or guilty or hopeless all over again. This is the danger, then, in asking too many questions. You cannot control the answers. You cannot unhear the things you have already heard. You cannot unknow the incredible sorrow you caused your mother.

"Failure to thrive" is what the doctor said, three words flicked like sand into my mother's ears. Taking shape inside her, docking on her deepest insecurities. If her baby fails to thrive, she will take it to mean only one thing, that she has failed, too. Three words are enough to make a story. A story I will spend my life trying to override.

▣ FREEDOM

The news in the local paper on October 1, 1975, was significant enough to make the front page: fifteen refugees had arrived from the small Southeast Asian country of Cambodia and had moved into a duplex on Walnut Boulevard in Corvallis. We were sponsored by two local churches, which pooled their resources to bring in all of us—my immediate family, Grandpa Sin, cousins and aunts and uncles. We were the talk of the town—the first Cambodians to settle amid the city's corn and fruit fields and its thirty-five thousand mostly white residents. We had arrived three months earlier, in summer, when the lingering scent of strawberries and ryegrass mixed with Willamette Valley loam infused the air.

Corvallis was and still is a tapestry of endless farm fields in a valley illuminated by golden wheat and knobbed with low hills. It anchors the valley, a wide belt of fertile fields that stretches from the state's biggest city, Portland, south to Eugene. The fields, the hills, the lushness of the land reminded my parents of home, of their village in Cambodia, which glistened green with rice paddies and palm trees that arched up into the sky like fishhooks waiting to bait the next sunset.

For my parents, there was comfort in agricultural abundance. They felt hopeful, just looking around. If there were fields, there was work, the kind that depended not on degrees and English words, but on how much and how long you could tolerate the blazing sun, a bent back, thorns pricking your fingers. In the coming summers, my family would be working those fields, picking blueberries, strawberries, tomatoes, raspberries, boysenberries, chasing crops from the top of the valley to the bottom as the harvest season stretched across sultry months.

Our duplex had three bedrooms and a bathroom and a backyard big enough for my siblings and me to run laps and catch each other. Ma was amazed by the electricity and plumbing when our church sponsors gave us a tour of our new home. In Cambodia, she and Pa used kerosene lamps to light their way and she cooked all of our family's meals over an open flame. In Corvallis, Ma learned how to turn the light switch on and off, how to flush the toilet, and how to turn on the electric range. She watched as a church lady rotated a knob and a ring turned different shades of red, a deep heat emanating from the strange coil, hot as coals.

The first time Ma tried to make a meal for us, she nearly burned the house down. Ma had pulled a whole fryer chicken from the refrigerator and placed it directly onto the burner, figuring the red-hot ring functioned just like fire. She watched and waited. The chicken skin started to burn, and then she saw flames and plumes of smoke billowing into the air. Then came a sudden, piercing sound . . . Deet! Deet! Deet! Deet! Pa raced around, a wildness in his eyes, trying to stop the noise. When he found the source, a small white disc on the ceiling, he jumped on a chair and yanked it off, then tossed it into the trash.

"That was a stressful time," Ma told me. "I didn't know how I was going to feed my family."

She learned.

Our town had mainstays like Burton's diner downtown, where bankers, farmers, and workers from the Sunny Brook creamery squeaked into vinyl seats and ordered fried eggs, flapjacks, and coffee darker than the oil that dripped from our car onto the driveway.

Pa worked breakfast and lunch shifts there, washing dishes until Mr. Burton pressed a clean apron and a pair of tongs into his hands and promoted him to the grill, a moment that sits bittersweet at the stem of Pa's memory because he once wore a different kind of uniform—a set of crisp dress whites with three gold chevrons on his shoulder board and his name on a pin clipped to his shirt pocket, where he always kept at least one good pen. With his Cambodian navy uniform, he felt official, capable, confident. With his Burton's apron, he felt nothing.

"It was just a job," he told me, in a rare moment when Ma was taking a nap and he was puttering in the kitchen, re-gaining his strength from the trauma of an injured heart. He wouldn't let himself think about that other uniform, about the past. What good was looking back, he told me, when we were in America and we had to find a way to survive?

Pa's first job was to scrape off plates of food into a garbage can before spraying them down and sending them through the dishwasher. As he intercepted dishes that buckled and surged along a conveyor belt, he couldn't believe the waste. He never understood how people could throw perfectly good food away.

One time he came home, reached deep into his pants pocket, and fished out a folded napkin with a slice of meat tucked inside, a slick of grease staining his pants. He had rescued it from one of the plates with half-eaten eggs and toast on its way to the dish room.

He passed the napkin to Ma.

"What is it?" she asked, surprise and curiosity lighting her eyes.

"It's what Americans eat in the mornings," Pa said. "They eat it with eggs and they drink a lot of black coffee."

Ma unwrapped the napkin, carefully, like a gift, peeling back the napkin's four corners, one at a time. When she saw the meat, she held it up to the light, examined it like an artifact. Ma brought the greasy strip to her nose, sniffed, and turned it over. She crunched off a corner before lowering it to the kids.

"What is it?" she repeated, now giggling as she chewed.

"They call it 'bacon,'" my father said, smiling.

"Let's see!" my sisters and brother shouted, leaping for the bacon in Ma's hand. "Let us have some!"

My siblings took turns chomping off a bit of the crispy meat. They smiled as it shattered between their teeth. Everyone agreed it was delicious, this strange strip of pork, and then giggled at the curious foods Americans ate.

While Pa was at Burton's, Aunt Pech found work as a janitor at Oregon State University's health center, something Pa had encouraged because she was a single mother now and she had to find a way to support herself and Cousin Pi. Ma was relegated to the job of watching after all the kids, because someone had to. Except for Aunt Pech, Pa said it was a man's role to go out and work.

Grandpa Sin, Uncle Sovann, and Uncle Chan got work at a cemetery in the nearby town of Albany. They were driven through aprons of flawless lawn and perfectly positioned headstones, like dominoes set in an open field, and then deposited at the far end of the cemetery, handed shovels, and told by the funeral director, "Dig." But my superstitious grandpa didn't last long at that job, spooked by the fact that he was working among the dead.

Nobody yet knew that back in Cambodia, our relatives were digging graves, too—their own. After my family had escaped from Cambodia, our relatives were scattered to concentration camps across the country. They worked each day without pay, from sunup to sundown, surviving on a single bowl of watery rice soup. Soon, men, women, and children would drop dead in the fields, dying of disease, torture, and starvation. For others, a more brutal fate awaited. Khmer Rouge leaders would march people to the edge of a mass grave and kick or shove them in, dead or alive.

My family knew none of this in Corvallis, all the adults busy with a different kind of surviving. Surviving a new country and culture, and the inevitable, persistent homesickness that afflicts refugees.

As the adults dispersed each morning to their separate jobs, Ma started to get restless staying home with seven kids. We ranged in age from one to twelve years old, and Ma got dizzy keeping tabs on us all. When Aunt Pech came home on payday, shaking a thick wad of cash in her fist and beaming with joy, Ma couldn't help what she felt; she wanted to come home with money, too. She thought of those days back in Ream, when she and Aunt Pech counted the money my father brought home. She wanted the feel of cash in her hands again, the tangible evidence that her family was succeeding. And she wanted the freedom to go out and work, just like my aunt, uncles, and grandpa.

But Ma needed Pa's permission. She had been culturally conditioned not to make decisions on her own. If Pa was willing to let her work, she could work. If he was unwilling to let her work, that would be the end of it. It was his decision, not hers, to grant her the freedom to get a job.

Pa knew he was in a tough spot as the sole earner in our family, starting over in a new country. We didn't have the piles of cash we once had. In Corvallis, my parents lacked both a bank account and money to put in it. My father rode a used ten-speed bike to work, doubling up on jobs and going to night class at the local community college to learn English and get an accounting degree. Ma stretched the money he brought home by buying bruised fruit and about-to-expire beef, filling our freezer with every kind of cut.

One day, when she'd had enough of being left behind, Ma gathered her gumption and approached Pa.

"With two incomes, I can help pay for things. We can save for a house," she said. "At least buy food and clothes for the kids."

I imagine my father sitting at the dining table quietly weighing. He suffered from the same brittle ego and affliction of pride that affected most Khmer men I would come to know. In Cambodia, he had taken tremendous pride in being the sole provider for his family. The fact that Ma would even ask to get a job threatened the delicate balance between them. A tug-of-war ensued between the old life and the new, between freedom and control, upending the gender roles that had defined my parents' lives in Cambodia and their comfortable, familiar family structure, my father as the breadwinner, my mother as the homemaker.

"They're hiring where Pech works," Ma said. "She said the work is easy. She'll help me learn what to do."

Pa stayed quiet. Still weighing.

"What about the kids?" he said.

"It's a night shift," Ma said. "The kids will all be asleep. You won't even have to watch them."

Pa did not say no, because he couldn't. He knew he needed help, and it was hard to argue with Ma's angle.

When the weather turned, and all the trees around town lost their leaves, Ma reported for duty at the student health center at Bexell Hall, covering the night shift while Aunt Pech worked days. She was issued a white work uniform and a massive metal key ring with a set of keys that jangled in the frigid night air. She worked from 9:00 p.m. to 6:00 a.m., mopping, dusting, vacuuming, and arranging her way through the night—after doing the same at our house—as the rest of the city slept. She scrubbed toilets and floors, marveled at all the pretty things on the desks of the doctors. She had a job, her first paying job. She would get her own wad of cash come payday. The thought of it gave her energy and motivation to keep going.

Watching Ma leave at night sent me into a spiral of distress. I cried and begged to go with her, kicking at my father to release me as he held me at the door, my mother trying to soothe me.

"Stay here with your sisters and brother," she said. "When you wake, Ma will be home."

I shook my head no, my high ponytail swinging wildly side to side.

I stopped crying only when Ma gathered me up and brought me to the car, depositing me in the back seat. I watched out the window as she drove us through the flat country dark of Corvallis, down Ninth Street toward campus, our car cutting through tubes of lamplight that appeared and disappeared at intervals. I thought of how big our Corolla felt when it was just Ma and me. Relief and joy washed over me in those moments, alone with my mother. So many kids at home made it hard to get her undivided attention, so I soaked it up when it was just the two of us, keeping each other going.

At Bexell Hall, Ma sat me down at one end of the hallway. There was no one there, in that cavernous building in the dead of night, the silence a little bit spooky.

"Gohn, you stay here," she said. "Don't go anywhere."

I nodded my head, then watched as she unlocked a closet and wrestled out a vacuum cleaner the size of her body. She plugged it in, and as the machine whirred to life, the sound ricocheting down the hallway like a motorcycle whizzing through a tunnel, I felt two things at once: alone and completely safe. As she made her way, the red cord slithered and jigged behind her. She disappeared into one room before re-emerging and glancing back at me. And in those moments when I could not see her, I knew we were still connected. I knew that if I followed that red electric cord, she would be at the other end. Comforted by this knowledge, I lay down, closed my eyes, and fell fast asleep, my body flattening against the scratchy industrial carpet.

The condition for Ma's taking a job was that she had to get to work on her own. Pa was too busy to take her, so he taught her how to drive. But he was too severe a teacher. My father slapped her knuckles when she didn't turn perfectly and yelled when she applied the brakes too fast, jerking them both from their seats and sending them forehead first into the windshield, their seat belts the only thing preventing them from sailing straight through the glass. She bumped into curbs, and nearly backed into a pole. My father thwacked her knee and yanked the steering wheel, hard, before knuckling her on the head.

After a few weeks, she no longer wanted lessons from Pa. She snuck out at night alone and lurched toward Wilson Elementary School, a straight shot up the road. There, in the empty lot, she practiced pulling into and out of parking spaces, turning left in concentric circles before switching and turning right, and braking, slow and steady, the lone car careening across lamplight. She wasn't a great driver, lacking patience and situational awareness behind the wheel, and in later years, she was content to let Pa do the driving. But back then, she was good enough to pass her license exam on her first try.

"Not like your father," she told me, with a grin and a twinkle in her eye. "He had to go back and take the test again."

Once she knew how to drive, Ma seemed to go everywhere. She drove to work and dragged herself across the parking lot because it was hard to stay awake when her body screamed for sleep. She drove to the store and hefted home bags of groceries to feed her hungry family. She drove us kids to the strawberry farms in the shadow of Hewlett-Packard, where techies tinkered with electronics we couldn't afford. Once in a while, to keep us kids motivated in the berry fields, to reward us, she drove us to North's Chuck Wagon on Ninth Street, where we piled thick slabs of honey ham and baked potatoes and pasta salad onto our plates at the all-you-can-eat buffet.

And then, when she'd had enough of her life, when my father's temper flared, when the pressures of being a mother, a wife, a daughter, and a foreigner in a strange new land became too much, she got in the car and drove away.

One time, she took us kids with her. Another time, she went alone. Each time she came home, she was sullen for days, refusing to talk to anyone. In her departures, and in her reluctant returns, a new mark got stamped in me, forming a pattern increasingly intricate and interlaced with hers. When I got older, I started running away, too. Fast and far. And that was the danger of being compulsively drawn to freedom.

◧ BROKEN FROM RICE

For those first few years in America, I am hers. I eat only Ma's food. I wear the sarong my mother sewed for me, held up with an elastic band at the waist. I speak only Khmer, even as my siblings begin their transition, crossing the bridge further into English. They each come home waving artwork in their hands, saying words I don't understand in their alien language. I watch and listen, amazed.

Sope seems to learn enough English to make friends right away, but maybe not that many words are required to race BMX bikes and blast crab apples to bits with firecrackers. Chan learns enough English that she will haul home a bag of books and sit quietly in a corner, devouring one after the next like candy.

Sin learns enough English to read the labels on cans and packages, helping Ma decipher how to cook the foods dropped off from church friends, and to understand how the S&H Green Stamps program works. When Ma's booklet is full, she takes Sin to the IGA supermarket on Ninth Street to cash in the stamps for prizes. They bring home three white ceramic bowls with blue trim that make Ma's face light up with joy, her first new beautiful things in America.

I stick with Ma, because we still speak the same language, until my day of reckoning arrives.

The first time she drops me off at Little Beavers preschool, I cry and cling for my life. I coil my body tightly around Ma's leg "like a koala bear," she said. I sit on her foot, rigid with desperation.

"Ma, gome doh, khnohm aht nauv tey," I wail, in Khmer. Ma, don't go, I don't want to stay here.

"It's okay, gohn," Ma says, wiping the tears from my cheeks. The warm temperature of her hand calms me. "Don't cry. Look at all the little kids you can play with. Be a good girl, gohn, and go play. Ma will be back soon."

Ma lifts her leg to kick me loose, but I stiffen against her effort. I look up to see two ladies standing near Ma, looking sympathetically at her. Ma offers only a thin smile of embarrassment and tries once more to shake me off. And when that doesn't work, one of the teachers moves in to pry me off, one finger at a time, like peeling a leech off its host. I let out an earsplitting toddler's scream as the teacher spirits me away, my arms uselessly reaching out toward my mother.

Her back is turned. Just like that, she is gone.

"You wouldn't let me go," Ma said. "You were scared of the people. You were scared of the food. You were different from everyone."

"I was scared because I couldn't speak English," I told Ma, a little perturbed that that wasn't obvious to her.

"How do you think I felt? I didn't speak English and I had to go to work."

It hadn't occurred to me that Ma could have experienced

the same pain and disorientation of learning a new language and trying each day to adjust to this new world. That she might have been as scared as I was.

When I was a child, my need for Ma was vast. It is a natural thing to want to stay close to your parents when you are that young. But I felt something more, as if my mother and I were one. Her dreams were my dreams. Her fears were my fears. Her sadness was my sadness, too. I refused to be anywhere far from Ma, as if my existence depended on being within her line of sight, as if there were an invisible cord linking us that supplied me with reliable doses of her love. But something in me knew she needed me, too.

It was in the way she lugged me around—to the store, to her English lessons, to work, as if I were her security blanket. And in the way she reached for me whenever my father got angry and lashed out at her, as if I were her shield. It was also in the way she regularly reminded me that I was the smallest of her babies, the runt who always got sick, who needed constant care.

Eventually, a belief grew inside me: I was my family's weakest link. My mother's burden. And Ma, she was my protector, committed to my health and survival. So I remained always near her.

When I was two and then three years old, I would lean against her thigh as my father and siblings sat cross-legged on the mat unfurled in the family room, where we took all of our meals. I watched Ma distribute pieces of chicken onto the plates of our family members, placing the choice cuts on Pa's plate, then returning her focus to me, shredding a drumstick down to the bone and pinching pieces of meat with rice and soy sauce against her plate. The shape of a tiny volcano entering my open mouth while Ma fed me. Everything quiet except a crunching noise echoing in my ear: my mother chewing on chicken bones.

When I was full and I would shake my head no at the next bite, Ma would always beg me to eat.

"One more," she would tell me, "just one more bite. You have to try harder to eat more, gohn. Fatten up like your older brother and sisters. It hurts my eyes to see you so skinny."

And so I ate and ate, working to get big and strong to make Ma happy.

When I was four years old, I remember hiding behind Ma's legs when a screaming match erupted between my parents and my father leapt up with a knuckle ready to rap my mother's head. Ma tried but failed to dodge him. I remember her with her hands up, ducking, doing what she could to protect herself. I looked up to a scribble of arms and was tossed in the tornado of their kicking legs. I didn't know why they were fighting. But I stowed this moment away in my mind, the first seed of resentment toward my father. The beginning of my own rage.

I learned it doesn't hurt to be knuckled like that. Ma knuckled me, too. That time she was busy preparing dinner before she left for her night-shift job and I dragged a stool toward the high cabinets to reach for a glass. I asked Ma for help getting the gallon milk jug from the fridge. I poured myself a full glass of whole milk, and drained it. Then another, and drained that, too. After three glasses, a milk mustache drooped beneath my nose and I flexed my biceps for Ma to see.

"Ma, I'm getting strong!" I announced. Ma kept her back turned to me, stirring something on the stove, but I caught her nodding her head.

After the fourth glass, I felt my stomach churn and a fire race up into my esophagus and out it came, waves of vomit that erupted onto the counter.

"Stupid child!" Ma said, bounding toward me with a knuckle out. She knocked me once on the head before lunging for a dishrag to clean up my mess. "I didn't teach my kids to be wasteful!"

When she hit me, it didn't hurt at all. But pain is not the point. Shame is. The head in Khmer culture is sacred. To touch it is a sign of disrespect. It is said to bring bad luck to pat a child on the head because in doing so, you are taking that child's knowledge.

A mother knuckles her daughter's head to knock obedience into her.

A husband knuckles his wife's to show who is in charge.

A sharp shame burned in my chest for being so careless, for wasting food, for all those times I watched my father hurt Ma when I was too small to protect her. But I would be better prepared next time to shield her. As I was born in the Year of the Tiger, it is my duty to protect those I love.

◻

"How ah you?"

"I am fine, thank you. How are *you*?"

"I em fine, sank you."

I hear my mother struggle to pronounce words as I hide beneath the table where her English tutor presses a pencil above the letters as they go. I am three years old. The teacher is kind and tries to lure me out from my hiding spot with toys, magazines, children's books. But I won't go. I want to stay close to Ma, curious about these new sounds she is making.

"How are you?" so different than my Khmer language, where we greet each other by saying, "Yam bai hai ngo?" Have you eaten rice yet?

Khmer is a language of food, and food a language of love.

Two phrases are aches inside of me, figures of speech that make slow revolutions in my head: "datch bai," broken from rice, and "datch bourh," broken stomach; in a single word, starved.

Broken stomach, or starved, is an absolute, the end point of broken from rice. It is the thing I will come to learn later, when I first visit Cambodia. A phrase echoed among survivors: "So-and-so datch bourh." Broken from rice is merely a point on the path to broken stomach. It implies an inability to access rice, or the unavailability of it. A disconnect from the source. This is the thing I will feel acutely in America, a shock to the system my body still holds. It happens for the first time when a teacher leads me by the hand to the lunch table at Little Beavers. Before I know it, someone places a bowl of macaroni and cheese in front of me. Where is my rice and soy sauce? Where is my mother? I watch kids all around me merrily gobble up the orange goo, and I turn my head and retch.

The children cry out, "Ewww!" and I am plucked from my chair, whisked away to lie down on a cot and wait for my mother.

I will hear Ma tell Aunt Pech about it later that evening. Two mothers laughing at the ridiculousness of children. "Put can't be broken from rice," she will say. But even as a three-year-old, I know this is only part of the story. There is a bigger truth: I can't be broken from *my mother's rice*. I cannot be broken from her.

◻ SENG

Two years after we moved to Corvallis, the adrenaline and excitement of starting over began to wear, and the drudgery of routine entered our days. If there was a tension that had been building in our house, amid the jolts and surges of adjusting, if there was distress beneath the cheery smiles Ma and Pa wore to greet our church friends and neighbors, I didn't see it. I didn't know anything at all was wrong until the day Pa nearly killed my cousin.

The fight was over a football, over nothing really at all. One afternoon in spring, Sope and Seng were playing with a football, and Seng held the ball a bit longer than my brother wanted. He begged for it back, but Seng kept the ball. So Sope raced inside the house, crying, and Pa panicked.

"What happened?" Pa said, scanning my brother for injury, and when he found none, he asked again, this time yelling: "What happened?!"

"He . . . he took the ball," Sope stammered through his tears.

"What?" Pa asked. "Stop crying. What happened?"

When Sope burbled through tears that Seng wouldn't give

him his football, Pa flew into a rage. He called out for Seng to come inside the house.

"We were just playing," Seng insisted. "I was gonna give the ball back."

In an instant, what should have been a minor playtime squabble between cousins devolved into a nightmare that broke the tenuous balance of our new lives.

"I told you again and again not to act nasty to your cousins!" Pa screamed at Seng. He smacked my cousin across the face with an open palm, so hard his neck snapped back. "Do you know how to listen?"

When Seng fell to the floor, Pa yanked him back up to standing. He twisted Seng's left ear like an apple stem, then smacked him just as hard a second time.

Pa was standing in the center of the room, one hand tight on his nephew's shoulder. He shoved my cousin to the floor, leaning over the boy, then took him by an ankle and suddenly, up and up Seng went into the air. Pa was spinning, both hands holding on to one of Seng's ankles.

Pa's face was flushed with adrenaline, spit on his lips.

"What's wrong with you?!" Pa yelled, as he swung Seng round and round, every rotation bringing Seng's head dangerously close to the coffee table, to the sofa's wooden armrest.

There are things I remember vividly from that moment, smells and sounds and sashes of light leaking through the window. So much crying. Ma's screams. Aunt Pech's face, scrunched up in shock. Heads turning away. My cousin in motion, spun round and round like a single helicopter blade slicing the air in uneven rotation. The gush of air every time that body passed by, fanning the fears of my mother. "Stop," she said. "Put the boy down." But it wasn't nearly loud enough.

Another sound drowning out hers. The dull *fwump* of

bone on wood. A moan. Blood mixed with sweat mixed with spit. Everything flying in a crazy vortex that made no sense to me then and still makes no sense to me now.

And then it stopped. What was left was Ma helplessly sobbing, her face pressed against the side of my forehead. Her hot tears dripping into my hair. She pulled my face to hers, to keep me from seeing. Too late. There was my cousin, lying like a broken bird on the floor.

"Pa!" Ma finally cried out, her voice louder this time. "That's enough!"

Pa had dropped Seng onto the floor like a spent cartridge and stalked out of the room, exhausted.

Ma shoved me off her lap and leapt to the carpet where her nephew lay, his hands on his head, blood seeping through his fingers, the color of crushed berries.

I don't recall who took him to the hospital, but he came home with several stitches and my mother spent the following weeks applying cream and pressing a hot towel to his head, where a huge bump jutted out like a clenched fist.

Pa sulked around the house for days afterward, not talking to anyone. He should have ended up in jail but didn't. I don't know what he told the doctors, but it must have been a magnificent lie. After that, Seng left to live with Grandpa Sin and his family down the street before eventually running away from home and leaving Oregon and our lives completely.

When I asked Ma why she waited so long to intervene, I was saddened, but not surprised, by her reply.

"I was scared," Ma said, "if I tried to stop him, he would hit me, too."

Pa only got worse, his temper a trip wire strung around him, and we seemed to increasingly snag the line. When he was mad, he would unleash a verbal squall that sent us all running for cover. Our home became a war zone, Pa firing off mortar rounds, leaving shrapnel at our feet.

Things stayed like this for a time, my father exploding, all of us running for cover, until one day when he came home from work and did the opposite. He walked through our front door, shirtsleeves rolled to the elbow, streaks of ketchup and gravy staining his shirt, like blood and mud from a back-alley tussle, and collapsed to the floor. He doubled over on his knees. He alternately sobbed and laughed, heaving wildly as he bucked his head in the air and slammed it back down on the ground. He sobbed some more. At one point, he began pounding his chest with a clenched fist, blow after blow above his heart.

"My home! My money!" he cried out. "I had a job. I had money!"

Ma rushed to the ground, kneeling next to my father, a hand pressed to his shoulder.

"What's wrong?" she asked. "What's going on?"

She worried that a dark spirit had caught my father and if that were true, where would she find a kru in Corvallis to cast a spell and drive the spirit away?

Pa just kept sobbing. Aunt Pech called Kay Webb, one of our church sponsors who lived nearby, and a few other church friends, who rushed my father downtown. At Corvallis Hospital, he was issued a hospital gown and admitted into the psychiatric ward.

What happened to my father in that psych ward—how long he stayed, what he was treated for—will remain a mystery because he won't talk about it. I was three years old when he went away, and I was in my thirties the first time I tried to ask him about it. When he didn't answer, when I sensed I had stepped too far, I did not ask again.

At the time, Ma told us only that our father was sick. And that when he came home, we had to be on our best behavior so he could get better. Ma and Aunt Pech have dissonant memories of how long Pa stayed in the psych ward; one says two weeks, the other says two months. They agree it was a long time, however the math comes out.

"I just cried every day," Ma said. "I didn't know how I was going to work and take care of the kids on my own."

Back home in Cambodia, a human catastrophe was unfolding. Around the same time Pa suffered his nervous breakdown, halfway across the world in Pol Pot's Killing Fields, his father collapsed and never got up again. My grandfather Ta Khann, the rice farmer who spent a lifetime feeding his family and his country, died the way many innocent Cambodians would during the genocide: starved for a spoon of rice. Datch bourh.

I learned this story many years later, when I went to Cambodia and one of my cousins whispered it in my ear. She knew because she was there.

When my father returned home to us after his stint at the psych ward, he had changed. He was both there and not there, always on the periphery, always apart. For a while, he just drifted through the days, like a wandering soul. Like a ghost of a man.

We were cooking together in Ma's kitchen in Keizer when she told me the story of my father's nervous breakdown. I heard in her voice a compassion for my father she rarely expressed.

"I felt sorry for him," Ma said. "He didn't want to leave his country. He was trying so hard to start a new life in America."

She understood the deep grief and loss of being torn from

home because she felt it, too. My family had had a life of abundance in Ream, my father on an upward trajectory in the navy and our family becoming increasingly established. Everyone knew our name. In Corvallis, our family depended on donated rice, subsidized rent, and the kindness of strangers. We were on welfare, but only for six months, something Ma made sure to tell me twice.

"Write that in your book, gohn," she said. "We worked hard for everything we had."

Given our family's dramatic shift in fortunes, and Pa's breakdown, I wondered about Ma.

"How come you didn't have a mental breakdown, too?" I asked.

"If I broke down, like your dad, who would take care of you kids?" Ma said. She shook her head then. *That a difficult time. That a hard life.*

And I knew, without her needing to say so, the thing that all refugees know: that our parents suffer and sacrifice so that their children may have an easier, better life than theirs. And that those of us who come from war can never fully escape it. Chaos is the cross we carry.

There are two memories from my childhood that are stuck in my head. They play, like a loop, making me dizzy with second-guessing. I cannot jog them loose. The first is of our family working in the berry fields that surrounded our town, trying to earn a living. There wasn't much happiness out in the fields when the sun tried its hardest to burn a hole through your head and your whole body ached from being folded over for hours. We were just together, that's all. I clench that memory in my jaw, a bone I will never let go. Because I cannot imagine my life any other way, without those fields and my family in them, without that particular tenderness.

The second memory is the one I can do without, because in it, my family is fractured. I used to turn it over and over again in my head, trying to make sense of it, trying to remember new details that would help me understand, but no revelation ever came. The moment we fled my father.

I have very few visual memories of that time. Instead, I am left with the visceral. The feeling of being rushed by our mother to put on our shoes and dash out the door. The feeling of confusion and fear. And the motion of the car, the centrifugal force making my stomach churn as Ma turns sharply, the bumps in my body as we cross the railroad tracks, and the pull of velocity as we hit the highway, leaving Pa behind.

In my mind, we ran away from my father because of what he did to Seng, because that moment left us all both scared and scarred, the range of his violence on full display, leaving a mark inside each of us. We all carry our own mental snapshots of that day. But I am not certain that Pa's brutality against my cousin was why we left. There is nothing to inform that conclusion, no words exchanged between Ma and Pa, no cues or clues to back up this line of thinking.

When I recently asked my siblings, their memories of Seng's beating and why we all ran away from Pa are also a blur. Perhaps, like me, they have tried very hard to forget. When I asked Ma, she also told me she doesn't remember. I struggle to believe her. How can she not know the reason she took us from our father? But I have stopped asking, accepting a truth that I've learned from my journalism training: we cannot always get the full story.

I could not have known what lasting impact that moment would have on me. If I could not feel safe in our own home, within the construct of family, where in the world could I find security?

I remember waking up the next day and being with our family friends in Salem, playing on a tire swing tied to a high branch of an oak tree. We laughed and dashed across the lawn in a game of tag, and for a while, I forgot we had left our father. Until he showed up to reclaim us.

When I raced into the kitchen to ask for water, I saw him sitting at the table in a scrum of adults. I stalled there in the doorway, just long enough to get a glimpse of the faces, to know how serious the situation was, before the adults shooed me back outside. Ma dragged the back of a hand over her eyes to wipe away a stream of tears. My parents' friends looked at Pa gravely. He kept his gaze down. I glared at him for making Ma cry. Even though he didn't see, I hoped he could feel my rage as I stood there.

I don't know how long negotiations took, but Pa must have given our family friends and Ma the assurances they needed to hear, because that afternoon, we were back on the road home.

This was not the first time Ma fled from Pa, and it would not be the last. I had always assumed she took us with her every time, until I was much older and she told me about a time she walked out on us all.

She had had another argument with Pa and left to stay the night at our church friend Grandma Foster's house. Ma listened as the retired teacher who tucked tissues into the sleeves of her blue knit sweater and occasionally served as my babysitter consoled my mother and urged her to go back home.

"Grandma Foster made me tea and gave me a blanket. She said, 'Don't be mad with him. He's your husband. You have to work things out.' She said, 'Go look after your children.'"

When Ma told me how she walked out on us, I kept waiting to hear a hint of regret in her words, or shame or remorse, something to indicate she loved us even though she left us. But her neutral tone gave nothing away.

What kind of mother leaves her children behind? And what kind of awfulness makes a mother gather up her babies in the middle of the night and flee? One is an act of self-rescue, the other an act of rescuing others. How often was she torn between the two? Between a duty to herself and a duty to her children? A tension strung so tight that the cord was bound to break. I think about the many times I would feel this very same weight.

I grew angry and resentful at Ma. Not because she ran away without us, but because she wasn't sorry. At least she didn't say so. When I asked her why she left alone, she just shrugged.

"Your father, he's difficult," she said. "I just put up with it. *Married no fun.*"

Difficult, in the way a man lets loose his temper when his pride has been challenged. Difficult, in the way he can no longer control his wife or his family because he is in America now, and his power has been diminished. Difficult, in the way he made a war within the walls of our home after we had already escaped the war in our country. I was his daughter and hers, but I felt like a soldier on a single mission: to always protect my mother.

None of my siblings saw the things I saw behind closed doors, when it was just Pa and Ma and me, where I became witness to the reality of their marriage because there were too many kids and not enough beds and I was the baby, the one my mother chose to tuck between her and my father at night. I shared their bed until I got too big, then Ma made me a make-shift bed out of a plastic fold-up lawn chair layered with army blankets and her quilts, which she wedged against the closet doors. I slept like that in their bedroom until second grade.

None of them knew about the times he hit her on the head for arguing with him. Or the time Ma gathered armfuls of Pa's clothes from the closet and dumped them in the dirt in the backyard, screaming her suspicions about some woman at his work.

None of them knew that in my twenties I had threatened more than once to call the cops on Pa for hitting our mother, one of those times because she had forgotten to pay the power bill. None of them knew because Ma didn't call any of them with her weeping; she called me, her baby, her protector, her confidante.

They also didn't know because I never told. There was a code of silence between Ma and me, that somehow I was protecting her by not speaking up, and somehow we were both protecting him, both of us becoming complicit in my father's violence through our silence. But why? Did I think my siblings would not believe me? Or did I alone want to be the one to rescue our mother, in a desperate bid to settle my debt?

I was four years old when I watched my father hurt her one too many times. When my own rage flexed into the room, claws out, startling all three of us. When I stabbed my father with a number-two pencil, newly sharpened.

I was drawing on the floor when the arguing started. Ma and Pa stood at the foot of their bed, on a long red shag rug in front of the dresser.

The pitch of their screams grew louder. I remember my mother's face, strained with hurt, my father's framed with fury. A second more, and my father is grabbing my mother by the shoulders, shaking her. He is standing in front of a small black-and-white TV with rabbit ears. Those rabbit ears in that warped moment protrude from my father's head like alien antennas. More seconds pass. My father's open hand flies up, high above his head. Ma turns her face against the coming blow.

I leap then. I don't feel myself move, but I am suddenly there, at the foot of their bed, my pencil gripped in a fist. As my father's open palm comes down in a raging slant toward my mother's face, my fist goes up, pencil tip out, a preschooler's spear. I scream from the depths, the primal, piercing kind of scream I haven't called upon since. I am angry and terrified and shaking.

In the arc of that scream, we collide somewhere in the middle, between his down and my up, close to my mother's face, and at the point of contact, time skids to a complete stop. A small blossom of blood sprouts from the left-hand corner of my father's palm, near his wrist. He turns, looks at me, stunned, and my mother turns to face me, stunned. I freeze, more shocked than either of them at what I have done. My father pivots to smack me instead, but my mother reaches me first, snatches me clear off the bed as her legs scissor us swiftly out of the room.

I've nursed that memory for years as the chief grievance against my father to legitimize the vast boundary between us. He hit us kids, and I didn't hate him. Only when he hit my mother did I feel the breadth of my own wild rage. Only then did I realize it was there all along, a faint roiling beneath my chest. I had always had an instinct to save Ma, never knowing from whom or what. Now I knew with a clarity that shocked and saddened me. I was saving her from him.

There would be other times, when I was older and too far away to intercept my father's blows. Those times she called me crying, telling me what Pa had done. That time I was living an eight-hour drive away, in Spokane, and wanted to call the cops, but she said no and hung up. The times in between, if anything happened, she never told me and I did not ask. I did not trust myself with knowing more.

I once told Ma that she didn't deserve to be treated badly by my father. She didn't respond. I understood, in the way she served her father and mine, in the way she often needed Pa's permission to do certain ordinary things like get a job, that this was not about what she did or did not deserve. It was about a culture that she felt bound to whatever the consequences. It was about duty, no matter the cost.

Even though her uncle raised her with different ideas, Ma returned to the belief that we are born already slotted into the positions we will be in for the rest of our lives, with gender roles that we are obligated to honor. If you were born a boy, you were prized and yet burdened with the task of carrying on the family name. If you were born a girl, you were doomed from the start. You would grow up and get married and live your life to serve your husband. She believed the only way to live honorably was to remain true to her Khmer culture, no matter what it required of her. Even in America, she believed this. She raised me to do the same.

Ma was so deeply set in her convictions, in her dependence on a cultural duty that she had fought against in her youth, that when one of my sisters expressed a desire to divorce her abusive husband, instead of encouraging her to seek safety, my mother tried to convince her to stay. Better to preserve our family's reputation, to save face, than to protect your own life.

It took me a long time to put the jagged pieces of Ma's story together, to understand that she never wanted the life she had. She tried to flee several times. But she returned every time. To her family. To her culture. To a relentless sense of duty, which was her albatross as much as it would become mine.

◻ IRONWOOD AVENUE

It was a dream: a three-bedroom, two-bath rambler in a lower-middle-class neighborhood in Corvallis, a few blocks from Wilson Elementary School, not much bigger than our duplex, but it had an extra full bathroom and a wraparound yard accessorized with native trees—Japanese maple, shore pine, Rainier cherry, Pacific crab apple, and birch—and it was ours. It was a small miracle, that between my father's nervous breakdown and our running away from him, my parents managed to rein in their focus to keep moving forward. Always reaching beyond the current moment. It was 1978 and I started to see more of my mother's smile.

Ma seemed to glow when she walked into the kitchen, conducting her own energy even when no appliances were turned on. There was a much nicer electric range than the one we had at the duplex, and more cabinets than she could ever fill. I liked the swinging saloon doors between the kitchen and front foyer. I wanted cowboy boots, a hat, and a holster just so I could swagger through like John Wayne, who I watched with wonder on TV. I wanted to be a cowboy, too.

"Sahat nah!" my parents' friends crowed on moving day. "So beautiful! You have the biggest, prettiest house of all!"

Ma's face bloomed with pride. Ma and Pa had started talking about buying a home not long after we moved into the duplex. The idea of renting made no sense to Ma. Every month you paid to have a roof over your head, but in the end it still belonged to someone else. She liked owning things outright, having the security of knowing something was truly hers.

By then, Ma had left her janitorial job at the student health center, and was working in the dining halls on campus cooking for students. Pa also got a better job than grilling hamburgers at Burton's. He pushed a cart up and down the hallways of the engineering firm CH2M Hill, delivering interoffice mail for almost a year until a respected church elder who knew someone in the accounting department recommended Pa for a clerk job.

Cousins came and went from Ironwood Avenue, filling our big house. Ma shuffled us around like musical chairs, by size more than by age, to make sure everyone had a bed, which meant almost everyone slept doubled up with someone else. But I was sleeping on the lawn chair in Ma and Pa's room. I liked sleeping so close to Ma, the better to protect her, even though my bent knee pushed through the plastic straps and the metal hinges poked my back.

Though our new house seemed to be a stabilizing force for Ma, there was still plenty of shouting. If my siblings and I fought with each other for too long, or if she got into an argument with Pa, she'd stammer through her tears, "Be careful, I'll run away and leave you all! I'll go live somewhere far away by myself where I don't have to deal with anyone."

Ma and Pa fought about bills and parenting and household labor, my mother gesticulating with a ladle and sometimes a butcher knife in the kitchen. Pa came home from work and barely interacted with any of us kids, leaving it up to Ma to juggle her own full-time job and do most of the cooking, shopping, housecleaning, and everyone's laundry.

There were other things. That time Ma screamed at Pa when he bought a gun, saying we didn't have the money and what was he doing buying a gun. Looking back, I realize that her distress was not about the money but about the gun. Less than a year later, she would jump on my father's back to wrestle the gun away from him when he threatened to kill a family whose daughter had pulled Chan's hair.

When I was seven, I stopped sleeping on the lawn chair in my parents' bedroom when a spot opened up on the full-size bed between Sin and our cousin Srey, who came to live with us for a few years when we moved to Ironwood Avenue. I wasn't there anymore to see my parents fight behind closed doors, but I knew it happened. Those times Ma emerged with a crumpled tissue in her hand, crying as she entered the kitchen to start cooking, or the opposite, when they fought so hard that Ma retreated to their bedroom and locked the door behind her to cry alone, I hated my father. She never did run away again, just threatened, but her threats were enough to make my hair stand on end.

Instead, she occupied herself with making our house a home. She shopped sales for furniture and made a garden in the backyard, where she grew chives, lemongrass, and chili peppers alongside zucchini, bell peppers, and tomatoes. She planted roses all around our yard, and when they bloomed— flares of pink, red, and orange all along our picture window—it made her smile. Pa bought paint and Ma equipped each of us kids and herself with a brush to give the house a fresh coat. She chose a cream white with brick red for the trim, quiet colors that camouflaged the chaos that sometimes still erupted inside.

I ran through the house with Chan like it was a playground. We danced to Abba, which Sin played on the record player in the living room, shaking our hips so fast, Ma laughed at the spectacle. Sometimes, just for fun, Ma got up and danced, too, tilting her head back and cupping a hand over her smile.

Chan and I did somersaults and cartwheels down the hallway and in the living room and didn't hit a thing. Mostly because there wasn't a thing in it, not at first. Ma and Pa eventually backed bookcases and hutches against the walls, and crowded corners with chairs. No more used furniture and pots and pans. They bought new beds, desks, lamps, a lawn mower, and a Sony color TV. There was even a beautiful teak six-seat dining table with leaves on each end that folded out to accommodate more diners. For a while, I thought we were rich. Ma filled an entire room of our house on Ironwood Avenue with houseplants like a terrarium—begonias, spider, cacti, dracaena, pothos, snake—which she carefully watered on weekends.

In just a few short years, we had traveled a few notches up the socioeconomic ladder, thanks to my parents' multiple jobs and the money we kids earned berry picking. We still ate all of our meals sitting in a circle on the mat on the floor, so Pa turned the dining table into his satellite office. He bought a typewriter and set it down at one end of the table, where it sat for the next twenty-five years.

Cousin Pi came to live with us around this time. His mom, my aunt Pech, was struggling to raise a kid on her own while working full-time. So Pi came with us to the new house. I was thrilled. Pi was like a little brother to me, even though he was a full head taller and would grow taller still.

Something changed with Pa, too, when we moved into our new house. He came home one day and raised a basketball hoop in the driveway. In the evenings, he watered the lawn and bushes around our yard, wearing his sarong, even though we begged him not to. Our friends laughed at us for having a dad who wore a skirt. He knew we were embarrassed, but he was not about to change who he was to accommodate our shame. When he came home from work, he flexed his biceps so that Chan and I could loop our arms around them. He swung us as we giggled and held on. I saw him smile when he motioned for Sope to pass him the basketball so he could take a shot.

The house on Ironwood Avenue did something to us kids, too. We each started coming into our own. Sope made fast friends with boys on our block, and Sin learned how to bake zucchini bread, even though she was only in the fifth grade. Chan took up part-time residence in her friend's backyard, where she swung herself high on the swing set for hours and hours while Cousin Pi and I rode my bike and played kick-the-can and hide-and-go-seek with the neighborhood kids.

Our home began to buzz with visitors as more Khmer families immigrated to Oregon, seeking out my parents for a range of help and advice. My parents had been among the first to settle in Oregon, so they became viewed as the elders in the Willamette Valley's Cambodian community as other families followed, through the 1980s and 1990s, until the valley's Cambodian population grew to several hundred families.

Sometimes our visitors overlapped, one family passing the next at our front door. They came with trays of apples and oranges, tins of butter cookies, moon cakes, and bags of jasmine rice.

"We barely have to go to the grocery store," Ma said, her face spangled with light, knowing our family's favorable status was solidifying in Oregon's Khmer community.

A rare weekend passed when we didn't have visitors who squeaked into and out of the nice sofas in the living room, the ones Ma covered in plastic to keep new. Word spread quickly in the Khmer community that my parents knew how to get a driver's license, apply for food stamps, search for doctors, and file taxes. Ma and Pa had already done it all, which made them experts in the minds of other Khmer families.

They carried to our front door plastic folders full of forms they did not understand, with abbreviations that spanned the alphabet: DMV, IRS, IRA, DS-260, W-2. Our house hummed with the energy and fellowship of a community center.

Ma inevitably called out for me or one of my older sisters, rarely our brother, to bring tea and sweets, snacks designed to hold our guests over until she could slip into the kitchen and cook a proper meal.

Even though it made her tired, all that cooking, all those hours sitting next to Pa while he offered advice, she did it because that was what Khmer women do.

Our phone rang just as often as our doorbell. Ma and Pa were the first to know when one of the Khmer kids in Salem or Portland got locked up or knocked up and dropped out of school, their parents calling Ma and Pa for advice on how to control their children. Ma used these phone calls as moral teachings.

"If it was my kid," Ma would say to us, after relaying to

me and my siblings the complete contents of these crisis calls, "I'd die of heartbreak."

It was as if, in the Khmer community, mothering was a sport, and Ma wanted to win. So she took great pains to guide us properly.

In Cambodian culture, the rules of engagement varied, depending on whether the relationships were lateral or vertical, and sometimes it was hard to keep track of all the cultural rules. You bent your body low when passing elders and always served them first. If you were a child, you were not allowed to voice opinions or make decisions. If you were a girl, you cooked and served the men, the elders, and the guests. And talking back to your parents was the sin that would send you to the seventh level of hell.

I watched how Ma interacted with her own father and absorbed the cultural cues she gave me. Although she was more than seventy-six hundred miles and an ocean away from Cambodia, distance could not erase the expectations she had of herself as a Cambodian wife, mother, and daughter. And the fact that Grandpa Sin lived nearby and visited frequently was the leash that tethered her to her conventional roots.

It confounded me how little Ma and her father actually spoke to each other, considering how often they were in each other's presence. She talked to Grandpa through us kids.

"Ask your grandpa how much cream for his coffee," she would tell me, even though Grandpa Sin was sitting a few feet away and could hear the question perfectly fine. "Tell your grandpa someone from church is coming by to see him." Grandpa nodded when he received instructions or information and relayed his own replies back through one of us kids.

Whenever Grandpa came to our house, I watched as Ma rushed and fussed around the kitchen to make his favorite food—rice soup with salted fish—before he had a chance to ask what was for dinner. She set the food on a round metal tray and dispatched me or one of my sisters—rarely Sope—to deliver the food to him while he sat at the dining table, propped up on a waxed wooden hook cane, waiting to be served.

"Why doesn't Sope ever have to bring food to Grandpa?" I asked Ma.

"I do!" Sope said.

"No you don't," I barked back.

"Yes I do," my brother insisted. To prove his point, he leapt from the sofa and rushed to the kitchen to bring a glass of water to our grandfather.

"Stop fighting," Ma scolded us. "Everyone has to help."

"Sope never does anything," I complained to Ma.

"That's because he's a boy," Chan said.

Growing up, I always believed we catered to Grandpa because he was old and Ma taught us to always respect our elders. That was one reason. The other part was purely an accident of birth: he, like my brother, and like my father, was male, and to be male in Cambodian culture meant a life of being catered to, of bearing the sole responsibility of bringing money home to support your family. It meant you could do whatever you wanted and answer to no one if you drank or hit your wife or kids, or, as in the case of both Grandpa Sin and my father, if you made your way into the arms of other women.

Sope got a free pass on kitchen duties and a new car with leather trim when he turned sixteen. He got to have girlfriends and spend the night at his friends' houses. He, like all Khmer boys, was a special thing in our culture—a prize that called for celebration—whereas a girl was a burden, a liability, a loss. A girl would grow up, get married, and leave to care for her husband and his family. That was the trade in Cambodia—a water buffalo for a daughter-in-law.

Except that's not how things ended up for Ma. She grew up and got married, but found herself in charge of taking care of her father. Ma loved Grandpa because he was her father, but she did not like him. She told me this one day on the phone, when I couldn't make it to Keizer to talk in person. Ma said her father was dangerous, disloyal, a deadbeat. She would never forget or forgive how he had treated Grandma Nhim.

But that stern, uncaring, and unkind figure my mother painted was not the man I knew. My grandpa fished butterscotch candies out of his front pockets when he visited, holding them high above his head to let my siblings and me leap for them. When I was in my twenties, I would often drive him to the mall. We walked arm in arm as he greeted by name the vendors in their booths and the saleswomen at Nordstrom, his favorite store.

"Pick one thing, anything you want, I'll buy it for you," he said. But I just smiled and never let him.

I understood my mother had an uneasy relationship with her father, a situation made clear by the things they said and didn't say to each other, and how they never touched or hugged, but she set aside any ill feelings she had for him in his dying days. It was Ma, rather than either of her two younger sisters, or even her younger brother, who took an unpaid leave of absence from work and installed him in a wheelchair-accessible ground-floor apartment, where she cared for him round the clock until diabetes overran him.

When I asked why she did this, given everything she had told me about their relationship, she was impassive.

"He was my father," she said. "I was the daughter."

She was not the oldest one in her family. But the feelings

of obligation, of duty, those feelings of responsibility to take care of everyone as she had done in Cambodia, followed Ma to America, where she taught me, through her stories and sayings, how to be dutiful and virtuous, too.

Ma disdained public emotional displays and any behavior that brought shame to the family. Telling someone "I love you" was a waste of words: "We just act love." She emphasized family over everything else, and constantly enumerated what she believed were immoral acts. Living with a boyfriend or girlfriend, getting divorced or pregnant out of wedlock, doing poorly in school—these were things that badly damaged a family's reputation.

She addressed topics like drugs, gangs, and teenage pregnancy on an as-needed basis, when there was a current example to point to and say, "Don't do that."

Ma did not address topics like being gay because back then, there was no one to point to and say, "Don't do that."

I grew up believing that being gay was bad, even without Ma explicitly saying so, because the bullies at school slung the word like a slur: "You're so gay!" During recess, the kids played "Smear the Queer," where they ganged up on and tackled whoever was holding the ball. I played, too, not knowing any better. Not knowing that one day, I would be the one to get smeared.

But I also knew I didn't have anything to worry about. Ma had said I would grow up and have a husband. So I counted on it. I trusted her with the kind of blind faith you have when you step into a crosswalk. You won't get hit, so long as you stay within the lines.

Somehow, with all the comings and goings in our house, Ma also managed to stay caught up on the daily tribulations of her children's lives, simply by listening and observing. She knew when Kevin Rhodes followed me and Chan home from Wilson Elementary School and threw rocks and big chunks of bark at our backs and threatened to cut us with a knife. She told us then, "When he walks one way, you go a different way. Stay away from people who only want to make trouble."

She knew where to find my oldest sister when she had graduated from high school and secretly followed her friends to the Mount Hood ski resort outside of Portland, where they got summer jobs. Ma and Pa were nervous about their oldest daughter being so far from home, something they considered improper for a young, unmarried Cambodian girl, so they drove along unfamiliar, zigzagging mountain roads slicked with snow and ice to bring her home.

Ma watched all of us kids with a long gaze meant to keep us safe and protected, and at the same time designed to keep us under her thumb. It both unsettled and comforted me.

"You know the pineapple, how it has so many eyes?" she once asked me. "I'm just like that. There is nothing I can't see."

Her message was clear: her field of vision was wide. Don't even think about doing anything to embarrass the family.

Ma's tireless gaze meant she also knew whenever I was sinking into a depression, which happened every few years, or when one of my sisters was struggling through a pregnancy. She called and consoled us at exactly the right moments. A mother knows when something is wrong.

One time, when I was in my early twenties and living in Seattle, she called and confronted me about dating a black man.

"This is not our culture, Put," Ma said, her voice kinked with concern. "We don't mix with black people."

"Ma, that's racist!" I yelled into the phone. "We're Asians living in a white world. You should know better."

"It's not racist," Ma said. "It's how our culture is. You're Khmer. You should know better."

"How do you know who I hang out with?" I asked Ma. Chan, who I was living with at the time, swore she hadn't told.

"I know everything," Ma said.

The pineapple's eyes were not only multitudinous, they could also apparently see across great distances. Of course, she didn't know everything. Her seeming omniscience was only one of the things about my mother I got wrong.

I was wrong to think her love was limitless and unconditional, and that she loved being a mother because why else have so many kids? I was wrong to believe that she was fearless and would always fight for us. I did not know she was also often afraid, that she was capable of being selfish.

Only now do I see how we teetered on our own pedestals, our images fragile behind the gloss and shine of success. There was the pedestal Ma made to balance our family on, hoping to preserve our family in favorable light, and the one I made in my mind to put my mother on, striving to collect her affections. We wanted to be worthy.

We had a new home, fancy furniture, a car, and a color TV—accoutrements of middle-class life that earned my parents the praise and envy of others. My parents were re-establishing themselves, both in America and within our Khmer community, and Ma was fiercely determined to maintain our good reputation. I got swept into the effort of perpetuating a public persona of perfection, interminably terrified of attracting the pineapple's discontented gaze.

◻ LIBERATED BY LANGUAGE

I could not sing my ABCs when I found myself sitting in Mrs.
Hedges's kindergarten class at Wilson Elementary School.
The sounds got stuck whenever I opened my mouth. Ma did
her best to make sure I was put together well—dressing me in
a pair of pants and a clean shirt that either had been donated
to us or she found at the downtown charity Vina Moses, and
trimming my bangs as straight as she could. But there was no
hiding the major flaw about me when I was five years old—
I still could not speak English.

My classmates belted out the alphabet with exuberance and
abandon, encouraged by Mrs. Hedges, who walked around
to each quad of desks and smiled as she guided the children
along. When she got to me, she made sweeping gestures with
her arms, as if trying to charm the sounds out of my mouth. I
shifted in my seat, too afraid to make eye contact.

I watched my classmates make sounds I didn't know how
to make. So I just sat there at my desk, head bent, my body
quivering as I cried.

Mrs. Hedges must have taken pity on me, because in the
afternoon, she motioned for me to step outside. I went out

into the dimly lit hallway and found my sister Sin standing with her friend.

"What's the matter?" Sin asked, bending low to look me in the face. "Why are you crying?"

"I want Ma," I said, wiping my eyes. Sin was sort of like Ma, a conscientious stand-in whenever our parents were at work. When I was a toddler and she was only eight years old, she toted me around on her hip. But I wanted our real mother.

"Ma is at work. She can't be here," Sin said.

I cried even harder. I wanted Ma to rescue me. I would have been happy to never go to school again.

Then Sin's friend whispered something into her ear. My sister's eyes lit up as she pulled on a necklace she was wearing—a string of plastic green beads whose shine was dulled by the low light of our school's dank corridor.

"See this necklace, see how pretty it is," Sin said. "I'll give you this necklace if you stop crying."

I did not yet own any jewelry besides the two gold hoop earrings Ma had pushed into my ears when I was a baby. I finally nodded, and Sin beamed as she pulled the necklace off and slipped it over my head.

"Remember, no more crying."

I lasted a day. For the rest of the week, Sin was summoned nearly every day to the nurse's office, where I sat sobbing into my sleeves.

"I spent half my fifth grade in the nurse's office with you," Sin told me recently. "Talk about separation anxiety!"

My unease started to settle with help from Mrs. Hedges. She leveraged her patience and persistence to dismantle my insecurities and build in their place a confidence that carried me through the rest of the year. For that, I loved her. During individual reading time, she came to my desk and helped me with the alphabet. The following week, she raised flash cards in front of me and helped me pronounce words, single syllable and short, like "cat" and "run." Halfway through the year, my English was hobbling along at best, but I sang the alphabet louder than anyone.

By the first grade, my vocabulary had improved, and I found my confidence. I still wore the necklace Sin gave me but didn't need to. I no longer cried. Mrs. Yoshimura read Dr. Seuss in class, and something about rhyming words caught me. I was hooked. Poetry was the kind of ordered lyrical language that made sense to me, like the Khmer language I spoke at home. That year, I checked out every rhyming book I could find in the library.

It seemed once I grasped English, I could not get enough of school and I also could not shut up. When Ma drove us around town on errands, I read every billboard, street sign, and business sign out loud. "S . . . t . . . op," I said, sounding out the red sign to myself before announcing it to Ma. "Ma, anung tah, Stop!"

I counted to ten at the top of my lungs until my siblings wanted to choke me.

"Put, shut up!" Chan said as I called out the names of businesses on Ninth Street.

McDonald's, Toyota, Bi-Mart.

"You shut up!" I shot back.

Avery Square. Campbell's. Taco Time.

"Just talk to yourself. We don't need to hear you," Chan said.

But Ma wanted to hear me. I know because when I said words out loud, it made her smile.

"That's good, gohn," Ma would say, beaming with pride

whenever I spied a word and enunciated it. "My daughter is so smart."

Soon, I was speaking English with my siblings. Then I started speaking English to my parents, even though they replied in Khmer. Looking back, I can't pinpoint the moment when the last Khmer words disappeared from my tongue and English words rolled around in my mouth in their place. Ma must have sensed the shift underway. She tried to reverse the trend and offered to pay me and my siblings twenty-five cents for each day we spoke Khmer at home. A highly lucrative deal when set against our two-dollar-per-month allowance. None of us took her offer.

How could I know then that language was the thing that would set me free? That in that moment when English began to overtake my Khmer, I was starting to travel away from my mother and my culture, entering an in-between world from which I would not reemerge? One foot in each culture, Khmer and American, too young to know that when a language leaves you, it might never return.

That year in Mrs. Hedges's class was both a beginning and an end. The end of my complete reliance upon Ma, and the beginning of something that must have caused her great fear. It was then that I realized I could survive without her, and that Ma realized something, too: she was losing her baby to America.

Arby's. Schuck's. Gables.

◻ A QWAK, A QWEN

Who wants to know about the Blind Man and the Disabled Man?
Quit fighting and move over so other people can sit on the sofa.
You have to learn how to share. Ma will sit on the floor over here.
I have room to spread out. And all of you can hear me.

There were two villagers, the Blind Man and the Disabled Man.
Both of them were beggars at the market. The Blind Man couldn't
see and the Disabled Man had no legs. Positioned across the street
from each other, they were unable to move. The Disabled Man
watched as people were coming and going from a distance. Very
few people were coming through the walkway where the beggars
were. So one day, the Disabled Man had an idea.

"Hey, Blind Man," the Disabled Man said, "bend down and I
will ride on your shoulders. I will be your eyes and you can be my
legs. Together, we can move around."

The Blind Man, sensing the potential for benefit, did as he was
instructed, lowering himself so the Disabled Man could climb atop
his shoulders. After that, the two beggars moved as one. In that

way, they were able to be more efficient collecting donations. They worked together as a team to their advantage.

Do you understand what this story is trying to say, gohn? We have to be smart to get ahead in life. When we work together, we can move forward and have success. There are a lot of stories about A Qwak and A Qwen. I will tell you some other ones later.

That's enough for now. It's late. You need to go to sleep. Tomorrow we have to wake early to go to the fields.

◧ PICKING SEASON

We picked berries every day of every summer, except Sundays, when I was a kid. We started with strawberries out at Kenagy's farm, before those cool early months of summer gave way to sun-plumped blueberries over at Wilt's, south of town. We picked at Wood's, Tweedt's, Pimm's, Anderson's, and Vancleave's before the bushes gave all they could and we moved on.

Raspberries and boysenberries came next, and sometimes we picked snow peas, green beans, and peaches, or gathered garlic and filberts scattered in dry dirt. One time, and just that once, we picked daffodils for a penny a stem. Ma didn't like us doing that job because it required using paring knives, which we angled at forty-five degrees into the earth to sever the stem. She deemed that job too dangerous, worried one of her kids would come home with a missing digit. And what would the Americans think of her then?

By late August, when picking season tapered off, there were still cherry tomatoes that we followed into fall. We rejoiced then, at that first perceptible drop in temperature and days that darkened faster, because that marked the end of picking season, of mud-caked knees, knotted lower backs, and fingers alternately stained red, blue, and deep green.

Ma liked working at Kenagy's best because Mrs. Kenagy paid us in cash, which she dispensed in a cartoonish blur of action from a wooden ticket booth set between the parking lot and the fields. Ma liked watching Mrs. Kenagy lick her thumb and reach into a plastic bank bag to count out crisp bills, which she pressed into the workers' hands, looking them in the eyes with a slight nod as if a fine deal had just been made.

I liked Mrs. Kenagy, too. She balanced herself on the back of a moving farm truck on the last day of picking season and passed out milky-sweet, delicious Creamsicle bars to all the workers. I followed her with the other kids like she was the Pied Piper. We ran and laughed and reached out for a treat as the truck inched across the field, coughing exhaust and dust in our faces. I crave those bars to this day, especially when it's blazing hot and there's work outside to do.

Our house had a tabletop rotary phone with a long cord capable of strangling all of us kids in one go. It was plugged into a jack in the kitchen and when it rang, the whole house shook. Ma always called out to Sin to answer since she knew the most English. Sin would answer and then call back out for either Ma or Pa, who would shuffle over from whatever corner of the house they were in. The person on the other line, if they were still there, had to then parse through my parents' broken syntax and the accent they would never fully lose, even forty years later.

One evening after dinner, one of the farmers in Independence, a town even smaller than Corvallis, wanted help in his fields. We got a lot of calls from farmers each summer, once they heard about us. Ma operated as our manager, so these particular phone calls exclusively went to her. She decided where, when, and for whom we would work. She made the kind of collective family decisions that Pa might have made if we had been in Cambodia. If he felt upset by the shift in responsibilities, he never said. He learned to sidestep some things in order to just keep moving forward. He was occupied with his own jobs, so he left Ma to take full command of our summers.

She operated with the kind of street savvy that maximized our profits and minimized our exposure to unkind or unfair farmers.

"Wayne Anderson says your kids work hard," Mr. Jacobsen said. "We could use some extra help out here."

"Oh, thank you," Ma said, beaming into the phone. She loved it whenever someone complimented her kids. "How much you pay?"

She could tolerate farmers who were mean but not the ones who paid poorly.

"Same as Wayne," Mr. Jacobsen said. "Whatever he pays, we'll pay."

Mr. Anderson paid twenty cents per pound; in a single morning, a good morning, and if we were picking blue crop, which came quickly and cleanly off the stem, we could each pick 250 pounds by lunch. As a family, we could haul in a full ton of blueberries a day if we worked straight through, from sunup to sundown, my mother pocketing five hundred dollars in cash at the end of each day.

Given the choice of letting us kids have the rest of summer off or extending picking season at another farm, Ma extended the season. The next morning, we drove twenty-two miles on Highway 99 toward Salem. We worked those fields for several days, as hard and fast as we did at all the other farms, filling up Mr. Jacobsen's shed.

One evening, Mr. Jacobsen called to say he was changing how he paid, moving to hourly; he offered us minimum wage.

Ma frowned when she hung up and told us the news. Minimum wage back then was $2.90 per hour. We had only worked at places that paid by the pound, which was one of the reasons why Ma and Pa liked America. The harder you worked, the more you earned, the better quality of life you could buy for yourself. Easily, we picked fast enough to triple minimum wage. Mr. Jacobsen must have done the same math Ma did.

So Ma came up with a plan.

"Go slow," Ma said, a big grin spreading sweet as coconut cream across her face. "Pick for fun, just enough to make two dollars and ninety cents, then you can play or rest under the shade and wait until the next hour."

I thought Ma was the cleverest person in the world, just like the animals in the stories she told us late at night.

"I won't be cheated by someone else," Ma said in instances like these. "We have to work hard and live smarter."

A few weeks later, Mr. Jacobsen reverted back to paying by the pound when he didn't get enough berries to fill his shed. We picked up the pace again.

In the fields, my family wore secondhand jeans with sticky set-in stains, plaid shirts chewed and grimed at the cuffs, and galoshes that revealed tube socks, doubled up for comfort, with holes in the toes. Each morning was the same. We got dressed, reported to the kitchen for breakfast, and loaded into the car, zombie-like and without complaint, not because we enjoyed working, but because we understood in basic terms that this was our life. During the school year, we played the same sports, complained about the same teachers, and ate the same nachos sludged with orange cheese our friends did, but we understood we were different.

While our friends at school played various summer sports and went to Girl and Boy Scout and music camps, we woke at 5:00 a.m. most summer mornings, with a gentle scratch at our backs from Ma, who was up by 4:00 a.m. making our meals. She was the first to wake, the first to disperse our home's cold overnight air as her bare feet shuffled across the cold linoleum kitchen floor between stove and fridge to make our breakfasts and lunches in one go.

We left for the fields when it was still too dark to see anything besides our breath straining through the dense fog that clung to the valley and didn't lift until well after sunrise. It was so cold our teeth clattered, and the dew on the leaves soaked our sleeves as we reached into the strawberry bushes to claim the juicy red jewels. Ma said, "Keep moving to keep warm," and so we did.

Ma prioritized feeding her family above all else—the greatest demonstration of love in Khmer culture. Lunch was sometimes rice with stir-fried beef and pickled mustard greens, or a loaf of Franz white bread with packaged lunch meat. Ma prewashed and preportioned iceberg lettuce and sometimes tomato slices so we could build our own sandwiches. I rarely bothered washing my hands, too hungry and impatient to wait as my sisters poured tap water from a recycled plastic soda bottle to rinse their hands. I ignored the black fingerprints smudged on those nice, pillowy white slices of bread and the gritty crunch, plowing through my sandwich like I hadn't eaten for days.

More often, Ma packed us sardine sandwiches, which she called "survival food" because sardines and rice were all we had to eat on the boat when we left Cambodia. She used a loaf of thick French bread that she had dispatched one of us kids to get from the IGA supermarket the day before—at exactly 4:00 p.m., when the price was cut in half to fifty cents. Ma slit the belly of the bread and spooned canned sardines inside, the tomato sauce soaking the crust, then stuffed it with her own homemade carrot pickles, cilantro, and sriracha hot sauce. She counted heads and cut the resulting hoagie evenly, with a long serrated knife.

We did not starve in those fields. Ma made sure of it. But sometimes she underestimated our appetite, or tried too hard to be economical. I kept it to myself whenever I was still hungry after all the food was gone. There was no point in telling her. It would only break her heart.

I was always the first to finish my food, and I glanced around to my siblings and cousins longingly to see if anyone might leave me a crumb. No luck. Invariably, Ma would eat a few bites of her sandwich, announce she was full, and then pass the rest to me. My face lit up with joy as I nibbled away while my siblings glared at me for taking our mother's share.

Lunch lasted fifteen minutes, in the shade of the biggest bush if we were picking blueberries, or on the shady side of our car if it was strawberries, where you got to rest your back against a wheel if you were fast enough to call dibs. To sit for a minute and collect some of the coolness concentrated in the shade when the valley still held the heat of the day is a sensation that ripples through me even now—a moment of peace and stillness that I cling to.

In Corvallis, we never got the kind of heat other places get, the kind that smacks you in the face when you open the door. But when you spend enough hours roasting in the fields the way we did, the heat starts to hurt and the sun slaps a stubborn stain on the nape of your neck that doesn't fade until winter. That tan made us look even darker—a condition that persistently troubled Ma. Dark skin gave us away as the laborers we were. In Khmer culture, dark skin signaled you were so poor that you spent your days exposed to the sun. Lighter skin signified wealth, a life spent indoors, presumably with an office job.

"I won't let anyone look down on me," Ma said, even if it meant sacrificing comfort in order to uphold appearances.

It sullied a person's reputation to be so dark. For Cambodians, being light-skinned was praised and respected. Being light-skinned *and* fat was the ideal. Fat meant wealth, comfort, and power. Skinny signified poverty and deficiency, in health and home.

So, Ma implemented a ban on T-shirts during picking season. She insisted we wear long-sleeved plaid shirts with a popped collar and sombreros with a string strap loose beneath our chins so we were always shaded in those open fields. We wore this outfit every day, even as temperatures soared into the eighties and nineties.

Sometimes, the berry seasons overlapped, and our parents would shuttle my siblings and me across town from one field to the next. We worked until dusk brushed the fields in a half-light and there was a silence about the land. Time stood still before bunching up at the end of the day, when we hustled to fill the final crates and buckets. Those were long days, and hard. You could hear a parade of feet drag like bricks across the gravel lot to our penny-colored Toyota Corolla, where all of us kids jammed into the back seat and Ma went up front, sitting shotgun next to Pa behind the wheel, and we peeled out toward home as the last light drained from the cobalt sky. It was beautiful, there in the Willamette Valley, but most of the time we were too tired to look.

Early on, when I was too young to distinguish ripe berries from unripe, my siblings were the ones who trudged quietly from our car to the weigh station to collect empty crates and a crate cart while I stayed hooked to Ma's hip, pressing my face into her coat collar to keep my nose warm and to breathe all of her in. Her smell was of damp wool and Folgers instant coffee with cream and sugar, and beef Top Ramen noodles, which she made us for breakfast because it was fast and cheap and she could bulk it up with thinly sliced sirloin and julienned green beans. Those smells fused together into a cloying funk that comforted me. Hers was the smell of home. A scent that seems to have somehow bonded permanently to her skin because when I sit near her now, I swear I can still smell it.

When I was too little to reach across a strawberry row on my own, I crouched close to Ma, the mud-caked wheel of her crate cart clipping my ankle as Ma nudged it forward. She taught me how to search for the biggest, ripest strawberries, and I held up each of my finds victoriously, like I'd plucked a ruby from the mines. When she shifted, raising the metal handle of the cart and scooting it and herself forward, it was my signal to shift, too. We moved like this day after day, for what would turn into years, inching toward daybreak and better light together.

The first thing I learned in the fields from Ma was how to contribute to our new lives in America, how to be worthy of my family.

She taught me, by the simple fact of who she was, about the dignity of labor, about enduring and working together and keeping quiet if I was cold or hungry or hurting, because to complain was to admit one's weakness in a family firmly fixed in survival mode. I learned that family, not feelings, comes first. That if one of us failed, we all failed, and if one of us succeeded, we were all successful. In that collective mindset, borders blurred.

"One chopstick is easy to break," she said. "But a handful of chopsticks together is strong. It is harder to break." I kept my head down and my hands rummaging through vines, our family moving across the fields as a unit.

She taught us that the world could be cruel, and it was our job to put our best selves forward. Which is why Ma was not only diligent in keeping us from getting too dark, she also was obsessive about keeping us clean.

We were newcomers in Corvallis, and Ma tried to ensure that no one in town had a reason to judge us. At the start of summer one year, she issued each of us a pair of yellow latex gloves to protect our hands from the deep pink stains of strawberry juice. We wore those gloves religiously until the farmers complained and said we couldn't use them anymore, told us the plastic was bruising their crop, which made Ma huff in displeasure. Most of the time, we were picking juicers anyway, so what did it matter what the fruit looked like when it was about to get ground down into pulp? But she couldn't or wouldn't protest, lacking either the guts or enough English words to state her case, so Ma invented other ways to keep us clean.

She figured, if bleach could whiten our father's undershirts, why not try it on our skin? I can still smell the noxious fumes rising out of a bowl of 50–50 water-and-bleach mix that Ma made us soak our hands in before the first day of school, to wash away the last stubborn hints of summer. Tomato tar was the hardest to remove. It left a film on our fingers and under our nails, tacky as superglue. Ma told us to be careful not to splash any of the bleach mix on our clothes, and be sure to rinse our hands thoroughly afterward because the bleach would burn our skin. No matter how hard I rinsed, the flesh between my fingers would turn scaly and flake off days later anyway. It was a necessary misery in Ma's mind. She was terrified of being judged, locked within a Khmer culture where children are a direct reflection on their parents. If my siblings and I were viewed as "dirty," it meant that Ma had failed as our mother to keep us clean. So we plunged our hands dutifully into the bleach.

The fields attracted mostly immigrant families like ours—Khmer families from other parts of the Willamette Valley, a few Mexican families, even a Russian family. We competed mostly against the Khmer families for the best rows and the most berries picked. At the end of the day, my mother chatted casually with the other mothers at the weigh station, comparing notes and feigning modesty as Ma proudly fanned out our fully punched weigh tickets, plucking hanging chads from the cards.

"If we do something, no matter what, we do it to win," Ma said, as we piled into the car. "Be number one!"

There were white kids, too, bused in from nearby towns. I never understood who paid for the buses and why, because the kids acted like those fields were a playground. They got into berry fights and took long, lounge-about lunches. They sneered at us, complained we were taking all the empty blueberry buckets. My siblings and I sneered back, and continued picking for our living.

Desperation was the divide that separated us from the white kids. For them, leaving the fields at the end of the day empty-handed had no bearing on whether they would have food on their tables. For us, leaving the fields each day with a pocketful of cash meant we might one day catch up to where the white kids and their families already were—safely ensconced in the middle class.

It was one thing to be different from the white kids. But to be different from the other kids in my own family was a deeper humiliation. The pollen that polluted the summer air was murder on my lungs, triggering asthma attacks that left me wheezing for hours. Out in the fields, Ma snapped a blue medical mask over my face to keep the allergies at bay. Ma wore a mask, too, because she suffered from hay fever. Even though I had company wearing that miserable mask, I still protested.

None of my siblings had to wear it, which made me jealous.

"You're different from them," she said when I protested. "You're vulnerable to illness."

"I don't need it," I said, swatting her hands away as she approached me from behind, holding the elastic band of a mask taut in her fingers.

"Don't be stubborn, Put," Ma said. "Do you want to suffer?"

With or without that mask, I felt dejected. Once, when a group of the white kids saw me, one of the scrawny ones pointed and snickered, "The strawberries must be sick. She needs to operate quickly!"

The kids burst into peals of laughter as they stood at the top of my row. I heard them still laughing when they walked to their side of the field.

Ma must have heard and seen those kids, because the next day, she took a blue bandanna and tied it around my face, tight.

"Try this," she said as she cinched two ends into a knot at the back of my head.

I'd seen a few of the row bosses wearing handkerchiefs around their necks. To collect the sweat that drizzled down from their brows when the heat of midday bore down. I don't know if the handkerchief worked better to keep the pollens from entering my lungs, but I liked that I didn't stand out so much. At least I thought I didn't.

"Now she's robbing the strawberries!" a different white kid said as he slinked by.

I pulled the handkerchief down from my face so that it slung from my neck, the way the row bosses wore theirs. By the afternoon, I was wheezing so hard, Ma ordered me to go sit in the car.

That evening, when she saw how quiet I was, and aloof, she issued advice for me, loud enough for the rest of my siblings to hear.

"Don't bother with what the other kids think or say or do. Keep your head down. Ignore them."

I was in the family room with my siblings, and though my eyes were on the TV screen, my ears were tuned to Ma's evening advice channel. She said my siblings and I were not like the lazy American kids in the fields. She said those kids would not get far in life and that I should not expend any more energy on worrying about them. Then she concluded with the same prescription for a successful life she always gave—part plea and part warning.

"Gohn, aign camh rien," Ma said. Study hard. "Sralang bong pahon, mai ouerv." Love your siblings, your mother and father.

She repeated this particular pair of notions of working hard and loving my family so frequently over the years that they became primary impulses in me. The loyalty I learned to have for my family muted my ability to be loyal to myself.

I made decisions based not on what I wanted but on how my family would be impacted by my choices, how my actions would reflect upon Ma.

You lose track of who you are in this kind of upbringing. You are connected and defined by those who raised you, becoming the sum of your ancestors behind you and your elders beside you. There is no "I," my mother seemed to say in her teachings. Only "us."

Ma's need to keep a close watch on me rivaled my own need to be near her. Because of what she called my "weak constitution," she never let me stray too far. She worried I might have an asthma attack somewhere beyond the radius of fast help, and then what was the point of surviving a war?

But she couldn't keep me near forever. Once I was liberated by language and the ability to communicate at school, I ran rough and wild. Let loose onto the schoolyard, I could be counted on to collect scrapes, scratches, and bruises of various sizes. I played only one way: hard. Which made it easy to sort my clothes from my sisters' when the laundry was done. While my sisters somehow kept their clothes looking practically new, I worked my outfits hard. A pair of pants with holes at the knees. Mine. A purple dress with a grass stain on the ruffled hem. Mine. Shirts torn at the sleeve, mismatched socks, sweaters pilled at the ribs. Mine, mine, and mine.

After a while, my parents seemed to lose track of me in the mix of our lives and too many children. I played with boys, because they were always skidding at odd angles on the hunt for bugs, bark, or rocks—whatever latest acquisitions could elevate their home collections of specimens. Or, they would be competing to see who could climb the jungle gym fastest. I was good at these things—the hunting, the climbing—and the call to adventure compelled me more than dressing up baby dolls in miniature clothes. I came home with dirt on my shoes and clothes, in my hair.

Early one morning at the start of first grade, Ma helped fit a red dress with a gingham pattern and a pleated waist over my wiggly body. I hated dressing up.

"Why do I have to wear a dress?" I asked Ma.

"Because you need to look pretty for the pictures. Now hold still," she snapped.

"It's too tight," I whined as Ma gave a harsh tug at the neckline and zipped the back of the dress. I gasped at the sudden squeeze.

"You only have to wear it for one day," she promised.

I calmed down because I believed her, and harnessed my energy to get through the rest of the day in the scratchy dress and white stockings, so tight I was convinced every last breath would be squeezed from me before the day was done.

Ma tamed my unruly hair into two braids that she tied together with a red rubber band at the back of my head and ran the palm of her hands under the bathroom faucet before applying a little dampness against my hair to hold stray strands in place. Meanwhile, Chan had already gotten dressed and looked polished and perfect. She gathered her hair into a taut ponytail, using cotton scrunchies that matched the color of her dress.

Sin and Sope had already left for school, so I walked the four blocks to Wilson Elementary School with Chan.

At recess, some kids I didn't know were playing tag and I joined in, hoping to make friends. When the bell rang, and the kids dashed to class, I ran too, and caught the heel of a boy's black dress shoe mid-stride. I flew and fell flat on my face, skinning both hands and knees. I didn't know it yet, but I also scuffed my nose. A teacher pried me off the asphalt, dusted me off, and sent me on my way.

Except for a burning sensation at the tip of my nose, I was barely aware of my injuries when I smiled brightly into the camera for my class picture.

At home later that day, when Ma scanned me with her eyes, I knew I was in trouble.

"What happened?!" she asked, dragging me by the shoulder down the hallway back to the same bathroom where she had carefully dressed me in the morning.

She took a damp rag and pressed it against my hands, knees, and nose, and the pain that bloomed from that contact shocked me into tears.

"I was just playing with some kids and fell down," I said. "I was rushing to class."

I emphasized the last part, hoping she would pick up on the fact that I was actually in a hurry to go learn. She wasn't impressed.

"Why can't you play normal, Put, like your sisters? Do you see them coming home with rips in their clothes and blood on their bodies?" Ma admonished. "Why do you have to play so hard, gohn? Learn to be more like your sisters."

But even then, I knew I was manifestly unlike my sisters. I was more like my brother. I wore torn blue jeans and T-shirts and climbed trees when no one was looking. My brother and sisters called me "tomboy" and laughed out loud. Ma laughed along with them. Pretty soon, Ma started calling me tomboy, too.

But she didn't laugh at the scrape on my nose. She had made me perfect that morning. I had ruined my class pictures, and by extension, I put a gash in Ma's illusion of perfection.

She didn't talk to me for days. It was this kind of quiet violence I feared most.

In my class photos from the school year 1980–1981, there I am with the scuff on my nose, a flaw I could not conceal. But there is also an enormous smile on my face. Scuff or no scuff, I had just run around the playground free, having all the fun in the world.

I was too young then to understand that what people thought about us mattered so much to Ma, that guarding our family reputation was a habit she watered and pruned until it grew so big it took over our lives. It was easy enough to erase the picture of our poverty with a 50–50 mix of water and bleach. But how could we hide the fact that we were refugees learning to live in another country? That we occupied two worlds and the hardest thing was to figure out where and how we fit in?

I learned early on that perfection was the price for Ma's affection. And so I strove to be the best student, the fastest picker, the most dutiful daughter. I didn't question Ma. I did as I was told. And that first tang of shame that came from falling in the playground and skinning my nose stayed stuck, like the Sunday psalms we murmured at church, at the back of my throat.

Every fall, I waited for Halloween. When I was in the first grade, I had begged my sisters to help turn me into Popeye. I paraded around our house, flexing my biceps with a plastic pipe hanging from my lip. In the second grade, I was the Fonz, wearing Pa's black dress shoes, even though I was swimming in them, and pulling one of Pa's white T-shirts over my skinny frame. I had a jacket and a switchblade comb that I slid in my back pocket and produced the minute a homeowner opened their door and we shouted, "Trick or Treat!"

Even though I had to state my identity after combing back my hair in elaborate strokes, I still grinned with pride. I was the Fonz. I felt spectacularly cool.

Long after Halloween was over, I still carried that switchblade comb in my back pocket and pulled it out in dramatic fashion to comb my hair. I laughed out loud at how funny I was. When I did this in Ma's kitchen, she shooed me out.

"Tomboy!" she snapped at me. "Go do that somewhere else."

I pushed past her through the saloon doors and went outside to find my brother. Having a bike meant that I could

keep up with Sope, who rode a red BMX bike Ma and Pa had
bought new at the PayLess store near our house. Ma rarely
bought us toys. She said we didn't have the money. But when
we moved to Ironwood Avenue, she bought Sope a new bike,
because he was a boy, and she bought me a used bike from a
garage sale, because I was the baby. Chan and Sin eventually
got their own bikes, too, but only after protesting.

Sope rode his BMX all the time, popping wheelies and
riding up and down bark piles. I followed, in hot pursuit,
more interested in the games he and his neighborhood bud-
dies played than hanging out with my sisters.

I rode and rode after him, until a new family moved in
down the street, and a girl with blond curls who lived there
caught my complete attention.

She had a bike, a strut, and a stutter. She wore what I
wore: blue jeans, T-shirts, tennis shoes. When she played
basketball, baseball, and wall ball, she played better than the
boys. When she walked, I sometimes wondered whether her
pigeon-toed stride made her faster or better or cooler than
the rest of us on the block. And when she spoke, she talked
tough, even though her stutter threatened to suffocate every
word she uttered. It made me like her, before I understood I
liked her. I was seven years old. Watching her I wondered, was
she a tomboy, too?

Amber McMichaels was my same age and lived with her
family where our street T'd with hers. She presided over a
younger sister and brother. All three were towheads, the kind
of blinding blond that made you wonder whether they had
come from a sun-dusted state like Florida or Arizona. I never
knew. They just appeared one day on bikes in our neighborhood, ordinary as plum blossoms.

Soon, we started walking to school and eating lunch

together, and playing in each other's backyards. When neighborhood bullies mocked Amber's stutter, she shouted back: "I-I-I-I'm g-g-g-going to k-k-k-kick your ass!" These were not just words. She would chase the offender down the street, grip him by the collar, and start kicking his ass, literally.

I felt something for Amber that I couldn't name then, something urgent and deep. I didn't understand it, why I liked her differently than I liked my other friends, why I liked her better. I was confused. So I tucked my feelings away and just stayed friends with Amber. We rode our bikes together and I stood back and watched, afraid and awed, as she whipped every last ass of our neighborhood bullies.

◻ TOO AMERICAN

I was too young and too absorbed in my own dramas to know how stressful starting over was for Ma and Pa. As they hurried from jobs to home to English classes and night school, exhaustion nipping at their heels, I dreaded the start of every new school year.

I braced for every homeroom teacher to trip on my name, forcing me to poke my head up and enunciate it loudly for everyone to hear. I slunk in my seat at the inevitable jeering from my classmates that followed. Each year the same desire crossed my mind to change my name to something familiar and ordinary, like Patty.

Despite my growing English vocabulary, certain things made me know I was different.

In Mrs. Yoshimura's class, we started each day with a hand over our hearts, our bodies straight and tall as we faced the American flag hanging in the corner. I had learned the Pledge of Allegiance the previous year, and was proud to be able to recite it.

As I began the pledge, I spied Mrs. Yoshimura weaving her way through the desks and before I understood what was happening, she was upon me, her body bent toward my ear, her hot breath on my face.

"You don't have to say the pledge if you don't want to, Putsata," she whispered, and walked away.

She went back to her desk, where she picked up where she had left off in her own recitation, leaving me hot with embarrassment. Why had she singled me out?

Looking back, I see it for what it was, an intended kindness on her part. But at the time, it was confusing. She hadn't whispered into any other students' ears. Was I not American?

It was then when I began to wonder where I came from, why I was so different.

In third grade, I marveled one day at the magic of the eraser to disappear any mistakes I made on the page. To my eight-year-old mind, if the rubber eraser could wipe clean mistakes on my worksheet, then perhaps it could wipe away my color. I put the eraser to my arm and began rubbing vigorously until Mr. Nordyke made his way over to me, his eyebrows arched in concern. He whispered in my ear, "Don't do that, Putsata."

So I stopped, feeling ashamed for being caught trying to erase myself rather than work on my handwriting. Later that day, when I looked at the spot I tried to rub clean, there was nothing there but a red welt that went back to being brown.

If I could not hide the color of my skin, I also could not hide the fact that my family was poor and couldn't afford the latest fashions my friends wore. Ma let us buy exactly two back-to-school outfits each fall. I worried my classmates would notice that I did not own enough clothes to wear a different outfit every day of the week. Instead, I alternated between one pair of slacks and one pair of jeans, with tops swapped with my sisters. I also worried someone would notice the reason I constantly tripped in the hallways was that my shoes were a size too large, which was the way Ma insisted on buying them, because we were growing quickly and she didn't have the money to keep up.

And then, at the end of each school year, when the friends I had managed to make excitedly prattled about the summer camps they would attend, I lied. I said my summer would be low key, hanging out at home in front of the TV, even though I knew just as soon as the last school bell rang, I'd be slumped down in the dirt in the strawberry fields. It was hard enough to navigate the social hierarchy of jocks, nerds, geeks, and loners. To be a refugee kid in a nearly all-white town only doubled the isolation.

Our parents sent us to Sunday school at Calvin Presbyterian, one of two churches that had sponsored my family to come to Corvallis. I dreaded wearing a dress and sitting in those backbreaking wooden pews while Pastor Peter Hutton droned on about eternal life by salvation. But going to church was never presented as a choice. It was a chance for my parents to repay the church for helping us start our new lives.

"The church members found us jobs and they brought so much food that filled our fridge," Ma said. "I felt we owed them something. So I let my kids go to their religion."

Ma's and Pa's lives revolved around the Buddhist notion of sang khun. An act of kindness triggers an obligation to repay that kindness in spades. This principle would take root at the center of my life and grow to crowd out every other notion I had of being good and worthy. I grew up Presbyterian because my parents felt they needed to sang khun.

My siblings and I sat politely in the pews and mumbled our way through the psalms, which felt like loose rocks leaving my lips, chipping teeth along the way. Whenever Pastor

Hutton called upon his congregation to join him in prayer, I bent my head and closed my eyes along with everyone else. I wasn't very good at praying, so I spent the prayers with one eye open, spying on the families who sat in clusters, three generations in a row. I wondered whether one day, I'd bring my future husband and kids here, too. Whether I would spend my whole life in Corvallis the way so many members of our church did.

But there was also this: my siblings and I were the only nonwhite members of our church. We were and always would be the obvious absence or presence in a predominantly white town. That meant we could never skip out on Sunday service without being noticed.

Meanwhile, Ma and Pa stayed at home and lit incense and prayed to the devadas as they spoke to our dead ancestors, asking for good fortune and good health.

Ma and Pa were willing to sacrifice some things for the sake of assimilating, but they drew the line at their own religion. For them, Buddhism went beyond belief; it was how they ordered their lives. They strived to live correctly, to make merit so they would be reborn with virtue in the afterlife. They believed in karma and reincarnation, while my siblings and I were asked to pray to a white guy on a cross to grant us entry into heaven. When I finally understood that the Lord, if you believed in him, would provide, I began praying vigorously—for Fun Dip and Tootsie Pops, and toys and games. It never worked. So I stopped praying and put my faith in other things, like the stories Ma told me.

Rice was the shared religion in our house, and we ate it devoutly with our mother's stir-fries and vegetable-dense soups—spinach with Cambodian-seasoned pork meatballs;

hot and sour soup with a flotsam of fish, tomatoes, and pine-apple; chicken curry with nubs of potatoes and carrots the same size as the stones we carried in our pockets down to the creek to sling at minnows skimming the surface.

Ma reigned over the rice pot, and whatever she made we ate, because it was delicious. But we loved American food, too. We still wanted to go to Pizza Hut and Arby's because that's where our friends ate. And all of us knew that fitting in was a careful calculation of what you wore, who you hung out with, and where and what you ate.

When McDonald's finally arrived in town, it was the event of all events. We played rock, scissors, paper, designating the loser as the one to climb out of our bedroom window after our 8:00 p.m. curfew to sprint over to McDonald's to get those crisp apple pies still piping hot in their cardboard sleeves. It was a luxury we risked a chopstick beating for. We scrounged enough coins from our father's pockets or from selling empty soda cans collected from the workers in the fields to fund our apple pie addiction, consuming more of those deep-fried treats than our hearts were made to handle. And if my parents knew, if they guessed we were sneaking out, they didn't say. We were all locked in the conspiracy of becoming American together.

We spoke English to each other and to our parents, even as they answered us back in Khmer—a language I always thought sounded sad and pretty, and came into my ears like a beat I could tap two fingers to. By second grade, the cadence of my mother tongue, all those Khmer words I once knew, began to dissolve, until the only language I spoke was English, having perfected jutting out my bottom jaw and rolling my tongue to form the "r" in "Robert" and "rabbit." It never occurred to me, until I went to Cambodia in 1990, that I was something more than American, that it was possible to be more than one thing.

When I was older, and strangers asked me, "Where are you from?" I told them, "Corvallis." Because, up until age sixteen, when I went to Cambodia for the first time, Corvallis was the only home I knew. I knew the person asking was angling for an origin, something to explain my name and the color of my skin. Strangers would say, "But your English is so good." I agreed. I often thought it was better than theirs and sometimes said so. I shut down pushy people by saying my parents were from Cambodia. I didn't say I was Cambodian. Back then, still desperate to fit in, I distanced myself from a country that had flashed dimly in the background of my life.

By the time I started fourth grade, Ma started accusing me and my siblings of being too American.

"They're following America again," I'd hear her tell her friends on the phone if we begged to order pepperoni pizza or expressed a preference for hanging out with our friends rather than staying at home with our family. We were "following America" when we wanted name-brand clothes, or a Swatch watch, when we listened to U2 and Bruce Springsteen, and when we asked to have birthday parties or go on overnight school field trips.

Watching our transformation into American kids, Ma tried to sway us back to our Khmer side. In the evenings, when we were together in the family room fighting over which sitcom to watch, she made her demands.

"One of you, I want one of you to marry a Khmer," she said. "Decide among yourselves who it will be. I don't care who. I just need one."

Her words were part warning, part desperate plea. All of

us kids would be marooned on the brown brocaded sofa in the family room, half listening to Ma and half tuning in to our favorite evening sitcom, *Diff'rent Strokes.*

"We're not old enough to get married," Chan said.

"Why do you want us to marry a Cambodian when we live in America?" Sope added.

I chimed in, forming a united front with my siblings against our mother: "We still have school!" I chirped.

Ma persisted through our protests as Sin aimed the remote control at the TV screen and scrolled mindlessly through the dozen or so cable channels we had to catch a few minutes of other sitcoms.

"You children, what the hell do you know," Ma hissed, swearing whenever she got too frustrated with us. "In Cambodia, they marry young in arranged marriages. Girls don't have a choice."

We all turned to Ma, our brows arched in disbelief. Being forced to marry a stranger was beyond my comprehension. Everything in America was about choice: how we dressed, what we ate, who we hung out with at school.

Ma barreled on.

"I want one Khmer in-law who knows our culture, how to take care of parents when they get old. You children don't know anything. Don't put me and your pa into a nursing home when we get old. I'd rather die."

My mother believed that if one of her kids married a Khmer, it greatly reduced her chances of ending up in a nursing home because Cambodian people did not believe in sending elderly parents away but rather took them in and cared for them until they died. More than that, Ma wanted us to marry someone Khmer as insurance that we would maintain a connection to our culture.

Living in a country that was not her own, Ma sheared off so many corners of her Khmer identity that she clung, stubbornly, to the few loose strands she could control, like food and Buddhism. And, if she could, her children's marriages.

For Ma, an arranged marriage was the ultimate form of cultural preservation, and a necessary strategy for continuing the family line. With its weeklong lineup of rituals and rites, a traditional wedding would allow Ma to cement her identity as a Khmer mother in the community.

So desperate was Ma to salvage the custom of arranged marriages in America that she resorted to bribery.

"Who wants money?" she asked one night, and we turned to her at once, our ears bending toward her words.

All of us did. When we were growing up, Ma never gave us any of the money we earned picking berries. So when she offered to pay us if we agreed to an arranged marriage, she suddenly had our complete attention.

"Whoever gives me a Khmer son-in-law or daughter-in-law," Ma said, "I'll give them money."

When we asked how much, she was vague and refused to name an amount. So we snickered, rolled our eyes, and swiveled our heads back to our TV shows.

I didn't know why Ma was so eager to arrange a marriage for one of us kids. It sounded like a weird concept to me, to marry someone you did not choose for yourself.

My ideas of marriage were shaped by the romances I saw play out on *Days of Our Lives* and *Dynasty*, and later, when I was a teenager, as I watched my friends grow giddy when they heard that a boy liked them.

I didn't get that same thrill when I heard that Ethan Hauser in my homeroom class liked me. I thought maybe I just didn't like him. Maybe there were better boys. Or maybe I just wasn't old enough to like anyone. I didn't know then that there were things I hid from myself.

My sisters and I understood, by the things Ma told us and taught us, that as Cambodian daughters we were fated for only one thing: we would grow up, get married, and raise kids. Like she did. Like all the generations of Khmer girls before us did. I was terrified of deviating from that path, terrified of making the wrong move and causing my mother so much anguish it would do her in.

My sisters somehow let our mother's accusations and disappointments dissolve from their lives. As an adult, when Chan was invited early in her career in academia to speak at an out-of-state education conference, leaving her new husband behind at home, Ma didn't mince words.

"Only prostitutes travel alone," Ma told her. "You're married now, Chan. Khmer girls don't act that way."

Chan was unfazed.

"Well, we're not in Cambodia," Chan told our mother.

And when Sin announced after college that she planned to move to Nebraska with her boyfriend, who later became her husband, my mother turned her back and sobbed.

"It shouldn't be like that," she told Sin. "Khmer girls stay close to their families."

It was improper, Ma said, for Khmer girls to live with their boyfriends.

My sisters continued to cross lines that, for a long time, I was too terrified to even approach, worried I would upset our mother. But I was in awe of my sisters for being unafraid to live their lives. I hated that it hurt our mother to see her children behave in ways she found morally unacceptable, but at the same time, I was rooting for my sisters, knowing that their willingness to push the boundaries might open opportunities for me to assert myself, too.

Even though Ma accused us of following America, she was also following America. She wore bell-bottoms with turtleneck knit sweaters and had her hair cut and permed at the Perfect Look salon, near the IGA market, where Chan's winning coloring contest Easter bunny was once prominently taped to the window. Ma was the first in our family to get full-time steady work, and the first to introduce our family to foods like lasagna, meat loaf, and roast beef sandwiches, which she cooked on weekends. She cut coupons, learned to quilt, and pushed her daughters to do well in school. And she taught us the value of an education, that if we had a degree, we could land better jobs than scrubbing toilets and washing dishes, like she and Pa had.

That she wore pants and knew how to drive was not in itself remarkable, but it was astonishing given where she came from. Women in Cambodia don't do any of the things my mother did, something I learned when I first visited our homeland. But we lived in America—a situation Ma also exploited to her best advantage.

She pushed the limits of how to behave, toeing her way to the margins of cultural norms for women in America, like driving and having a job outside the home, but somehow still preserving a strident fidelity to our Khmer culture. It was a fuzzy line to straddle, for her and for us.

We were all of us American. The difference was a matter of degrees. Cambodia was a mention and a meal, it was a language so lyrical it sounded like birdsong. But it was never fully mine.

◘ BLUE LETTERS

For two full years after we moved into our new house in 1978, my family had something close to happiness. Two years when the tragedy of Cambodia was still unknown. Two years before our lives, and the number of people in it, would shift once more. Two years before the first blue letter appeared in our mailbox.

Pa was the one who fished it out, an airmail express envelope, weightless as a dried maple leaf, postmarked Thailand. His hand trembled, like he was holding an explosive, when he brought it into the house.

In 1979, the war in Cambodia ended. A trickle of news filtered out about the horrors that had unfolded over the course of four brutal years. While my family was picking berries in the fields of Corvallis, our relatives were harvesting rice and digging irrigation canals as part of Communist leader Pol Pot's plan to turn Cambodia into the rice capital of the world. His plan depended on slave labor, forcing my relatives to work without pay and on a starvation diet of one cup of watery rice soup a day. Nearly two million people perished. Many of my relatives were among them. Ma and Pa were on a mission to know who was still alive.

Pa made a flyer in 1980, pasting a photograph of himself in one corner and Ma in the other, with a brief description of our family and our address in Oregon. He printed the flyer in bulk and recruited the help of a missionary in Portland, who had planned to visit the refugee camps along the Thai-Cambodian border, to distribute the one hundred copies he had made.

The first letter arrived that same year.

"Brother," the letter writer stated, "do you remember me?"

Uncle Chamroeun, my father's half brother, wrote in detail about all of our relatives he knew who had died and listed the ones he believed were still alive. He wrote of his own struggle to survive the genocide.

Ma gathered all of us kids into the family room so that Pa could read it out loud. I remember the moment only vaguely. I remember with greater clarity what happened next.

There was a shift, dramatically swift. Ma stopped filling our home with furniture and started filling it with family. In 1981, Ma and Pa helped sponsor Uncle Chamroeun, his wife, and his daughter to immigrate to America. Two years later, in 1983, my cousin Motthida, orphaned when her parents died in the war, arrived with Aunt Vuthy, whose husband was led away by Khmer Rouge soldiers after he got caught stealing a potato for his hungry, pregnant wife; she lost the baby, too. A few years after that, in 1986, my father's mother, Yay Yeim, was the last passenger to step off the airplane at Portland International Airport, toting only a wicker basket that contained her betel nut and a pair of worn-out plastic flip-flops that had somehow held up through a multiday journey through the jungle to reach the Thai border.

Our relatives came through our front door hungry and haunted. Ma seemed to live in the kitchen full-time, dashing from her mortar and pestle on the counter to the stove, where she stirred enormous pots of soup.

I thought it was fun, to have so many new family members in our lives. By then, Cousin Pi had gone back to live with his mother. Motthida filled in behind him and came to live with us permanently. Yay Yeim stayed, too.

From my relatives, we learned bits and pieces about what had happened to them in the genocide. And then a movie made clear the depth of the horrors. In 1984, after Mo joined our family, Pa drove us to a movie theater in a Portland suburb, near where Aunt Vuthy shared an apartment with Grandpa Sin. I danced around the house with anticipation, eager to experience the cinema for the first time.

Our parents told us we were going to see a film about Cambodia called *The Killing Fields*.

We sat in a single row, and when the lights came down and the first images flashed onto the screen, I was captivated.

The movie chronicled the life of a Khmer journalist and fixer for *The New York Times* who was caught in the genocide. He ultimately escaped, fleeing through the jungles of Cambodia to reach the border of Thailand. In one scene, where the protagonist, Dith Pran, catches a gecko that he will later gulp down to supplement the Khmer Rouge's starvation diet of rice soup, I felt something inside me sink with despair. And in another scene, during his daring escape, I gripped the slim movie chair armrests as Pran tripped into a muddy field of skulls and bones. I registered the shock and terror on Pran's face and felt the chill he emitted on-screen.

When the movie ended, my siblings and I filed out of the dark theater and schlepped toward the car. I felt angry, sad, betrayed by our parents. Nausea pushed up my throat as the theater doors flung open onto a lamplit parking lot and we made our way to the Corolla. I leaned against it, waited for our father to unlock the doors, and felt like we'd just staggered out of a car crash.

On the drive back home to Corvallis, a feeling came at once, so powerful it shocked me. I was furious at my parents for taking us to watch a nightmare that was true, not knowing that they were reeling, too.

It was as if we knew almost nothing about Cambodia and then suddenly knew everything all at once. Mo was a part of our family now, having fled an awfulness that lived in her solemn eyes. And then there was this movie, depicting a world that lacked humanity. And that world belonged to us.

The onslaught of information jolted me to my core. This was Cambodia? Why didn't they tell us?

My siblings were stunned silent, too. We never discussed the film as a family, nor did my siblings and I ever talk to each other about what we saw. I couldn't believe it was real. And I couldn't know then that the story I watched unfold on the movie screen is the story I would come to hear, hundreds of times over, from nearly every Khmer person I would meet. A difficult and profound realization struck me at once: I come from this, an entire nation of survivors.

I felt something even then, being witness to someone's life story on the screen, that I could not name, some flicker of emotion inside of me. Why was I alive when so many Cambodians died? I did not know that this was the beginning for me, that what I felt leaving that movie theater was the first sprout of survivor's guilt, shooting its way through the dark.

Two years after we watched *The Killing Fields*, my grandmother, Yay Yeim, came through our door. Much like Dith

Pran, my grandmother had trekked across Cambodia and across the Thai border before coming to America. Unlike Pran, she was seventy-six when she did this. For five days, she crossed jungles and mountain ranges thick with understory and infested with land mines, tigers, and Khmer Rouge soldiers. She hired young village men—with money my father sent in advance—to carry her on their backs when her legs gave out and her feet, clapping in a pair of tired plastic flip-flops crosshatched with cracks, began to blister. She eventually arrived at a Thai refugee camp, where my father tracked her down through a humanitarian aid agency and brought her to America.

My parents didn't tell us her story. I read it in the local newspaper the next day. It had always been that way with them, easier to tell a stranger difficult things than to be vulnerable in front of their own children.

They were a bridge—Yay Yeim and Mo—connecting me to a place that still remained largely in my imagination. But the world that my grandma and cousin came from was so much darker than the fables and folktales Ma told me. Their stories had to do with death and loss, with suffering and hardship. I couldn't wrap my head around them.

I tried for a long time to forget about *The Killing Fields*. We tried to adapt with two more people in our home. And in the coming years, our family would make room for dozens more. We made multiple trips to Portland International Airport to collect the latest round of relatives whom my parents sponsored. They emerged from their flights with the same weary expressions, their eyes vacant and cored. Those were genocide eyes. They had seen too much, held everything and nothing at once.

Ma added more scoops to her rice pot to feed the flow of

family. Just as Ma and Pa's house in Ream had brimmed with thirteen people at one time, so, too, did our house on Ironwood Avenue. Pa tried to alleviate the overcrowding by converting half of the garage into a fourth bedroom. My parents bought a Chevrolet Astro van, which they used to transport rice from the stores and relatives to and from doctor's appointments, English lessons, and job hunting.

More blue letters arrived. I turned eleven years old, then twelve, spending middle school passing notes in my homeroom class with a boy I liked and learning how to ride his skateboard. I turned thirteen and then fourteen. And the letters, like the years, kept coming.

At the time, I didn't fully understand what they were. I just thought they were evil for what they did to my mother. A couple of times, I tried to hide the letters between bills and supermarket circulars.

Each time, I watched as Ma sat at the kitchen counter and read the latest letter, holding a hand over her mouth to muffle a gasp gathering in her throat. I put a hand on her leg, tugged a little to let her know I was there. But she just walked to her bedroom and locked the door behind her.

I followed every time. Waiting, in case she called for a glass of water, or tissues. In case she needed me. I sat hunched at the end of our hallway and didn't leave until she stopped crying. I didn't need to press my ear to the door to hear it, because the sound was loud enough on its own. Her heart, breaking.

I asked Ma recently if she ever wanted to say no to the requests that came with every letter—please send money, please help me get to America. But she was too railroaded by guilt.

"I felt sorry for our relatives," Ma said. "They survived the

Khmer Rouge. I would rather suffer so that they didn't suffer anymore."

And that meant we suffered, too. More people meant more laundry, more dishes to wash, and more vegetables and meat to buy, prep, and toss into Ma's wok for stir-fries, Ma constantly calling on me and my sisters to come to the kitchen to help even though, most of the time, I just wanted to go outside and ride my bike. We gave up the space and privacy we had enjoyed for a few short years to accommodate our relatives, to make room for their stories and sadness, too, my siblings and I sharing our limited toys with younger cousins and teaching our aunts and uncles basic English. We understood that our relatives had come from someplace difficult, and we understood, when Ma nudged us to take our relatives to the store or the park to play, that our job was to help provide them a little bit of joy.

We continued to work in the fields, leaving footprints and seasons stacked behind. All the years of my youth passing in a blur of morning fog and afternoon haze, and my sense of duty to take away my mother's sadness deepening. Watching Ma, I learned the burden of fierce family love, that she would do anything to help our family and relatives, and I, as her daughter, would have to follow suit. As more family joined us, I understood that it was my job to help take care of my relatives so that none of us in our extended family would break. And this is how it happens, how you start to lose yourself behind the needs of others, spurred by survivor's guilt and driven by duty.

PART III

DOUBLE DISPLACEMENT

◻ THE RETURN

She roasted a twenty-five-pound turkey, and a spiral honey ham, and then she made scalloped potatoes, green beans, cranberry sauce, and rolls. By 1990, our family had grown so large with relatives from Cambodia that feeding all of us was no different than feeding the students she cooked for on campus: Ma made everything in vast quantities, stirring curry with a paddle in a pot big enough to bathe in.

It was Thanksgiving, and Ma made a point of initiating our relatives to the traditions of their new country.

My sisters and I, sometimes with Cousin Pi, spent the morning peeling russet potatoes the size of our shoes that Ma cut into quarter-inch-thick coins and then fanned into casserole pans for her legendary scalloped potatoes. She made an enormous salad and dispatched Pa to Richey's IGA supermarket for dinner rolls and jug wine. That was the American menu.

At the same time, she babysat an enormous pot of chicken curry on the stove and strained vermicelli noodles in the sink. Somehow, she also found time to make a hundred egg rolls, with help from my sisters, who had the patience and skill to roll them perfectly tight. My aunts brought sirloin steak salad and *num bao*, pastries filled with pork, and a huge pot of *samlaw caw-goh*, Cambodia's traditional beef stew with lemongrass and carrots. My sisters and I stayed for days in the kitchen with our mother, washing, cutting, stirring, slicing, while Sope watched TV. I sometimes snuck into the family room to watch with him, but Ma called me back to the kitchen. And if she ever saw all of us together, perched on the sofa, she swatted at us and we scattered like flies buzzing off a hunk of meat. She chased us to go do homework or housework. It hurt her eyes, she said, to see us sitting around.

Before we ate, Pa went around collecting small samples of each food Ma had prepared and placed these on a round metal tray with incense sticks and candles. Ma called us all into the living room, where Pa had set the tray on a hutch, and we prayed. Mostly Ma and Pa and our aunts and uncles and grandpa prayed. But as my father recited his Buddhist chants, calling on the spirits of the ancestors to come and join our feast, Ma glanced sideways at me, my mouth not moving, which Ma took to mean I was not praying like everyone else.

"Pray, gohn," Ma said. "Call upon your ancestors."

When I glanced to my right, I saw Mo's eyes closed tight, concentrating. Chan, Sin, Sope, and Pi stood respectfully, mouthing something to themselves. I did not know who they were praying for.

"I don't know who to call," I whispered to Ma.

Her glance turned into a glare, one that said I should know better, pained that I didn't.

"Call upon the dead, your relatives and ancestors who died."

I didn't know anyone who had died. But I knew Mo, and I knew that her parents had died because Ma tried to shut me up when I inquired one time why Mo got a new doll and my sisters and I didn't. So I called out to Mo's parents. I didn't know their names, so I just said, "Auntie and uncle, come join our feast," over and over again, my mouth moving and the pineapple monitoring me out of the corner of her eye.

We stood at the altar longer as the eighties turned into the nineties, the number of names of family members who had died in the genocide having multiplied. Pa became breathless when he called out so many names, and started to do them in rounds, pausing to catch his breath and careful not to miss anyone. Ma called out names, too, but her voice was garbled from weeping.

In the summer of 1990, when Ma had had enough of the blue letters, she switched gears. Instead of praying year after year, instead of waiting for more letters and more lists of the dead, she went on a mission: to locate the living.

Ma walked through the front door one evening, her white chef's smock stained with tomato sauce, and announced she was going home. Her voice was sure and urgent. An old worry buried in my bones bloomed and burst in my head. This is it, I thought. She's finally leaving us and won't come back.

My anxiety receded when Ma cast around for a volunteer among us kids to go with her to Cambodia. She was specifically recruiting for a sidekick capable of multitasking, someone who could help fill out travel forms because she didn't know enough English, and also help support Grandpa Sin and Yay Yeim, because they were going on the trip, too.

Sin and Sope had already graduated and left home by then, leaving me, Chan, and Mo. Ma reasoned that since my sisters were seniors, she didn't want to interrupt their studies and potentially delay their graduation.

So Ma chose me.

I was ecstatic. I had joined my high school's journalism class that year, and had dreams of one day becoming a foreign correspondent. Now, as I entered my junior year of high school, I'd have my first international byline with a story from Cambodia.

Chan and Mo understood Ma's decision, and though they didn't express outright happiness for me, they also didn't make me feel bad. Within a few years, Chan would take her own trip to Cambodia with Ma and Pa, and several more years after that, Mo would relocate to Phnom Penh to work for the United Nations.

Ma said she gave me the job of her travel partner because she was confident I could catch up easily with school. She also told me that since I was just a baby when we left Cambodia, she wanted me to make memories of my own in our homeland.

And then she told me the thing I had waited all my life to hear, the thing I desperately wanted to be.

"You're strong," Ma said.

After spending so many years hearing stories about how I was always sick, how I was so weak, I soaked up Ma's affirmation that I was strong, that I was clearly useful and had something to contribute to my family. She gave me a job I found critically important: to help my grandmother and grandfather carry their luggage.

At Portland International Airport, Pa sat off to the side with Ma, a plastic business envelope in his lap.

"When you get to Bangkok, this is the address of the U.S. embassy," Pa said, pressing a sheet of paper toward Ma. He had typed out a contact sheet that detailed our entire itinerary and important addresses and phone numbers of the rare relatives in Cambodia who had cell phones.

"Here's your hotel," he said, holding up another sheet. "Here's your ticket," he said, holding up a photocopy.

Ma nodded absently. She was barely listening, too nervous and excited to pay attention. She smiled and joked with Uncle Sovann, who had come to see us off. I loved Uncle Sovann. Before he and his wife had their own kids, he took me to their apartment in a Portland suburb on weekends and spoiled me with pizza at Chuck E. Cheese and candy-by-the-pound at the mall.

Now I leaned down to their five-year-old daughter, my cousin Malis, and cooed into her ear, "One day you'll go to Cambodia, too."

We flew into Phnom Penh on a twin-engine plane with rusted bolts and hinges. Mist spewed from the vents and made Ma clench my hand, a look of terror dashed across her face. This was not her first time flying. But it was the first time in fifteen years she was going back to her country.

I had been on an airplane once before, in 1975, when Ma carried me in her arms as we boarded a flight from Subic Bay, in the Philippines, to California, where my family got processed as refugees at Camp Pendleton Marine Base, near San Diego. But I was a baby then and had no memories of that trip. Now I was more curious than afraid about flying. I was nervous and excited, too, about going to a land that had existed, to me, in my mother's stories, in my relatives' sad eyes, in the cinema where I saw my first nightmarish glimpses of my homeland.

The plane sputtered and choked its way through the clouds so loudly on our descent into Phnom Penh that I could barely hear Ma when she suddenly let go of my hand and reached across my chest, pointing out the window.

"Look, Put, that's the Mekong River," she said.

I peered down onto a winding river the same mud color as the Folgers instant coffee Ma drank religiously each morning with a spoon each of cane sugar and powdered creamer.

They say the Mekong is the only river in the world that naturally goes both ways, reversing course twice a year, challenged to know which way to go when the monsoons create so much excess water that it has no choice but to flow from south back to north. And on this reversal, an entire country depends, pushing the river's carp and catfish up and down the waterway and giving the villagers who live along its shores something to survive on.

"Lots of fish in there, all kinds," Ma said. "Riel fish, that one they use for prahok. Catfish, big as my thigh."

Prahok, the stinky pickled fish that Ma used in great quantities as the base of almost every soup she made, and that made us kids pinch our noses and run around the house screaming in disgust. For Ma, prahok was the essential Khmer ingredient, and she had a glint in her eye any time she talked about it.

Ma began to fidget in her seat and take deep breaths as the flight attendant, a Laotian woman who seemed to choke on the Khmer words clanking out of her mouth, announced we would be landing soon. I kept my gaze locked on the land, my eyes adjusting to the alternating hues of brown, green, and gold. Endless acres of rice paddies spread out like squares of carpet patched with seams of irrigation ditches, and the golden spires of pagodas jutted up from between palm trees with fronds dancing in the breeze, lifting and rising like helicopter blades—a land cut through with the purest light.

It was all new and beautiful and I felt my heart surge with anticipation of the great adventure ahead.

It wasn't until we hit a furious patch of turbulence that

rattled our food trays and the luggage bins overhead that I turned to catch Ma weeping. She wiped a stream of tears with the corner of a white handkerchief that she had taken from a pocket of her Gucci purse.

"This is our home, Put," she said, honking hard into her handkerchief. "This is where we're from."

But how could I call a place home when I had never lived there? And if Cambodia was my home, then what was America?

When the plane landed, my uncle Sol waited for us at the bottom of the stairs, standing poised on the tarmac as we stepped off the plane. His job as a mechanic at the airport gave him the special privilege of going directly to the parked plane to retrieve us.

Stepping off the plane felt like entering another world. A wall of heat hit me so hard I stumbled backward and the supercharged sunlight scorched my eyes, making it hard to get a good look at Uncle Sol. He was my great-uncle San's son, the first of many relatives with whom Ma would reunite, and whom I would meet for the very first time. Ma fell into his arms like cut timber when she saw him. The last time they had been together, he was just a boy.

In the span of fifteen years, boys became men. Men became fathers. A new generation of family members waited to meet us.

Uncle Sol hired a minivan taxi to take us to our hotel in the city. On the way to Phnom Penh, we passed buildings pockmarked with bullet holes and mothers crouched in ditches bathing their babies in water the same murky brown as the Mekong River. I watched out my window as people rode bicycles with furiously flapping chickens strapped to the back rack; old men in plastic sandals and grimy shirts pedaled ladies home from the market, leafy greens and fishtails flopping from baskets cinched between their legs; and entire families of five or six people balanced on a single moped.

As we got closer to town, I watched a little girl, who looked maybe four years old, pick up a half-finished cigarette someone had tossed to the curb. She brought it to her lips and left it there, hanging. That was the first thing in Cambodia that struck me as terribly sad.

Uncle Sol installed us at the colonial Sakol Hotel, with its tall and narrow paneled French doors and trifold-shuttered windows. The hotel was anchored on the southeast corner of the Independence Monument, erected in 1953, when Cambodia won independence from French colonial rule.

In 1967, on one of the corners opposite the hotel, Ma had caught a glimpse of Jackie Kennedy on a state visit to Cambodia, riding in the back seat of a black Mercedes sedan, waving with a gloved hand. How elegant, these Americans, Ma had thought then. She never imagined she'd one day live among them.

Eight years later, in 1975, Khmer Rouge soldiers paraded around the same monument, pumping AK-47s into the air, and evacuating the city just as my family, living then on the southern coast of Cambodia, fled.

Uncle Sol helped me carry all of our luggage up narrow stairs to our second-floor room, twisting his body to accommodate the weight and awkward bulk. Between us we had packed eight suitcases, because the airlines allowed two free pieces of checked-in luggage per person. Five out of eight were filled with gifts for relatives—men's dress shirts Ma bought at JCPenney, sweatshirts, candy, Tylenol, aspirin, Oil of Olay, lipstick. One suitcase contained clothes for Ma, me, and Yay Yeim; one was filled with my school textbooks, notebooks, highlighters, and pens; and one was all for Grandpa Sin. Uncle Sol left our luggage in a nook near the door and said he would come back later.

He didn't come back, but a revolving cast of other family members did. Before we had a chance to relax and unpack, I heard footsteps echoing up the narrow stairwell. The door slowly inched open to reveal a montage of curious faces peering in at us, as if we were animals in a zoo. There was Ming Pheaktra, Uncle Sol's wife; Yay Leour, Uncle San's wife; and my cousin Beih. Ma pulled them into her arms before releasing them into our room. Everyone squeezed each other's bellies, cheeks, and arms before embracing in another round of hugs.

Outside our window, down below on the street, I heard a motorcycle rev and a loud male voice boom up to us, followed by the sound of someone crashing up the stairwell. I turned in time to see a tall, trim figure with smudges of black hair dye along neatly sheared sideburns fill the doorframe. He wore wire-rimmed glasses, black pants, a freshly ironed dress shirt, and a thick black belt cinched around his waist. His enormous sandaled feet slapped the ground with every step and his cologne shoved into the room right after him. He came through the door cackling and would later leave that way, too.

Ma turned to him, and her face lit up with a joy I hadn't seen before. She waded through a sea of arms and legs toward her uncle San, the man who raised her and whom she loved more than her own father.

"Pou," Ma said. Uncle.

"What's this I hear about Americans visiting Cambodia?" Great-Uncle San said, letting out a deep belly laugh.

He had been asking this question to everyone en route, from the guard outside the hotel to the front desk receptionist, before climbing the stairs to find us. He let out another loud cackle that practically made the room shake. "It's broadcast all over the news. I came to see with my own eyes who these Americans are."

He was a jokester, and I quickly learned that laughing out loud was the way he dealt with the memories of war.

Ma began sobbing into Great-Uncle San's shoulder, the way she did with Uncle Sol, with big, heaving gestures. Great-Uncle San's face creased with emotion as he held Ma and patted her on the back. Fifteen years of separation caved in on both of them.

"It's okay, gohn," he said, his face cramped with the effort of holding back his own tears. "No need to cry. We're all here now."

As I watched my mother fall apart in her uncle's arms, I instantly loved this man without even knowing him. I loved him because she did.

It took her a minute, but when she finally composed herself, Ma looked her uncle up and down, taking all of him in, assessing where the war altered his contours.

"Uncle, you're too skinny," Ma said, pinching for pounds around his waist that she struggled to find. He let out a ripple of giggles, as if someone had just tickled his belly.

"And you, gohn, you are so fat. Look at all the meat on your bones! Is everyone in America fat like this?"

Everyone laughed, including Ma, and she smiled at his compliment. In Cambodia, "fat" is high praise, a sign that you come from wealth. It would take me years to fully grasp this.

Throughout the day, more family members arrived and our room brimmed with bodies. First, second, and third cousins, aunts and uncles by blood and through marriage, close family friends. People leaned against every inch of wall, squatted on the tile floor, draped two or three on a single chair. Several joined me on the bed where I was taking it all in.

From across the room, I watched as Ma talked animatedly with her family members. They would talk fast and laugh long and everything was loud until it wasn't and the voices dimmed down to a near whisper and the tears welled up from the eyes of everyone squatting around Ma. I would see Ma start to weep then, and before I could pass her tissues, her weeping would turn into sobbing that shook her whole body.

All of this laughing and crying confused me, but I had no time to process. In the midst of all this, my cousins and aunts tried to feed me, as if I, not they, had been starved.

Each of our family members brought an assortment of fruits to our hotel room, most of which I'd never seen: thumb-sized bananas, lychees, mangoes, palm fruits. I quickly learned their names and what I liked best: mangosteens, with their soft, pearl-white flesh packed inside a hard black shell, and rambutans, the red oval fruit with its spiky, rubbery shell that looked like something from a child's toy box. There was fresh coconut that Ming Pheaktra took to with an enormous butcher knife, chopping off the top and jamming a straw in before passing it to me. There was jackfruit, with its soft perfume, and the infamously stinky durian, plus cassava and sugar cane peeled and cut into inch-thick rounds. I understood then that Ma being a food pusher was not merely her personality, it was the way of Khmer women.

All that fruit brought an overwhelming scent of sweetness into our room, compounding the weight of the already humid air.

In case we were still hungry, my aunts and cousins toted tiffins with steaming jasmine rice, watercress soup with tamarind, dried salted fish, and stir-fry chicken with ginger. One of my aunts brought two river lobsters, curried with shallots and lemongrass, which she spooned out for me to eat with Cambodia's ubiquitous rice soup, babar. I looked around as everyone looked at me, self-conscious about being the only one feasting as my aunt urged me on. I later learned that none of my relatives ever ate these lobsters because what I eventually gobbled down in three bites cost what most of my relatives earned in a month.

It was embarrassing, all this food. And I began to wonder if this was more food than some of them had seen in a long time. I spied a few of my younger cousins eyeing all the food, and when no one was looking, I repackaged some of it for them to take home.

Though I was somehow related to everyone in the room, they were all strangers to me, just as I was to them. So I sat at the edge of my bed and just waited to see who would come through the door next.

My cousins came to me, as did my aunts and uncles, to look closer and to try and speak to me. I was an oddity, an object on display. And though I reflected a sense of familiarity to them, I was manifestly unlike them. The only things I seemed to share with my relatives were the color of my skin and hair and the shape of my eyes and lips. I had arrived in Phnom Penh with permed hair, wearing Sin's faded Levi's and my brother's T-shirt, with a yellow Sony Walkman hooked to my hip that played a cassette on a loop of the Corey Hart song "Never Surrender." My cousins all had straight hair and wore sarongs, the traditional colorful skirts worn by both women and men.

Each person examined me, running their gaze over my face as if to find something of themselves in me. Cousin Khmau, who was roughly my age, pinched my cheeks so hard I thought my bottom jaw would fall right out. Aunt Cheam hugged me so tightly, I gasped for breath. Everyone touched my hair and chatted about me as if I wasn't there. Within the next several years, I would see many of these same faces again—in America. Part of my parents' mission was to bring to America as many survivors as they could who wanted to go.

"Does she speak Khmer?" one cousin asked another, glancing at me and then back at each other.

I could understand Khmer, because Ma spoke our language at home in Corvallis, but by then I was only speaking English. All my thoughts were in English. I regretted not taking Ma's offer of cash when I was younger to speak Khmer, embarrassed now that I could not communicate fully with my relatives.

"Why is she so skinny and her mom is so fat?" another cousin wondered. "They say she goes to school. All the girls in America go to school."

Then I spoke, and they all leapt back a little, startled.

"Doiche khneah," I said, pointing at the color on my arm, the shape of my eyes, the roundness of my cheeks. In my simple effort to connect us, I pulled up words from the depths of memory that I had never spoken but had heard Ma say and knew their meaning. "Same thing."

They repeated after me, "Doiche khneah, doiche khneah," and giggled into cupped hands and loose ends of their kramas.

Then, out of nowhere, Great-Uncle San was upon me. He was louder than anyone I had ever met before or since. He looked at me and chuckled, which made me chuckle, too.

"So this is what an American looks like," he said, and slapped me once on the back before sidestepping across everyone and walking back out the door, cackling all the way down the stairs to his motorcycle.

For the next few days, we barely left our hotel room as word of our arrival in Phnom Penh reached our relatives in the countryside. Some came by motorbike, others by over-stuffed taxis, and still others by two-wheel tractor pulling a wooden cart top-heavy with cargo: bags of rice and the passengers who slumped against them.

At night, after all our relatives left, Ma pulled thin strips of paper napkins supplied by the hotel, three or four at a time, from a plastic bag and pressed them to her wet eyes. But the napkins were so cheap and thin, like papier-mâché, that they would disintegrate in her fingers, leaving a shredded mess that littered the floor like confetti strewn across sidewalks slicked with rain. Sometimes Ma just stood in the bathroom and cried for a long time over the sink, washing her face as the tears streamed down.

When she came to lie down in the bed next to me, her eyes were red and swollen.

"I feel sorry for our family, what they went through," Ma said.

When I asked her what did, in fact, happen to our relatives in the war, she just rolled over and started crying all over again.

One day, we rented a minibus that quickly filled with family members who were cadging a ride back to their villages. We all endured the four-hour journey on bucket seats with torn cushions over broken roads to Chous village, where Ma was born. Though it was fewer than sixty miles, the minibus rarely went faster than twenty miles per hour because the roads, deeply scarred and ruined by war, were covered with craters big enough to swallow small cars.

After learning about so many relatives who died during the genocide, Ma insisted on holding a ceremony in her mother's village to honor them. She sent word in advance through another cousin for her sister, Aunt Samnang, to gather up the village women and make huge cauldrons of chicken curry and vermicelli noodles for a community feast. We brought several enormous plastic bags full of baguettes, nearly wiping out the morning supply of bread from a bakery in Phnom Penh that Ming Pheaktra said was the best.

When our minibus turned at an unmarked road between sprawling acres of rice paddies and began maneuvering the dusty road to Ma's village, children emerged like crabs from the rice paddies, screaming and clapping as they ran alongside us.

We stopped at a wooden house on stilts, its packed-earth front yard impeccably swept except for areas of dirt scratched by a roving band of chickens. A woman with sunken cheeks, skinny arms, and a severe gaze ambled to the minibus's door. Having survived the war, she was in no hurry now. I watched her through the dusty window of the minivan as she approached with suspicion in her eyes, as if we were a car full of strangers.

"Mee Nang!" Ma yelled, stepping out of the bus and facing her younger sister. "Why didn't you come see us in Phnom Penh like everyone else? You are so stubborn! You haven't changed at all."

My aunt was indifferent.

"Why didn't you come out to the village a long time ago?" Aunt Samnang said, matter-of-factly. "Everyone here has been waiting to see you."

The sisters hugged and looked intently at each other, surveying how fifteen years and such disparate lives—one of war and suffering in Cambodia, and the other of peace and plenty in America—had changed them. Ma didn't cry. She must have run out of tears from all that crying at the hotel. Or she must have figured she needed to put on her big-sister hat, because she planned on spending the next several days convincing Aunt Samnang to go to America.

Relatives swarmed to see me when I emerged from the minivan. I said, "Jim reap sour," a simple hello, to everyone I met, and smiled, lacking the vocabulary to say much else.

Ma had explained to me on the airplane trip to Cambodia that the customs of our people involved cremating the dead and placing the ashes in a family stupa, a concrete mausoleum erected on the grounds of the village pagoda. Our family's ornately carved stupa, with a crenellated top that reminded me of a miniature version of a pagoda, was built a long time ago at the edge of a small pond where dragonflies perched on lily pads, shaded by the thin canopy of a tamarind tree.

We sat on the floor of the Chous village pagoda, the inlaid tiles cooled by crosswinds, our legs folded and feet to the side or behind—never pointing to the Buddha, Ma told me upon entering—and waited for the seven monks on the raised dais to begin the ceremony. I pressed the palms of my hands together, mimicking the prostrated posture Ma and our relatives held, and kept my head bowed as the monks chanted. The hum of their incantations calmed something inside me, as if these prayers, though I did not know the words, were a specific vibration my body already knew.

When the head monk flicked holy water on my head, I didn't know what it meant but felt the significance of the moment, of being blessed in my mother's village by a monk who had survived the genocide. I felt the weight of the culture and customs and a way of being that Ma and Pa had tried desperately to cling to in America.

In that moment, I understood why, when I was growing

up and my parents sent me and my siblings to a Christian church, they stayed home and lit incense, holding fast to their Buddhist traditions. In Cambodia, life followed the beat of Theravada Buddhism. More than a religion, it was a way of living. Everything centered on honoring one's elders and preserving good karma for the afterlife. To my parents, doing good by others and making merit was in their blood. Which meant it was in my blood, too. There was something serene and sacred about these ceremonies, about the chanting and incense smoke wafting overhead like spirits dancing. A particular cadence tucked into my DNA. I exhaled long and deep and felt for the first time an immaculate stillness inside me.

After the ceremony, more than five hundred villagers gathered in an open field to feast on the chicken curry Ma had commissioned from the village women. While our relatives squatted in an open field and slurped noodles and the sun pounded down mercilessly, Ma discreetly pulled out a leather bag, which I had observed her guarding nervously from the day we left Portland International Airport.

It was full of bricks of cash, several thousand dollars in crisp U.S. bills. When she reached in and handed me a stack, I stared at the money in my hands for a long time, a school of thoughts swimming across my mind. I thought about all those backbreaking days in the strawberry fields. All the money my siblings and I made and never got to keep. All the times Ma said, "We don't have the money," when we asked for clothes or cool gadgets or toys. Here we were, in the middle of a village whose name I could not pronounce, with our savings in a single bag, and Ma was poised to give it all away.

Ma's voice snapped me out of my reverie before self-pity and resentment had a chance to hook my heart.

"This is a celebration, Put," Ma said, a huge smile opening

up her face. "This is how we Khmer people do things. We do a big party and give gifts to our family and clan to thank them and show our respect."

Ma nudged me to start passing out the cash.

"Ten or twenty dollars to the elders, and one dollar each for the kids," Ma said, and then left me with the cash. Ma divvied what was in her leather bag among Uncle Sol, Ming Pheaktra, and Great-Uncle San to help ensure everyone got money. I used both of my hands, in a show of respect, to press ten- and twenty-dollar bills into ancient hands shriveled and gnarled by years of farmwork as each of the village elders I gave money to thanked me and gave me their own blessings.

On to the kids. Uncle Sol and I lined them up in a field to reduce the chaos and make sure each kid got his or her dollar. All the while, I was trying not to think of the wrongness of the situation—of this cash, the money my siblings and I had earned working arduous hours on the berry farms in Corvallis, now being handed out to our family in Cambodia. And the wrongness about the "rich" cousins from America coming to spread their wealth; meanwhile, we grew up in Corvallis believing we were poor.

I didn't question Ma about it then, careful not to spoil her moment. She was laughing and smiling, overjoyed at being surrounded by her kin. We were all having a good time until news reached the neighboring village that Americans were handing out money. More children arrived, ambushing us from all angles. In an instant, Uncle Sol, Ma, Ming Pheaktra, and I were surrounded by swarms of excited children clawing at our hands, which held the dollars. I panicked.

Across the field, I heard Great-Uncle San shouting.

"Everyone back away, that's it, step back. We're leaving. We have to leave now," he announced, his voice penetrating the syrupy air. Ma climbed back into the minibus, dabbing at her eyes with a krama and reaching out a hand from the open window to grasp the hands of some of the elders she didn't get to visit.

I was being pulled by an amoeba-like mass of kids and elders away from the minibus but suddenly felt someone grab my hand, and in the next instant, I was jammed in the back seat, the last one in before Great-Uncle San slammed the door shut and we sped down the dirt road back toward Phnom Penh, leaving everyone in a cloud of dust.

"That was fun," Ma said, giggling as she relaxed into her seat and recounted how she was so swarmed by villagers she could barely see, "and a little scary."

On the ride back to the capital, a family friend who had spent the day helping me record the ceremony on my camcorder told me Cambodia had suffered a lot, and that our people were still "waking from war." He was glad that I had come to Cambodia with the camcorder, so I could bring back video footage to share with my "American brothers and sisters."

"Remember what you can, child," he said. "This is a part of who you are."

Back at the hotel that night, I contemplated what he meant, trying to sort out what parts of me were Khmer and what parts were American. In that moment, in the country where I was born but from which I had been taken before I learned to walk, I felt acutely American. I couldn't speak my own language. I didn't know it was a sin to touch a monk until Ma slapped my hand away when I tried to shake the head monk's hand. I winced when someone handed me a skewer with a grilled frog splayed on it. For the first time, I was surrounded by people who looked like me, and I felt profoundly out of place.

The reunions were taking a toll on Ma and me. Mostly Ma. I couldn't imagine listening intently as each of our family members told her their own personal version of how they survived starvation and beatings. Ma became a confidante and counselor, and I worried she would break under the burden of so many sad stories. Every story was another twist of the blade in her belly. I didn't know how she was able to hold so many people's anguish.

"We have a good life in Corvallis," Ma said to me one night. "We were lucky we escaped."

Her solemn words tugged at me. The guilt they held did, too.

So many times, I had wanted to tell my relatives that things were not all that easy for my family in America, either, that Ma had her own struggles learning English, and getting a job, and figuring out how to feed her family in a country built on wheat rather than rice. That we went as a family from dawn to dusk to work in the berry fields to earn money—some of which my relatives were now holding in their hands. That my siblings and I watched helplessly as our mother locked herself in her bedroom, and through the door, we could hear her muffled cries. We endured hardships, too. But I didn't have the words or the guts to say this. We all suffered, just differently. The difference was only of scale. Ma and I were witness to their struggles and hardships, but they would never be able to see ours.

Ma and I decided to take a day off from receiving visitors at our hotel room and take in a few tourist attractions around town. The hotel manager pointed us to a museum called Tuol Sleng, where we could learn about the Khmer Rouge, and before he got a chance to tell us—or warn us—about the exhibits, we were already climbing into a three-wheeled cyclo, Cambodia's ubiquitous rickshaw, with a seat in front and the driver pedaling in back, moseying across town.

Tuol Sleng was a former high school in the Boeung Keng Kang III neighborhood of Phnom Penh, which the Khmer Rouge converted in 1975 into a torture prison where an estimated eighteen thousand people died in the regime's hallmark brutality. I felt a flash of fury toward Ma for not telling us about the war in Cambodia, for failing to prepare me for this moment. My parents had taken my siblings and me to see *The Killing Fields* when I wasn't yet a teenager, but there were no conversations afterward to help us process what we saw, what it meant for a country to go through genocide, and what it meant for us to come from such a history. It makes sense to me now, why my parents didn't talk to us about the movie, or their lives, or the war. Beyond their Buddhist religion, which urged forward thinking, they lacked the language of war and politics to translate events in our homeland for us.

As a child, you believe your parents know everything. As a teenager, I still believed this. I didn't realize how wrong I was, that my mother also did not know of the atrocities that had unfolded in Cambodia while we were in America. Everyone outside of Cambodia had been in the dark for four years as the Communists instituted an information blackout. No news or information went out of Cambodia during that time, and none came in.

Now, at Tuol Sleng, we were about to get doused with the wounding truth of our country's war.

The museum docent was a gentle soul who wore a damp rag at the nape of his neck and a safari hat with a chin strap that hung low to his chest. He unspooled some of his own story of surviving the genocide as he led us through the darkened rooms and hallways and into a courtyard where a high bar had been used to hang and torture prisoners. He spoke softly, as if not to awaken the spirits that might still linger there.

The rooms and corridors smelled of decay, and I felt a heaviness all around us, the stench of death looming thuggishly in the air.

In one room, black-and-white mug shots of the victims who died at Tuol Sleng lined every inch of wall. The look of terror and resignation on their faces haunts me to this day. Hope had no purchase here. The prisoners understood their fates, heard the anguished screams and crying of fellow prisoners being tortured and the eerie silence that followed. I saw an instrument with clamps meant to slowly tear fingernails from the flesh and another that crushed skulls inside a vise. I got dizzy looking at it all. The stench. The heat. The horror. I couldn't believe my eyes.

We walked through upstairs classrooms divided into crude prisoners' cells made of hastily laid brick. Each cell, the length of a coffin and only slightly wider, had a pair of iron ankle shackles and a military artillery box for a toilet. Two foreign journalists had died at Tuol Sleng, and when the tour guide told us the Khmer Rouge targeted journalists, teachers, and doctors, a chill slid down my spine. Rather than scare me out of a future career as a journalist, that moment only cemented my resolve to pursue it. People had died trying to tell the truth. I knew, in that moment, I would continue their work for them.

In a series of torture chambers on the second floor, I finally felt my legs give out beneath me, and my entire body convulsed at what I saw. I was certain my morning breakfast of noodle soup would come spewing out.

Each room had a metal bed frame, chains, and torture instruments discovered by Vietnamese troops when they invaded Cambodia in 1979 and routed out the Khmer Rouge. The Vietnamese had taken photographs of the person—or rather, corpse—found in each room. In one photo, a woman's mutilated, decomposing body hangs partly off the bed, her ankle still chained to the bedpost. A crow sits perched atop her belly, pecking at the exposed insides. I looked down at my feet and saw smears of dried blood peeling up from the floor.

"She was pregnant," the tour guide said evenly.

I gagged and was certain that if I stayed any longer in that house of horrors, I would surely lose my mind. Ma's face turned white as we traveled the haunted hallways of the school. She braced herself against a wall at one point, feeling shaky and faint.

We pressed on, slowly stepping through the courtyard, the classrooms—everywhere echoes of death.

In the room with all the faces, the rows and rows of black-and-white mug shots of victims, I glanced at Ma as she peered closely into each face, looking at every single photo. Only recently, talking together for the first time about that trip thirty years after that first return to Cambodia, did I ask what she was searching for.

"Why did you stay there, in that room with all the pictures, for so long?" I asked.

"I was looking for my brother," Ma replied. "He was a teacher, and I knew the Khmer Rouge didn't like anyone who was educated. They rounded up teachers and killed them first. I thought maybe I would find him there."

All these years, I believed that that trip to Cambodia in

1990 was for my mother to search for the living. Only now do I see that she was also on a mission to find the dead, to know what had happened to her siblings, her cousins, her aunts and uncles and father-in-law who had perished. Only now do I see the courage she must have corralled to steel herself, to once again look, as she did in 1973 when she peered at the bruised and battered corpses of military men brought back from the fighting, to see if someone she loved was among the dead.

In the end, the tour guide led Ma and me to a small receiving room, where he offered us tea and asked us to a sign a guest book.

"Foreigners like to come here," the tour guide said, "to learn the sad story of our country."

He didn't say it, but I took him to mean foreigners like me.

Tuol Sleng broke my soul. I could feel the million pinpricks of guilt, shame, and sorrow stab at my core. We had survived, while so many others had died. These emotions would eventually calcify in me, like a new bone, becoming a permanent part of who I am.

I had a new appreciation for my parents, for taking us out of Cambodia when they did. For giving up their life and country in order for me and my siblings to live in peace and have better opportunities in America. I also felt a deeper debt to Ma, for saving me. I wasn't fully sure yet what I could do to repay her. But I promised myself I would keep trying.

For the remaining days we stayed in Cambodia, I had nightmares about war and torture and would wake in a sweat only to find Ma vigorously snoring in the bed next to mine, the dust-covered blades of the ceiling fan rotating slowly above us, and the fruit my relatives had brought us staring at me from the corner like an indictment. While my siblings and I had a home and our friends and McDonald's apple pies, my relatives had been suffering unspeakable cruelty.

And then I thought of those moments when our relatives would lean in and speak in low tones to Ma, saying things that made her weep and shake. I finally understood, in the starkest of terms, what things they must have told her, what savagery she didn't want me to know about.

I lost my appetite for days after going to Tuol Sleng. Once my energy and good health returned, the visitors did, too.

One morning, as I lay on my bed with a blue highlighter in one hand and my U.S. history book balanced on my knees, we heard the lightest rap at the door.

Ma opened it and saw one of her second cousins, standing meekly, with a young man who looked to be a teenager, like me. He wore black cotton pants and a nice, crisp white button-down shirt, and he stood back a step or two behind Ma's cousin. His hair was moist, as though he had bathed just minutes ago, neatly combed to one side.

"I'm sorry to bother you, Bong," Ma's cousin said. "I brought my son. I wanted to ask if we could talk."

Ma glanced at the boy and half smiled. Then Ma glanced over her shoulder back at me before stepping out into the corridor, pulling the door almost all the way closed, and lowering her voice to a whisper.

"I thought you could meet my son," the woman pressed on. "Maybe there is a match. He's a good boy. He takes care of his family and works hard."

"Put is studying right now," I heard Ma say. "I'm sorry we can't talk now."

Ma's cousin tried to peer past her shoulder to see me and I pretended not to pay attention.

"You know, in America, the girls go to school and when they graduate, they get jobs, just like the boys," Ma went on. "It's not like here in Cambodia. They choose on their own who to marry."

Marry? Was someone asking to marry me? I shot up ramrod straight in bed and cocked my head toward the door, straining to hear better.

I felt the embarrassment and shame poke into Ma's voice as she tried to explain herself and defend me as her cousin insisted her son was a good student.

"He'll make a good son-in-law," she said.

"I'm very certain he will," Ma said. "It's just, the kids in America, the girls, they don't get married until later. It's a crazy thing in America. They choose on their own."

After a few more words were exchanged, Ma came back in and closed the door.

"Who was it?" I asked, as Ma veered toward our fruit supply to get a mango.

"My cousin," Ma said. "She wants you as her daughter-in-law."

She said it so matter-of-factly that I wasn't sure if she was joking, but I knew Ma didn't joke that way. A bolt of panic surged down my spine.

"I'm not getting married, Ma," I snapped.

Suddenly, I felt my heart plunge. For the first time, I grew suspicious of Ma's motivations in selecting me to go with her to Cambodia. I was angry and afraid, while Ma acted like it was no big deal, like everything was under control.

At night, my head spun with fear. I was only sixteen years old. What if she did marry me off? I would never see my family or friends again. I would be at the mercy of a stranger.

How would I even communicate with my husband when I barely spoke Khmer, and the words I did know hurled off my *rundath rung*, or "hard tongue," as my cousins called it. No one would be able to understand me, a feeling of deep isolation I had already experienced once before at Little Beavers when I couldn't speak English. I couldn't handle it.

The afternoon brought another rap at the door. Ma opened it to find a friend, who had also brought along her son. Ma offered this mother the same explanation, that things are different in America, not like in Cambodia. Girls in America are independent, she explained.

When this mother tried to suggest to Ma that, as a Khmer mother, she had the authority and prerogative to decide my fate, Ma stood her ground.

"Yes, I know," Ma said. "She is a Cambodian daughter, but she has grown up in America and adopted their ways. I have to let her decide."

She was saving me, and I didn't yet know why.

Before the trip ended, several more mothers would come to our hotel room, lining up in the hallway outside our door, each one propositioning Ma with an offer of a Khmer son-in-law. My body started seizing up at every knock on the door. And though each time, Ma gently explained I would not be getting married anytime soon, I began to worry that if the right relative or friend came along with the right boy, she would break down and seal a deal. After all, this was the woman who had first begged and then tried to bribe my siblings and me to marry a fellow Khmer, to keep our rich tradition intact.

For the next several days, I sulked and snapped at Ma, as if she had somehow betrayed me by even talking to the mothers.

"I'm not getting married," I repeated, my voice kinked with defiance. "You can't do that to me."

By then, Ma was tired of trying to manage my misery and finally put my anxiety to rest.

"Don't be crazy, Put," she said. "I'm not leaving you behind."

◻ DATELINE, CAMBODIA

There is a photo in my office, next to a picture of my mother on her wedding day, two images that hang in stark contrast to each other. This one is full color, a photo I snapped on the last day of our trip to Cambodia in 1990. Ma sits shoulder to shoulder with Great-Uncle San on a bench at the airport. He is waiting to send us back across the ocean, to America.

My mother's face forms a circle, round with happiness, her mouth wide open, laughing, and her uncle's face is broken in laughter, too, a joke they shared together, niece and uncle, to lighten the minutes before a teary goodbye. When I look at the photo, I see my mother as she must have been all those years before being burdened by marriage and then children and then running from war and starting anew in a foreign land. I see in her face the purest joy. To be home again. To be held by the gentle giant who raised her. Looking back, I wonder if she even wanted to return to America. If she might have preferred to stay there, in the land and amid the people she loved.

I smile when I look at that photo, wishing there was a way in America she could feel such weightlessness again.

I sometimes think of that first trip to Cambodia as a bridge: on one side, there is the teenage me, figuring out my place in the world and even within my family; and on the other, the person I would become. I didn't think of that trip then as being traumatic, because I didn't think in those terms when I was sixteen years old. Only looking back is it clear that trauma was already in me; the trip merely triggered it, setting in motion an arc into adulthood that would lead me again and again to my motherland.

It will take years, the rest of my life, to untangle my jumble of emotions around that one experience. But I know that in Cambodia, I found parts of me that had gone dormant. When I heard all my relatives speak our language, in a place where English could not impinge, I fell in love once again with the pretty words and sounds that make up my first language. I saw how my hunger for stories was rooted in my mother tongue.

I returned to school in October, when my friends were already decorating their lockers with cotton cobwebs, carrying pens with plastic pumpkin tops, and coming up with costume ideas. I made up absent days from my first month as a junior at Crescent Valley High School in different ways. My French teacher had required that I keep a journal written in French during the two weeks I was away in Cambodia. Another teacher let me make up missed exams after school. For the *Crescent Crier*, I merely had to start writing stories.

I wrote a short editorial about my experiences in Cambodia, but it barely skimmed the surface of what I learned there, how the trip had changed me. The person who had crossed the Pacific Ocean as a teenager and entered Cambodia was different than the one who exited and returned to her life in America. Something inside me got jostled, a deeper awareness of who I was, that I was more than merely American.

Before we left for our trip to Cambodia, I had let myself believe the trip would bring Ma and me even closer together. But it seemed to have done the opposite. A new, dangerous tension rose between us, and I struggled to keep my balance.

Ma became more impatient with me and my sisters, revealing a temper I didn't know she had. When she came through the door in the evenings after work, my sisters and I leapt from the sofa and hid in our bedrooms before she had the chance to accuse us of being lazy.

She would head to the kitchen and taste whatever stir-fry or soup one of us girls had made, and then cast her criticisms into the air like bread crumbs scattered to the birds, left for us to gather later.

"Too salty!" she screamed once when she dipped a spoon in a stir-fry of beef and pickled mustard greens that one of my sisters had made. Another time, when she sampled the lemongrass chicken soup I had made, she clucked her tongue. "Oh, this is too bland," she said. "I can't eat it."

She fought with Pa about bills. She fought with my sisters about their cooking.

And she fought with me about me. She scrutinized my hair, my clothes, my attitude. "Why can't you dress better, like your sisters?" she said one day. I was wearing my usual jeans with one of my father's white undershirts I had pilfered and a mustard-colored sweater. "Your sisters always brush their hair nicely. They wear pretty sweaters, not the rags you wear."

In the summer, she scolded me for wearing shorts she deemed too short, even though they came to midthigh, and oversized T-shirts, same as the other girls at school. But Ma never went to our school, so she didn't see how normal this was. She only knew how teenage girls in Cambodia dressed, with long skirts and shirts that did not reveal even a bare shoulder, maintaining their modesty.

"Look at your cousins in srok Khmer," Ma told me. "They wear pretty sarongs. Their clothes are clean and they even wear makeup. They find a way to look good, and they don't have any money. Please try harder to look nice, gohn."

I didn't stack up. It is easy as a teenager to ignore what your mother thinks about you. But it was different for me. There was that boat. There was that debt. I wanted to make her proud of me, but simply being myself, I was clearly failing.

I rolled up a sweatshirt and shoved it under my bedroom door so that she couldn't open it and see me cry.

She saw in my female cousins glimpses of the daughter she might have had in me, if we had lived in Cambodia. Maybe I would have been easier to tame and contain in Cambodia, conforming fully to our culture, because the Khmer culture would have been all that I knew. But I was in America, where the terms were different, where it was not only acceptable but encouraged for girls to be viewed and treated as equal to boys.

That trip to Cambodia made me acutely and uncomfortably aware of myself. I was no longer a girl but was beginning to back awkwardly into adulthood. I began noticing my own body and the dramatic changes underway. I hated what I was becoming. I hid my budding breasts beneath baggy sweatshirts and wore men's boat shoes two sizes too large, because they were on sale and because men's shoes worked better with my wide feet. I stuffed newspaper in each toe box to make them fit. I didn't want any of my sisters' hand-me-downs. Instead, I rooted around the back of my brother's closet—for cast-off T-shirts or old shorts that might fit me. I didn't dress like a boy, not exactly, because other girls at my school wore oversized T-shirts and even boxer briefs. I just didn't want to wear the floral prints or pastels that Ma favored.

No one seemed to care what I wore except Ma, and her nagging was wearing me down.

"Put," she said once, "why don't you wear some nice skirts? I'll give you the money to buy new clothes."

She must have been desperate. It wasn't like Ma to give us money.

"I don't want new clothes," I said. "There's nothing wrong with my clothes. If you care what I look like, that's your problem."

I slammed my bedroom door, which had the immediate effect of sending my father into a rage, and the entire house turned into a tempest.

Whole months passed like this: Ma coming home in a sour mood, me and everyone else who happened to be home diving for cover. Sin and Sope were the first to graduate and moved out as soon as they could, leaving me, Chan, and Mo to hide in our rooms. Yay Yeim just sat in a corner of the family room, chewing her betel nut, her lips smudged deep red like blood.

I never asked Ma about it, but looking back, I wonder how the trip to Cambodia impacted her. She was the one who absorbed her family's stories of struggle and survival, of torture and starvation, while I only heard translated bits and pieces through her. She cried the entire time we were in Cambodia, but when she came back to Corvallis, something had hardened in her. A deep grief that manifested as anger. And that anger seemed to swallow her whole.

I was also having a hard time adjusting back to my American life. There were things I couldn't reconcile. I tried to figure out: Were we poor or not poor? While Ma handed out bricks of cash to our relatives who had survived the war, my siblings and I got an envelope from the administrative office at school with our monthly supply of free lunch tickets tucked inside. For the better part of his senior year, Sope sold his meal tickets to other kids at a steep discount and took the proceeds to Pizza Hut down the road to offset the cost of his pepperoni pizza habit. He did this for months until he got caught and called into the principal's office.

Chan was so embarrassed to use her meal tickets, she often skipped lunch. Mo ate lunch surrounded by friends who also ate school lunches.

I was too hungry to be embarrassed. I stood in the lunch line every day, picking up lukewarm tater tots and cold baked potatoes too firm to serve as a reservoir for melted cheese and sour cream.

But did we need those free meal tickets? We thought our berry-picking money was going toward the mortgage and bills, food and our clothes. When we wanted to do things—go to the movies, get new shoes, have birthday parties at the roller rink, the way our friends did—Ma muttered the same refrain: we didn't have the money.

We did have the money. We'd had it all along. Ma had just saved it for our relatives who needed it more. It was they, not we, who had survived the war.

In recent years, as my siblings and I reminisced about our childhoods, I asked my sisters and brother: "Did you know Ma was sending our picking money to Cambodia?"

For a moment, I considered pulling up the calculator app on my phone.

"Don't do the math," Mo said. "Better not to know."

Sope shrugged his shoulders.

"I guess we didn't need the money," he said. "Our lives were okay."

I don't know how much our quality of life would have improved if Ma had spent more money on us—the money we worked to earn every summer—but after being in Cambodia and seeing how my relatives struggled, I felt ashamed for wanting new clothes and money to eat lunch off campus with my friends rather than eat in the cafeteria with my free lunch tickets, for wanting a Swatch watch and a home in Vineyard Mountain, the neighborhood just past our high school, where the rich kids lived. I felt guilty for everything. By then I had, for the first time, my own bedroom and bed. I had my mother's food. I never knew, until then, just how uncomfortable it felt to be comfortable.

Ma and I, we had become moody and mean. I fought with my sisters. And Ma fought with me. Pa was the only one not fighting with anyone, for a change, with all the women around him making so much noise. Looking back, it's so clear. We had both slid into a deep depression, Ma and I, each of us standing on the opposite edge of the chasm. We both became withdrawn, barely talking to anyone at home, much less each other.

I can now see that trip together to Cambodia for what it was. A return home, for Ma to reunite with her relatives who survived the war and for me to know my relatives, my country, and my culture. But it was as if, upon returning, the ground beneath our feet gave way. Our relationship, once sitting on bedrock, was pulled apart by plate tectonics of deep grief and a culture that gave us no outlet to convey the things we were feeling.

I never asked her, when we got back from our trip, how she felt about returning. We didn't share our separate and mutual experiences. Ma and Pa raised us to hide our emotions, to submerge them so they wouldn't get in the way of day-to-day survival in America. Sharing feelings and seeking counseling were American constructs, and Ma was not American. I watched what she did and I learned to push my messy mix of feelings down, too.

But by spring, a flotsam of sadness had surfaced. An ambush of emotions I could not hold back. Something inside me felt dark and dead. I didn't want to see my friends. I ate dinner alone, in my room. Two things had collided at once: my growing teenage angst, and the profound sadness of knowing I came from and was the product of a country racked by massive human slaughter. It was hard enough to go through the routine teenage struggle of trying to fit in. Harder still was trying to understand who I was in the context of belonging to two worlds, one of peace and the other of war—America and Cambodia.

I felt a profound hopelessness. When I began writing dark poetry about death and suicide, my friends told our high school counselor. When I told my counselor that there were moments I could not explain, where I felt an undertow of the deepest sadness and didn't know why, that I sometimes thought about killing myself, and also did not know why, she referred me and my parents to a family psychologist.

When we went to our appointment at the Corvallis Clinic, I felt the shame in Ma's eyes as we sat down in an unremarkable office and the psychologist closed the door behind us.

"Our culture is not like this," Ma said to the nice man, who sat with his legs crossed on a chair opposite the sofa where my parents and I sat, straight-backed and trapped in an awkward silence. "When we have problem, we fix problem in our family."

That is the only thing about family counseling I remember. That, and the fact that we never went again.

At home later that day, Ma cornered me in my room.

"Next time you feel sad, or you have a problem, just talk to me or your dad," Ma said. But in her deflated voice, I knew she didn't mean it. The language of feelings and emotions was not one we spoke, or even knew how to speak, in our home.

If there had been a way to tell Ma that her constant fighting with Pa was impacting me, each night as I closed my ears against their screaming; that Ma's relentless criticism of my clothes and my imperfect cooking was overwhelming me; that there was a particular chaos in me that had to do with what I felt for girls rather than for boys—if Ma had known these things, would anything have changed? When the pressure in my head mounted, I did what came naturally, what I had learned by watching Ma: I ran away.

One spring night, I drove north on Interstate 5 to my aunt Vuthy's apartment in Beaverton. By the next morning, Aunt Vuthy had talked me into going back home, assuring me my parents loved me. I knew this, but sometimes it took hearing it from another relative, someone close to Ma, to feel it.

By the fall, entering my senior year of high school, I ran away to my friend Aidan's house. After a few days, his mother persuaded me to go back home.

Ma and I fought some more.

We fought when she wouldn't let me join my school's track team and I did anyway. We fought when she wouldn't buy me a pair of running shoes, so I stole hers—brand-new in the box. When I ran through mud and could not return the sneakers to their pristine bleach white color, she took a knife and sawed them in half.

"How did I raise my kid to be so ungrateful?" Ma screamed

as she chucked the pieces of shoe off our back patio. She went to her room and sobbed. I shook with shame sitting on the sofa, too terrified to look up as she stomped down the hallway.

Even now, I still feel guilty for making my mother cry.

We fought when I stayed out late with my friends and she told me only whores do that.

I ran away again.

I thought I could maybe live with Sin my last year of high school, since she was attending Oregon State in Corvallis, but the night I showed up on her doorstep, when I saw the tight quarters she kept, I wasn't so sure.

Sin slept on the bottom of a bunk bed she shared with one of her friends, in an apartment off campus they shared with one other roommate. At least the bottom bunk was a full-size bed. I curled into a sleeping bag on the wooden slats. I wasn't sure whether Sin and her friends didn't believe in mattresses, or if they simply didn't have the money to buy them. Either way, it made me miss my comfortable bed on Ironwood Avenue.

The next night, over alfalfa sprout burritos at the vegetarian joint Nearly Normals, Sin tried to convince me to go home. I told her Ma had been acting strange lately. She was increasingly critical and mean and it was difficult to live with her and Pa since both of them were constantly fighting and I was fighting with her. Sin chomped into her burrito, a patch of alfalfa sprouts dangling from her bottom lip as she chewed.

"Ma is never going to change," Sin said. "She is who she is. You're almost graduating. Just focus on that. Get your diploma, then you can leave and you can do whatever you want."

"What do I do if I can't stand it at home?" I asked.

"Go study," Sin said. "I'm sure you can study at the library on campus. They don't check IDs. Just see how late it stays open and stay until it closes."

I worked as late as I could after school in Mr. MacPherson's journalism class and then in the evenings I punched in at Arnold Dining Hall, where Ma had gotten me and my sisters part-time work serving food. I took my books with me to campus, and after the last hungry student came through the cafeteria turnstile, I schlepped to the library and stayed until 10:00 p.m., when the lights flickered off, wing by wing, until the darkness reached me. Sometimes, if I still didn't want to go home, I plunked down in a chair in the student union and cracked my books open again. I saw Ma only a few hours a day at Arnold, and because we were working, we stayed out of each other's way.

Amid all the running away and juggling of jobs, I managed to keep up my grades and went to prom with Ethan Hauser, because he was the one who asked. We went on a triple date with my friend Jenny and my best friend, Kate. My sisters joked that I had a boyfriend. I denied it. I couldn't tell them whom I really liked.

Kate and I had known each other since our freshman year. She sat next to me on the first day of French class. The next year, we also had history and English class together. Kate had a car, and after school, she carted a bunch of us around town—to the Dairy Queen at the strip mall down the road from our high school or downtown to have a slice of pepperoni at American Dream Pizza. On weekends, she invited people over to her house to watch movies. I always went.

I don't know when the shift happened, but in our senior year, I started to see Kate differently. When we sat on the floor in a circle once in French class, Kate sat down next to me. Her hand brushed against my hand and I felt an immediate electric shock travel up my arm and buzz my brain. I jerked my hand away.

"Oh, sorry," she said, when she saw me react.

"No, I'm sorry," I said. "Here, let me move."

I scooted. But sitting that close to her, all I could feel was heat crawling along my limbs and my whole heart about to burst.

Whenever I was with her, my head spun with confusing and conflicting thoughts and my heart pumped so much blood I was sure I'd lose consciousness. It wasn't real, I told myself, those crazy feelings I had for a girl. For my friend.

I didn't know then that what I was feeling for Kate was a crush. I didn't want to know that about myself. It wasn't real and it wasn't right. It wasn't what Ma would want. Ma had already told me, when I was growing up, what my future would look like.

In her kitchen, while my sisters and I cooked alongside her, she often told us, "When you have a husband, you always need to have a hot meal ready." She said "husband." Which is what she had. Which is what I would one day have, too. So I rode out the rest of my senior year, clutching that word "husband" as if my life depended on it. I counted the days to graduation, when I could finally be free.

I applied to Oregon State University, the University of Oregon, and Pennsylvania State University. I got accepted to all three. I told anyone who asked that I wanted to go to Penn State for the journalism program. The truth was, I followed my finger on a map to the farthest place from Corvallis.

But I knew I could not afford out-of-state tuition, so I shoved my Penn State acceptance letter into a drawer.

Then Ma started her campaign, the same one she had tried on all my siblings before me.

"Stay close," Ma said. "You don't need to go so far to study in college. You can stay home and eat Ma's food. It will be better than dorm food you eat somewhere else."

"But you cook dorm food," I said.

"I'm just saying you don't know who's going to cook *your* dorm food."

She had a point. Ma's food, whether she cooked at home or for the students on campus, always tasted delicious. I couldn't say the same about some of her colleagues' food.

Even though we had been fighting, I still loved Ma and still wanted to be as near to her as I could. It wasn't just about the food. I knew she was worried about being alone with Pa, and I felt the need to protect her. Though they continued to fight, I didn't see him hit her again during my high school years. But I had my own room. I was no longer witness to what happened when they closed their bedroom door. I recognized that for Ma, even having one kid at home was a buffer between her and Pa.

I could not leave, but I also could not stay.

I didn't belong in Corvallis and I knew it. The city was too small for my ambitions. I made a bargain with myself. Two years at OSU, and then I'd transfer to UO, an easy hour's drive away, in Eugene. When I told Ma that I was staying home and that I would go to OSU, she beamed and kissed me on the cheek. I knew I had made her happy.

"My daughter is a good daughter," she said. "You'll save lots of money staying at home."

In the end, the universe intervened. Just months away from graduating high school, I saw the news on the front page of the campus newspaper: OSU was facing a massive budget deficit. The journalism program would be completely cut.

I took it as a sign that the program I intended to pursue

was now obliterated from OSU's course offerings. I didn't feel as bad about leaving Ma, convincing myself that a good journalism program was my priority.

In June of 1992, I graduated from Crescent Valley High School, the last of the Reang kids to come through, collecting honors and awards that I handed to Ma. My grades, and recommendations from my teachers and school counselor, were good enough to help me secure enough scholarships and financial aid to pay most of my way at the University of Oregon.

That fall, I packed my alarm clock, poetry books, empty journals, and cassette tapes into egg crates. Ma and Pa drove me south down Highway 99, past Wilt's blueberry farm, where we worked, and Mary's Peak, where I hiked, and Abby's Legendary Pizza in Junction City, where Ma and Pa had taken us as a treat when we were younger.

After they helped me settle into my room in the international dormitory, I walked Ma and Pa to their car. An emotion surged from my gut up through my throat as Ma pulled me into a hug. The sharp bite of guilt.

"Take care, gohn," she said, her voice already cracking. "Study hard. Eat plenty."

We were once a family that grew and grew, and then shrank as all the kids moved out. Now it was just the three of them, Ma, Pa, and Yay Yeim. When my parents disappeared around the tennis courts to their car, when the coast was clear, I sat on a bench and began to cry. Even now, I don't know who those tears were for.

Eugene was not far from Corvallis, but it was one more step away from Ma, toward a version of myself without her.

▣ RUNNING

The University of Oregon has one of the greenest, cleanest, prettiest campuses I have ever seen, with five hundred species of trees, many of them rare and majestic, from all over the world. I did not get to sit idly beneath them. Once in a while, I wanted to lounge in the shade of those trees, the way I saw other students do. But I told myself there was no time to rest. I wanted to get my degree and get a job. To my mind, college was a slingshot that would propel me into a journalism career.

I took everything I could from college and gave a little bit back, too. I ate my way through the cafeteria like a termite, stopping for nothing. My friends watched and wondered how it was possible that I ate twice as much as they did—a plate of spaghetti, a salad, and a turkey sandwich and chips, plus the tallest soft-serve I could make without it tipping over—in the same amount of time as they ate their normal human serving size meals, and not gain a single pound. I shrugged my shoulders and dashed off to my next class.

In the adrenaline rush of living on my own, I signed up for every dorm-organized trip—whitewater rafting, mountain biking, bowling. I took karate to learn how to fight and teamed up with Kim Nguyen, a photographer for the *Daily Emerald*, the campus newspaper, to start the school's first-ever Southeast Asian Student Association, even though there were only six of us and Chan was one of them. But mostly, I kept my head down and worked.

If college is where one is meant to test the limits of his or her own stamina, I found mine my sophomore year. I majored in journalism then stacked a second major in English literature on top of that. Chan had helped me get a work-study gig at the Office of Academic Advising, and after a few weeks, I realized I could use some advice myself.

Chan was able to get me in to see Bunny, who mostly dealt with older students. I wanted to see her because people in the office said she was the best.

Bunny was thin and lithe and power-walked past her fellow runners at marathons. I often saw her on campus, disappearing in the milliseconds between blinks. That kind of speed appealed to me; this woman had places to go. I felt assured she would understand the reason I was there to see her, the thing I wanted to know:

"Is it possible I can finish early?" I asked.

I had been doing some rudimentary math related to my scholarships and financial aid. I figured if I was able to graduate a year early, I'd save several thousand dollars in tuition and living expenses. I had two goals when I started college: to not ask Ma and Pa for financial help, and to get a degree without going into debt. I thought if I could do this, Ma would be proud.

Bunny pulled out a notepad and scrawled some numbers on it.

"It looks possible," Bunny said, glancing at my transcript

and the numbers she had written down. "But advisable, that's another question. You would have to really push yourself."

"I think I can do it," I said, triumphant.

Bunny paused for a moment and looked at me.

"Why are you in such a hurry?" she asked. "Maybe you should take some time to enjoy college."

I didn't know how to explain to Bunny that I had always been in a hurry. All my life, I was in a hurry to grow up and do everything, the way I watched my mother do. I figured the faster I could get through college and start my career, the faster I could earn my own money and live independently. My life had quickly become one big hustle to prove to myself, and to Ma, that I could make it on my own, that I was no longer that weak and vulnerable baby on the boat who always needed her mother.

Each semester, I registered for every graduate-level course I could, since those were mostly three credits, rather than the two I could earn from undergraduate classes. To accommodate the fullest course load, I took evening courses. When I wasn't in class, I was at the Academic Advising office answering phones, filing, and directing students to their appointments. And when I wasn't there, I was at the library studying for exams, sandwich crumbs snowing down on my lap.

But there is a cost to so much running around. I started to do poorly on exams and fell asleep during class. I felt a pressure build inside, like something in me was about to break. I cried through a full afternoon. And then a day. A day became a week. I stayed in my room, unable to take a step anywhere beyond the bathroom, beyond our dormitory floor. My roommate talked to the resident adviser. I worried I was going to fail my classes. I worried I would be too ashamed to ever go home again.

Before I knew it, a campus police officer was at my bedside late one night, talking me out of slitting my wrists, called by the RA when my roommate alerted her.

I thought of Ma, how her hope had saved me when I was a baby. How had I arrived at this place of hopelessness? And what would she feel, knowing I had squandered the second chance she gave me?

As I stared into space, the campus officer crouched near my bed, talking to me gently, like a friend. He stayed awhile, and before he left, he insisted on one thing: a promise that I would not harm myself. I agreed, not for his sake, but for Ma's. Guilt can be the thing that makes you want to die but can also be the thing that forces you to live. I felt guilty when I thought of how hard she fought to keep me alive, to help me thrive. How dishonorable it would be to betray her best efforts at mothering.

Chan was called to my dorm, but I didn't want her to see me so broken. She sent a message through my roommate that I could call her anytime if I needed anything. She must have called my childhood friend Emily, who lived in a nearby dorm, because the next day, Emily was at my door. We had been friends since first grade, and though our lives had diverged by the time we got to college, she was still my good friend, the person who, at the time, knew me best.

We walked to the creek where couples rented boats and rowed lazily beneath willow branches draped over the water's edge. We scrabbled over a cluster of boulders and each claimed a spot.

"So what's up, dude?" Emily asked. "What happened last night?"

"I don't know," I said, staring blankly at the water. "I've just been super stressed. Class, I guess. Maybe it's too much."

I told Emily that I was trying to graduate early and maxing out on credits each term. I told her if I graduated a year early, I wouldn't have to ask my parents for help. Since I was little, Ma had watched me cautiously, worried I would get sick or have an asthma attack, worried always about my well-being. College was my first chance to show Ma I didn't need to depend on her anymore.

Emily said she understood, but saw beneath my blabber.

"You're always overachieving," she said. "It's like you're constantly running. You've been running since we were kids, Put. Dude, aren't you tired?"

When I was in fourth grade, I went to Emily's house after school one day to play. She had a room of her own, full of toys and stuffed animals. She had her parents and only one brother, and there was a different energy at her house than mine; there was calm. I told her I wished I could live with her. So we plotted. I would run away from home and live in her closet. Each night she would eat half her dinner and then smuggle the other half to me. It seemed, at the time, a better way to live than being at my own house, overrun with people, my parents constantly fighting.

"You're running in circles," Emily finally said, as we walked back to my dorm. "It's like you're running from yourself."

I didn't know what she meant.

A few days later, I saw Chan and told her I didn't know what had gotten into me.

"Please don't tell Ma," I begged my sister. "I don't want her to worry."

"Have you talked to a counselor?" Chan asked. "Maybe that will help you."

I don't remember who I saw at the Student Health Center the next day, but I must have spoken to someone, because after that, I went back to my dorm room with a bottle of pills rattling in my hand.

Despite my talk with Emily and my sister's urging me to drop some of my classes, to spend more time mountain biking and rafting, activities I came to enjoy, I was unwilling to relinquish my plan of graduating early. Instead of slowing down, I sped up. I doubled down and recommitted to studying harder.

The campus paper, the *Daily Emerald*, was hiring, so I applied, thinking that would lift my spirits. But I was a sophomore, competing against dozens of juniors and seniors jockeying for a limited number of newsroom spots available. I put my name in the ring anyway. When one of the *Emerald* co-editors later saw me in class and told me I didn't get chosen, she urged me to apply again when I was a junior.

I didn't wait around. I landed an internship at the *Corvallis Gazette-Times*. Ma beamed when she got home from work one evening and saw that I was home for the summer, even though I didn't share her enthusiasm. But there were no other options. By then, Sin had moved to Nebraska with her boyfriend. Chan stayed on the UO campus in Eugene for her summer jobs, living in her car to save money. And Mo and Sope were each living in their Greek houses on the OSU campus.

Ma's smile sagged when her gaze landed on my jeans, ripped at the knees.

"Put," she said, "you have money to buy nice jeans. Why are you still wearing rags? You look like a homeless person."

"Because that's what I wear, Ma," I said, closing the door on her.

As the years went by, I understood the deeper meaning behind Ma's obsession over appearance. She flat-out said so one time.

"Who's going to want to marry you, gohn, dressed so basic like this?" she asked.

Everything I needed to know was contained in that single criticism: a mother helplessly grooming her daughter for marriage, suspicious that her daughter is engaging in subterfuge.

"Then I guess I don't need to get married," I snapped back, and I knew, from the instant I said those words and saw Ma's stricken face, that I was breaking her heart.

For the rest of the summer, I tried to avoid her, filling my schedule with back-to-back jobs. I hadn't been to the berry fields in a couple of years, but I was planning to live off campus in an apartment with Chan my junior year of college, which, by Bunny's math, would be my last. I needed to earn extra cash. So I hustled from one job to the next, just as I had watched Ma do. I woke at 5:00 a.m. and was out in the fields by 6:00 a.m. I worked at Anderson's blueberry farm, north of town, for two hours every morning before rushing home, showering, and driving the opposite direction to reach the *Gazette-Times* newsroom by 9:00 a.m.

In the evenings, I punched in at Arnold Dining Hall on campus, tied an apron around my waist, slipped on plastic gloves, and served up Ma's special of the day. I went home only to sleep.

I got paid better than minimum wage in the summer of 1993 when I worked in the *Gazette-Times* newsroom. My salary was $260 per week, which was $6.50 per hour, which was about $2 per hour more than what I made serving on the lunch line at Arnold. I could make just as much in the fields, $50 in a single morning if I hurried. But berry picking was not a career, no matter how much it paid. I threw myself fully into my newspaper job.

In the mornings, my editor, Barb, assigned me whatever

story was left after the veteran reporters had their pick. I crisscrossed my hometown, covering crime and rodeos and the increasing embrace of mechanization by farmers bent on profit-making.

But there is one story I will never forget. A story that put me back in touch with one of the original farmers we worked for, the one Ma loved and admired the most: Mrs. Kenagy.

The local chapter of PFLAG (Parents and Friends of Lesbians and Gays) was setting up a hotline in Benton County to support families, and when Barb gave me a list of PFLAG parents, I was shocked to see Lois Kenagy and her husband, Cliff, on the list. I felt as if I had stumbled into some intimate knowledge about the Kenagys that I wasn't supposed to know, that I had inadvertently trespassed on their private lives.

I took a deep breath and dialed the number Barb gave me. I figured since Mrs. Kenagy knew me and my family, she would agree to be interviewed by me. But when I called, she didn't say yes right away.

"We're still dealing with this," Mrs. Kenagy said. "I don't know if Cliff wants to go public with this."

When the Kenagys began to reveal to family and friends that their daughter was gay, members of their Mennonite church shunned them. So did some relatives and their peers in the community. They had been involved in PFLAG for two years before I called them. But being open with people close to them about having a gay family member was different from broadcasting it to the entire community in the newspaper.

"Okay," I said, not wanting to press the first farmer my family ever worked for. "Maybe I can call back and check in with you tomorrow?"

When I called the next day, Mrs. Kenagy had only one thing to say.

"When can you come over?"

At their house, Cliff brought out a photo of their daughter, Susan. The photo looked like a family studio portrait, like the ones my family got from Olan Mills or Sears. There was a glaring hole cut out from the photo, where someone's face had once been.

"So who was that?" I asked, pointing at the hole.

"That's our daughter's partner," Mrs. Kenagy chimed in, and as she said it, Mr. Kenagy's head drooped. I started my story with him.

If someone had asked Cliff Kenagy 10 years ago if he knew a gay man or lesbian, his answer would have been a confident "No."

But roughly a decade ago, he learned that his oldest daughter, Susan, is gay.

His first reaction was that he had somehow failed in raising his four children. But that feeling didn't last long, he said.

"I recall telling her I would love her regardless. I would accept her unconditionally."

Cliff was the one who cut that hole in the family photo, and as I watched him hang his head, I felt ashamed for prying into such deep and personal grief. I didn't ask when or why. I understood. Eventually, the Kenagys made it their mission to help educate others about gay issues. Mrs. Kenagy stopped going to the Mennonite church that shunned them. Together, Lois and Cliff started a religious support group for parents of lesbians and gays.

As I listened to the Kenagys talk about their experience, I felt a dull pulsing in my head and beneath my ribs. A voice inside me wouldn't stop repeating as I tried to focus on my interview. *Tell them. Tell them.*

I cleared my throat, but the words stayed stuck. I was afraid. Afraid of what it would mean for me. For Ma and me. I still lived under her roof and tried to please her. It was easier to live in that liminal space of half-truths. So I left the Kenagys' house with a notebook full of words and two stories: one story for the next day's paper and another I couldn't yet tell.

I don't remember if I told Ma that I'd interviewed Mrs. Kenagy. If I did, I probably fudged about the reason, worried she would be horrified that I had interviewed her favorite farmer about something so painful and private.

I don't remember telling Ma much of anything about my life that summer, mostly because I was hardly home. And whenever I was, I stayed in my room. I read or wrote poetry until Ma got home from work. I shuddered when I heard the front door open and close, then Ma's footfalls down the hallway to her room, where she changed out of her cook's smock into a pair of sweatpants and a cotton blouse. She barged into my room on her way back down the hallway.

"What are you doing, Put?" she would ask, poking her head in the door as she held it a crack open. "Why are you always hiding?"

I didn't say.

In the fall, when the trees started to lose their color and the fields around Corvallis lay fallow, I moved into a duplex with Chan and one of my best friends from high school, Alna, who had transferred that year into UO's business school.

On the weekends when she didn't have a shift at the dining hall, Ma and Pa drove to Eugene to deliver a box of Ma's homemade food that would last us a couple of weeks. Alna's mom also made food—aloo bhindi, curries, basmati rice—which she brought back after her weekend visits home. In between, we made ramen with an egg and green beans or broccoli, the way Ma used to make it. Sometimes dinner was rice, soy sauce, and a handful of dried shrimp or Ma's pickled plums. We learned to survive.

One weekend, I cadged a ride home to Corvallis with Alna and got dropped off at Arnold Dining Hall. When Ma saw me, she whisked around from the kitchen to the serving counter, pressed a tray into my hands, and steered me into the lunch line, swiping her own meal card through the register.

"That my daughter," she said, to a new cohort of young servers and work-study students. "She at UO in Eugene. She come to see me."

It wasn't enough for Ma to simply give me a tray and let me choose my own food. She piled everything in sight onto my plate. Meat loaf. Green beans. Steamed corn on the cob. Pasta. The different plates of foods hung precariously over the lip of the tray.

When we sat down in a corner, at a table with Ma's co-workers, Ma didn't eat. She was content to just watch me.

"I already ate earlier," Ma said, when I offered to share my food. I wondered what she had eaten. Chicken bones again?

I kept my visits short, worried that the longer I stayed home, the more time Ma had to criticize me for how I looked. I retreated back to Eugene as quickly as I could, back to my ticket to the wider world: journalism class.

When I started my Advanced Reporting class, my teacher, Bob Welch, pulled me aside one afternoon. He knew I had interned at the *Gazette-Times* and that I was already working on the school's magazine.

"You know, they're hiring at the *Register-Guard*," Bob said. "They've got two part-time positions, night shift. You'd be the only one in the newsroom. But it'd be good experience, and probably good pay."

"I don't think they'll hire me," I said. "I couldn't even get a job at the *Emerald*."

"You've got a summer internship. That's more than most of the people who apply for these part-time jobs," he said. "You should at least apply."

I wore khaki slacks, a polo shirt, and penny loafers to my interview because they were the nicest clothes I owned. When the city editor asked me why I wanted the job, I said, simply, "I love telling stories." I talked about growing up girded by my mother's fables and folktales about Cambodia, how a well-told story had the power to not only captivate but change people's minds and attitudes. I wanted to make that kind of magic.

When I was offered the job, I jumped up and down in our duplex and nearly broke through to the bottom floor. When Chan came home and I told her about it, we both laughed out loud that the campus newspaper didn't hire me, but the local newspaper, where so many of my peers in the journalism school aspired to work, did.

Ma and Pa bought me a brand-new blue Honda Civic when I told them I'd landed my first real job. When they handed me the keys, Ma said it was a late payment for all those years in the berry fields. I didn't know if I should laugh or cry.

Chan had met her boyfriend, Todd, her freshman year. But I didn't think about dating. I thought about all the classes I still had left and how not to fall asleep for my early-morning classes after I'd spent all night at the *Register-Guard* newsroom listening to the police scanner and cruising all around town to cover car crashes, crimes, and fires.

The stories I wrote at the *Register-Guard*, and most of the stories I had written the previous summer at the *Gazette-Times*, I forgot about as soon as they appeared in print. But there was one story that haunted me, that would not leave my mind: the story of Mrs. Kenagy coping with having a gay daughter, and the photograph of Susan Kenagy posing next to a woman with her face cut out. I didn't want to be that empty hole in a family photo.

For a full year after writing about the Kenagys, I felt like I was being hunted by an old emotion. I kept up hectic school and work schedules, refusing to let myself slow down. I spun through my days, waking up early for my first class and then going to the Academic Advising office in the afternoon before one or two more classes that ended in the late afternoon. I left campus by 6:00 p.m. and gulped down dinner in a few bites before driving downtown to the *Register-Guard*, where I followed breaking stories until midnight. My next class was eight hours away, which I split down the middle: four hours for homework, four for sleep. I wouldn't stop.

I worried that if I stopped or slowed, I'd have to turn around and confront that feeling—the same one that stalked me the night I wanted to kill myself the year before. The feeling I got when I skinned my nose in the first grade and ruined my class photos. The feeling that came when Ma bleached our hands at the end of picking season, to hide the dirt and the evidence of who we really were. I would be confronted with shame. I would be forced to face the person Emily said I was running from, forced to confront the fact of who I was.

I was gay.

◻ HIDING

I knew when I wanted to dress like my brother rather than like my sisters and preferred playing with his action figures and toy trucks. I knew when I always wanted to walk to school with my friend Amber, who lived down the street, and concocted every excuse to extend our play time together.

I knew when my friends had crushes on the male camp counselors during our fifth-grade field trip, while my crush was on Nesika, a high school freshman with chestnut hair she kept tied back in a ponytail who was the camp counselor in charge of the girls. She pricked her finger when she tried to affix a safety pin to my necklace with beads that spelled out my name, then sucked the blood that burst from the wound. I knew nearly nothing about her, but I loved her.

I knew when an electric shock coursed through my body when I sat next to my best friend in high school, and her hand brushed my hand and I jerked away, as if I had just touched fire. I knew who I was, since I was a kid, and in a way, when Ma called me "tomboy" and laughed along with my siblings, I wondered if maybe she knew, too.

I stayed in hiding through a summer internship at *The*

Oregonian in Portland, where I stifled a crush on the mentor assigned to me. I stayed in hiding for another year, through a dream job in a nightmare location at *The Spokesman-Review*, in eastern Washington, where depression tracked me for days. It was there in Spokane where I sat in the back row of a Lutheran church, where I had gone because it was closest to my apartment, and listened to the pastor speak about the evils of homosexuality. I decided then and there if God did not accept me because I was gay, I had no business sitting in his house.

But something about that sermon, about the shame it nudged to the surface and the uneasiness I felt being gay and Asian and living and working in a city so close to the Aryan Nation compound, seared me. My identity was shaken once more. I looped a leather belt over the closet rod in my bedroom one late night to test its strength against my weight, but once again thought of Ma, how she struggled to save me, how I must learn to save myself.

I hid until the fall of 1996, when Seattle finally flushed me from cover.

◨ RING OF FIRE

When I moved there in the fall of 1996, Seattle was still basking in the hipness of grunge. My friends and I went to the Sit & Spin lounge to do laundry and drink beer, and to the Crocodile to listen to up-and-coming garage bands. On payday, feeling flush, we sat on the rooftop of the Camlin Hotel and drained highballs and Manhattans, one after another, as the sun sank in the west, vanishing beyond the Puget Sound and behind the Olympic Mountains. Microsoft was the big game in town for technology, its headquarters hunkered amid towering pine and spruce trees on the east side of Lake Washington. And soon, Amazon would take over the Pacific Medical Building atop Beacon Hill, hovering over Interstate 5, its industrial lights flaring against the dark.

I was hired at *The Seattle Times* with a cohort of other budding journalists, all in our early twenties. We were Asian American, African American, Native American, and Latino. We were gay and straight. We were all from someplace else. And we were hungry for the next big scoop, for our names on the front page, top of the fold.

In the newsroom, the air was charged with a frenetic

MA AND ME · 221

energy that turned even the idle activity of smoking into sport as reporters competitively chain-smoked in the dank door-ways of the stone building. I caught a lucky break in January 1997 working a weekend shift when a quadruple murder shook the close-knit enclave of Bellevue, across Lake Washington from Seattle. The story made national news when two teenage boys were arrested; our newspaper at one time as-signed seven reporters to the case. Mine was a constant by-line, ultimately catching the attention of a local literary agent who urged me to write a true crime book.

By the spring, I had signed a book deal with a major New York publishing house. I was twenty-three years old. I called Ma to tell her the news, which she in turn broadcast to all of our relatives and her friends in Oregon.

"My daughter is famous!"

The irony of my situation didn't escape me. I came from a country of mass murder only to arrive in America and into a career that channeled me toward writing a book about a multiple murder. I could not escape the constant reminder of senseless deaths.

In Seattle, I was suddenly surrounded by cool people my age. After speeding through college mostly alone, I finally had a seemingly endless supply of new friends to hang out with.

Keiko was my first friend in Seattle. She smoked Camel Lights, and when I watched her one night exhale with a con-trolled elegance, I was already in love with her. She wore keys that clinked on chains around her neck when she sa-shayed through the newsroom in her thrift-store fashions. And when she talked about her sources and her stories, she cussed with casual defiance.

She was a classic brand of journalist, and I knew I would never be like that, but watching Keiko made me realize how easy and important it was to be comfortable in your own skin. She was a Jersey girl, half Japanese and half black, and didn't care what anyone in Seattle or in the newsroom thought about her. If she was hit on at the bars and clubs we went to by a man or a woman, she was flattered just the same. If an ignorant person asked to touch her hair, she laughed in their face. I'd never met anyone like her.

The newsroom vibrated with the combined energy of other reporters of color who made no apologies about who they were. I saw more people of color in the *Seattle Times* newsroom than in my entire life in Corvallis. We debated over local draft beers about the world being a melting pot versus a salad. Nothing conclusive came of these conversations and I didn't care. I felt, for the first time, like I belonged.

Tyrone was the first gay friend I ever had. We met for lunch, and when Ty revealed that he was gay, I was immediately in awe of him. He often started stories with the words "My mama told me," and if you listened closely, you could still hear echoes of Kentucky tucked into his inflections. He had a boyfriend, and when he told me so, he said it so casually, it barely registered that this man loved another man. He said it as if it were the most ordinary thing.

I hadn't wanted to admit that I was probably gay, too, but I figured if I was going to reveal myself to anyone, Ty would be the safest person to tell. I didn't use the word "gay" when I told him. I had had crushes on guys in college. I didn't know what exactly I was, so I said I was bisexual. It felt more safe to me than true at the time. Being bisexual felt like familiar territory. I already existed in that middle realm between being Khmer and being American. I was okay with straddling sexual orientation lines, too.

"Oh, honey," he said, after I mumbled my way through

coming out to him. "Let's find you a girlfriend. That's the only way to know for sure."

I didn't know I wanted a girlfriend until I met Ty. In college, I poured my time and energy into school so I could graduate early. After college, I hustled at my internship and then later at *The Spokesman-Review* to prove myself a skilled reporter. In Seattle, there was an entire neighborhood dedicated to gay people. I could hold hands with another woman here and it would be perfectly normal.

We met one night after work at the Wildrose on Capitol Hill, a predominantly gay neighborhood of Seattle. The Wildrose was the only lesbian bar in town. I had asked Ty if he would teach me how to snag a girlfriend.

"First of all, you have to change your attitude," Ty said, laughing. "This is not open season on lesbians. We are not on a hunt."

It felt like it to me. As if I needed to develop the skills to identify the correct species for me—women who liked other women.

"Be casual," Ty said. "You want to give off a vibe that you're just here, hanging out, having fun."

I was not exactly having fun. I felt itchy in my slacks, J.Crew button-down shirt, and outdated penny loafers. Ty and I sat on swivel stools at one end of the bar, the place so dark I could barely see him, much less any potential date for me. I did see a few ladies playing pool and a handful more scattered at two-tops on the far side of the joint. I noticed I was the only one who was not sheathed in leather and ink, and who wasn't wearing combat boots. I wasn't dressed for going out because I didn't own going-out clothes.

It was my first time inside a gay bar, let alone one that catered to women. I hid my nervousness just about as well as my awkward choice in clothes. My legs kept moving, and I shifted constantly on my stool, swiveling left and then right, craning my head toward the door every time it pushed open and someone new walked in. I didn't feel casual. I felt completely anxious.

When a woman who looked my age, with short, brunette hair, blue jeans, and black boots, walked in alone and took a seat at the other end of the bar, I elbowed Ty. He sat calmly nursing a rum and Coke.

"That one," I whispered. "I like her. Can you go talk to her?"

Ty chuckled.

"What? No. That's your job, honey," he said.

"What do I do?" I said, trying not to look at her but not being able to help myself.

"Send her down a drink," Ty said.

I kept trying to catch the eye of the bartender to ask what the woman had ordered so I could send her a second round, but by the time the bartender came back around to us, the woman was gone.

"Shit," I said, "there goes my future wife."

I didn't go back to the Wildrose again for a long while. Instead, I poured whatever energy I didn't put into work into building a cadre of new friends. Slowly, I started to open up corners of myself I did not know existed. I had grown up in a predominantly white agricultural community in Oregon. Now, surrounded by so many people from other cultures and parts of America, I started to feel prouder of my immigrant roots.

My job at the newspaper also connected me back to my culture. I was assigned a story about a Khmer doctor in town who started a knitting club for survivors of the Khmer Rouge genocide. She hoped that if the women kept their hands busy, they would eventually begin to process and talk about their experiences of war. I was told that the women did not speak fluent English. And I did not speak fluent Khmer. So I called someone who did: Ma.

Ma was thrilled to be able to help me pursue my stories, even offering some of her own questions to add to mine. She was so excited for me that I wondered, if things had been different for her, if she had been able to do anything she wanted with an education, as her uncle insisted, would she have chosen to be a journalist, too?

I dashed through a list of questions I wanted to ask the women in the knitting circle, and asked Ma to help me translate. I told Ma my questions in English, and when Ma told me how to say the phrases in Khmer, I wrote them down phonetically. I clutched my list with me when I interviewed the Khmer women in a small storefront on First Hill.

The day the story came out, I walked into the newsroom and grabbed a copy of the paper as editors stopped to praise me. Another reporter could have done the story, but I was certain because I was Khmer and could close the communication gap between me and my interviewees, I got the best story.

I felt, for the first time since Ma and I had returned from our trip to Cambodia seven years prior and had struggled to see eye to eye, that we were finally finding common ground again. And bubbling just beneath the surface was the undeniable truth, a thought I had tried to banish when I went away to college: I still needed my mother, and she clearly wanted to feel she was needed, too.

In the newsroom, I quickly discovered that the boundless energy of my peers lasted deep into the small hours; they all seemed to be sleeping with each other. Among reporters, rumors raced from one cubicle to the next faster than the house fires we covered. I didn't know if anyone else at the newspaper was gay, but I made it known to my friends that I was available and interested in dating, just in case.

"I think you should meet my roommate," Wanda, one of the young photographers, said to me one day. "I think you two would get along."

Wanda lived with two female friends on the top floor of a duplex in the Lower Queen Anne neighborhood with a view of the Space Needle from the kitchen window. The next day after work, I followed Wanda back to her place.

We walked through the family room and past the kitchen, to a back bedroom where a woman was lying sprawled on a bed, her face hidden behind a magazine.

"Hey, Meg, this is my friend Put," Wanda said. "She works at *The Seattle Times* with me."

Wanda moved to the side, revealing me.

"Hi!" I chirped, my voice crackling with nerves.

"Put just moved from Spokane, but she's originally from . . ." Wanda turned to me. "Where in Oregon did you say?"

"Corvallis," I said. "That's where I grew up, but my family is from Cambodia."

Meg shot up from her lounging position on the bed and burst to the door to shake my hand. In her other hand, she held her magazine, folded over.

"Oh my god, this is so crazy," Meg said. "I'm literally reading about Pol Pot and the genocide in Cambodia. It's here in *The New Yorker*. Have you read it?"

I hadn't. Meg was beaming at the coincidence of the situation. She said she'd loan me the magazine once she was done.

She was beautiful, with wavy strawberry-blond hair and a

smile that seemed to emit its own light and heat. She worked as an editor for Sasquatch Books, a local publishing house. I took it as a sign that we met at the exact moment she was reading about my country's genocide. It was the summer of 1997. And I was in love.

Looking back, I should have anticipated the universe throwing a wrench at me. Three weeks after meeting Meg, I met a man who was so kind and handsome, it stopped me in my tracks. David was a friend of Keiko's, a reporter for the local NPR affiliate in Seattle. He held a house party and, not knowing Keiko intended to set me up with him, I invited Meg. There I was, sitting on a futon couch sandwiched between Meg and David.

Later, David and I met for tea and then lunch, and the more I talked to him, the more I started to feel that first woozy flash of a crush. I found myself in a tight spot. Her or him?

"Is it possible to fall in love with two people at the same time?" I asked Keiko.

We were lounging on her bed, in her studio apartment, staring at the ceiling.

"Sure it is," Keiko said, blowing smoke from a freshly lit cigarette. "I think you can love a lot of people at the same time. You just have to know what you really want."

I told Keiko I was dating Meg. And I didn't yet know what or who I wanted. Keiko suggested I be up front with both of them, and confess my dilemma: I liked them both, though hadn't yet kissed either. The mere thought of telling Meg that I liked a guy or telling David that I liked a girl made my heart race with anxiety.

When I presented my predicament to David, he seemed unfazed.

"Can you just date us both for a period of time, and then decide?" David asked.

He was serious, and I was a little bit stunned. I never imagined that that would be an option, to date two people at once.

When I presented my predicament to Meg, she was also unfazed.

"I'm sure you'll figure it out," Meg said.

But before I had a chance to date both of them, something else decided for me.

That weekend, Meg and I went to Capitol Hill, ducking into a gay bookstore and then eating avocado toast at a corner café where we sat pressed up next to gay boys who smiled and flashed us a thumbs-up. When we walked back to my car, Meg pulled me into a side street, pressed me against a brick wall, and kissed me. A jolt of electricity buzzed in my brain, down my spine, and to my toes. I had never been kissed like that by a girl, or by anyone.

We kissed on the sidewalk and in the stairway to her apartment. We stumbled up to her bedroom, where Meg undressed quickly. I stood, watching awkwardly, unsure of what to do.

"Do you need help?" she said, nodding at my shirt.

"Oh, no, I . . ." and in an instant, I was fully naked in bed with a woman.

When I broke the news to David that I had chosen Meg, a sadness flared inside. A feeling of betrayal. Of David. But also of Ma.

Ma had raised me and my sisters with the knowledge that we would grow up and get married and have kids, like she did. But ever since I'd left Ma, with that first separation in college, I tried to follow my own instincts and impulses. I tried to know myself apart from her. The physical distance made it possible for me to claim some emotional distance, too. Now that I was even further beyond her line of sight, I stretched. I was attracted to both men and women, so I stayed open to both genders. But after being kissed by Meg, I knew what I knew.

I hadn't come out to anyone in my family, but when Chan landed a job in Seattle and moved in with me, I knew I couldn't hide. I had already met Todd, her boyfriend, and I wanted her to meet my girlfriend.

We met for lunch in downtown Seattle, near the Russian export office where she worked. When our salads came out, I did, too.

"Just wondering if you heard me," I said between bites of salad. "I said I'm gay."

"Yes, I heard you. It doesn't matter if you're gay," Chan said. "It doesn't change anything."

Chan barely batted an eye and just kept crunching through her salad.

I took a deep breath and let it out slowly. I was grateful for Chan's reaction. I told her about Meg and that I planned to tell our parents and the other siblings individually. If no one else in our family accepted me, at least I had my sister.

A month after I met Meg, Ma called. I panicked and wondered if the pineapple was watching me, if she knew I was dating a woman. But there was an excitement in her voice.

"I have a concept!" Ma chirped into the phone. "They moved me to cook in a new building. There's Italian food, a deli, Mexican. And I have my concept."

"Ma, I don't know what concept you're talking about," I said. "Are you leaving the dorms?"

Ma explained how Oregon State University's housing

department, which managed student dining services, was renovating one of the bigger dormitories, and creating a food court where students could swipe their meal cards and choose what foods they wanted to eat. Ma was in charge of the Asian food.

"I have to make a name for my concept," Ma mused out loud. "What do you think of 'Ring of Fire'?"

Ma rolled around the name out loud a few times and I could feel her smiling through the phone.

"Dat da Ring . . . of . . . Fire!" she said in English, drawing out the word "fire" so that it sounded explosive on her outbreath.

"I like that name, Ma," I said, chuckling. "So what are you going to cook?"

"I'll have two woks and make stir-fries and soups. I'll make egg rolls, and the chicken you kids love to eat with rice," Ma said, her words racing into my ears. "I'll make the students all the food I made for you guys."

Ma kept talking as I sat on my sofa in the West Seattle flat I shared with Chan and gazed out across the Puget Sound. Ma talked about how her pay had gone up and how her old colleagues at Arnold were jealous that she had been chosen to operate a concept at the food court. I pressed the phone into my ear, wanting to take it all in—my mother, for the first time that I could recall in America, sounded happy.

An emotion washed over me all at once, bittersweet. I wanted to tell her, but couldn't, that I was finally happy, too.

☐ THE SUITOR

We had a habit, Ma and me, of talking on the phone every week, even when we were fighting. It started when I went away to college. Mostly, I called her, to check up and see how she was doing. Occasionally, she called me. If we didn't talk constantly, she would think I was dead. If we didn't talk constantly, I would think Pa was mistreating her. I understood the moment I moved out of my parents' home that this was an imperative part of being a Cambodian daughter—letting Ma know where and how I was at all times.

After I moved to Seattle, Ma and I kept up our weekly conversations. Only now, those calls shifted to the weekends, often after I had gotten home from hanging out with Meg. Because I never told Ma about Meg, she assumed I was single. I was twenty-three years old, already a year older than she was when she had her first child, when she found herself trapped in an arranged marriage because she had to choose between hiding out in the middle of a war and getting married.

So when she called one day asking if I remembered the

middle son of one of her friends, I rolled my eyes, already suspicious.

"Gohn," she said, "do you remember Thavy's family? They came with us on the boat?"

Alex Trebek's voice droned in the background. Even though Ma could not answer any of the trivia questions, she watched *Jeopardy!* every day for the sole purpose of getting an education.

"Of course I know them," I said. "Thavy and I used to play together when we were little."

Ma plowed ahead.

"You know Thavy's brother, Phearum, he just moved to Tacoma," Ma said. "Isn't that close to Seattle?"

My suspicions churned and churned. I knew where the conversation was going and tried to head her off.

"Not really," I said. "It's not that close."

"Gohn, I talked to his mother, and we thought maybe you two could meet," Ma said. "Just have lunch together. Just talk and get to know each other."

I wanted to kick myself. If I had been brave enough to come out to Ma, we wouldn't be having this conversation. I thought about Meg. I wanted to tell Ma then and there that I was gay. But the words failed to form on my tongue. Instead, I tried to find the quickest exit from the conversation.

"Ma, we probably don't have anything in common," I said. "And besides, I work long hours at the paper."

"Gohn," Ma said, "can you please just agree to meet him once? Is it going to kill you?"

And so I agreed, if only to make Ma happy. I knew I wouldn't like him in the way Ma hoped I would. I was already in love with someone else.

A few weeks later, Phearum drove north on Interstate 5

to meet me in Seattle. We had talked once or twice on the phone, awkward conversations where neither of us said much and covered the silences by negotiating logistics. We met for dinner at a Chinese restaurant in the International District and at the last minute, I begged Chan to come along.

"You owe me one," Chan said, as we got into the car.

I didn't remember much about Phearum when we were growing up. He ran around with his brothers and mine. If Phearum sensed my unease on the phone, it was exacerbated in person. Our conversation was stilted, punctuated by silences that seemed to stretch for minutes at a time. Chan probed for updates on Phearum's family and his new job, and he meekly asked the same questions back. Chan did most of the talking, and in that moment I loved her more than anything.

I called Ma before I had a chance to take off my shoes and coat as I flung myself through our front door.

"Like I said, Ma, we don't have anything in common," I said.

Ma was stubborn, same as me. She tried every avenue to persuade me to meet Phearum again, this time alone, and to spend more time with him. She appealed to my sentimental, duty-bound side that was relentlessly loyal to her.

"You know, we all escaped the war together, gohn," Ma continued. "His parents are good people. His family is all good. Ma would be so happy if our families joined together."

When she realized her plan to set me up with the son of one of her closest friends would not materialize, her voice flattened, deflated by failure.

"Ma wants to see you happy, gohn," Ma said. "You're getting old. Ma and Pa don't have too many more ideas for who you can marry."

"I don't need help, Ma," I said, careful not to squash her

good intentions. "There are plenty of people in the world. I'll find someone."

That night, I drove over to Meg's and collapsed into her arms. I fell into the deepest sleep.

I tried to visit Ma and Pa as much as I could, worried that Ma might be a little lonely now that all her kids were gone. I stopped at the International District in Seattle to gather moon cakes, sesame balls, and baguettes—the things I knew they would have a hard time finding in Corvallis. I went to campus to eat her egg rolls and stir-fried noodles at the Ring of Fire. Ma piled my plate high, double what she paid for. She held my arm as she walked me through the food hall, announcing to her colleagues, "This my daughter. She the baby one. She a famous journalist!"

"I'm not famous," I told them all as I walked by. "Just a journalist."

At home, over a dinner of rice and pan-fried fish with fresh herbs, I told Ma about some of the stories I wrote for the newspaper, how Chan and I were cooking some of her dishes in our apartment, and how I was meeting plenty of friends.

I omitted Meg from my conversations, even though I wanted to tell Ma that I had met someone who was kind, smart, and loyal—the sorts of qualities I believed she would like. It felt deceitful, to keep hidden from her the most important new aspect of my life: I had a girlfriend. But I was afraid. Afraid and guilty. I was raised to marry a man. I had fallen in love with a woman. I didn't yet know where I could safely stand between my Khmer culture and my American culture. So I stayed silent, and asked my siblings to keep silent, too.

I'll tell her one day, I told my siblings. When I'm ready, I will tell her. I insisted our mother hear it from me. But a year passed, and then another. I stayed hidden in my cozy swaddle of secrets.

For my family, it seemed as though bad news came as the price of good news. That the universe had concocted some terrible calculus for my family and could not simply deliver good news into our lives and leave it at that. It was as if a taut rope was strung in between, too much good news and we were snapped back to the bad.

Such was the situation in 1999, the year Chan got engaged and Grandpa died. Grandpa Sin's diabetes had started to plunder his body and by the spring of 1999, both of his legs developed gangrene. I drove to Oregon to see him shortly after his double amputation, a procedure that saved his life but ultimately extinguished his will to live.

He was heavily sedated when I walked into his room.

"Granddaughter," he said when he saw me. "Grandpa is not feeling well."

He shifted in bed as I reached for apple juice and brought it to his lips so he could take a sip.

"My legs," he said, "are they gone?"

I paused, choking back tides of emotion. All my life, Grandpa Sin was the explorer in the family. He rode the bus to every neighborhood of Portland, and in our early years in America, he rode a bike with one of my little cousins in the basket up front. When I moved to Seattle, he called Chan and begged her to take him to visit me. We explored Pike Place Market, slurping clam chowder at the waterfront and buying sesame balls in the International District, my grandfather poking his hook cane at trash along the sidewalk hoping to surface an abandoned coin. Those legs of his had carried him out of our burning country twenty-four years prior. Now they were gone.

"Yes, Grandpa," I said. "They had to cut off your legs to save you."

He stared at the ceiling, his face full of resignation as he reached down below his knee and patted down the sheets where there was emptiness beyond his knees. He kept patting the bed, as if his legs were merely misplaced somewhere and his fingers would surely make contact with them if he just kept searching. He gave up eventually, exhaled deeply, and lay back in bed.

I stayed at Grandpa's bedside for three days before I returned to Seattle. He told me stories about when he was younger and learned to speak Japanese because he worked with Japanese traders at the port in Kampong Som. He started counting to ten in Japanese to prove it. *Ichi, ni, san, yon, go* . . . collapsing his fingers as he went until he got too sleepy and started snoring.

When he woke again, we talked about our trip to Cambodia in 1990. The fresh papayas and mangoes. The delicious fish. I said I would take him back to our homeland once he was out of the hospital and felt better. We would return home together. He smiled as he drifted off into his next drug-induced nap.

Less than a month later, I felt a sharp pain shoot through my gut. I was in downtown Seattle in the King County Courthouse, covering the Bellevue quadruple murder trial. By then, I'd left *The Seattle Times* to work full-time on the book, which would be published two years later. During a break in the day-long trial, my friend at *The Seattle Times* saw me clasp my hands over my stomach and raised his eyebrow in concern. He gently took my mini cassette recorder from me.

"Just go home," he said. "I got you covered."

At home, I flung open the front door and felt nauseous. I glanced at the answering machine, a single red light flashing.

When I pressed Play, my mother's voice came through, flooding my apartment with her words mangled by her sobbing.

"Put," she said, "gohn, get your sister and come home."

Grandpa died on a Wednesday, twelve days before his eighty-eighth birthday in March. Less than one month after he lost his legs. As I watched the cemetery crew lower Grandpa's casket into the earth, I felt my knees buckle. Aunt Samnang had already collapsed on his coffin and crawled to the edge of the pit, one hand reaching in and clawing the earth as she screamed to be buried with her father. Ma was wailing so loudly, it echoed down the valley below.

Grandpa's death shook something loose in me. Before he passed away, he told me, "Always remember, granddaughter, we come from the good people."

What did he mean? What did he want me to know? I regret I never asked him.

We had promised each other we would take one more trip together to Cambodia. I never got to fulfill that pledge, and the broken commitment stung my lungs. I couldn't breathe.

Grandpa was buried in a plot of land overlooking the valley

of Portland's west-side suburb of Beaverton, where he spent his entire time in America. He had bought the plot years in advance, for close to three thousand dollars. I had always assumed that he would want to be cremated and have his ashes brought back to Cambodia. But he had fled Cambodia more than twenty years before, and somewhere along the way, he had come to terms with his existence in America. In the year before he passed away, Grandpa joined dozens of other immigrants at the federal building in Portland to answer three questions about American history and politics in front of a judge. When he answered correctly, he became someone new: an American citizen.

In my parents' Buddhist tradition, when a family member passes away, the surviving family must call forth the spirit of the deceased to release the living and step forward into heaven. This transition occurs one hundred days after death. The family makes offerings of food and accoutrements for the journey: a new pair of sandals, a blanket, and candles to light the way into the next life. In June, Grandpa would have been dead for one hundred days. In May, exactly one month before that posthumous milestone, Ma called.

"I'm going to Cambodia," she said, "to do the ceremony. Do you want to go?"

◻

It was just the two of us, this time, on the plane. Ma and me. I didn't have to pack a suitcase full of books because I was no longer a student. Instead, I filled two suitcases with gifts and medicine for our relatives back home. I hadn't imagined the next time I'd return to Cambodia would be both for my grandfather and without him. To go to the country of your birth on these terms puts joy so adjacent to sadness that they mute each other's edge. I felt an emptiness push into my core.

It would be my second trip to my homeland in less than a decade. In the intervening years, I had graduated from college, and landed both a job and a girlfriend. I was twenty-five years old and newly swept into a dizzying momentum, professionally and personally. I wondered whether Cambodia and my relatives' lives had changed, too.

We arrived in Phnom Penh just as the skies burst open with monsoons. When the rains came, it was as if, through a single slit in the sky, an entire sea crashed onto the land. I watched from the balcony as motorbikes stalled out in front of our hotel in the Boeung Keng Kang I neighborhood, where Uncle San lived. Only Land Cruisers with the blue United Nations logo on the door and black snorkel jutting up along the hood seemed to pass easily in the flooded streets. In a few days, we would take our chances with the downpours and gun it for the village. Monsoon or not, we had to send Grandpa to heaven.

Ming Pheaktra and the kids greeted us at the airport. Her kids had grown taller, creeping into preadolescence, along with countless other cousins I had met the first time I visited Cambodia. The city was progressing, too. Great-Uncle San's road and a webbed network of other minor neighborhood roads around his house had finally been paved. But in between rains, the dust still clung stubbornly to the roads' uneven edges. A collection of new restaurants and hotels had opened to cater to the country's burgeoning tourist industry. And fiber optic cables laid underground had brought dial-up internet, connecting Cambodia to the world in a way that emphatically announced progress.

Nine years earlier, when I was a teenager, I had navigated my country and my relatives with awkward apprehension, thrust into a culture I struggled to claim because it was both mine and not mine. When you live in one country but belong to another, your feet fall hesitantly upon the earth. I was a stranger in my own country, and there is no greater unease than feeling alone in the midst of an entire population that looks like you.

Back then, I had felt resolutely American. My perm, my faded Levi's, and the Sony Walkman hooked to my hip practically screamed it. But learning more about Cambodia in a college course in Asian American studies and being among a diverse group of friends in Seattle had inspired me to embrace my Cambodian culture. On this trip, I was determined to fit in as Khmer.

I wore a long skirt that went to my ankles and kept a krama with me at all times, slung over my shoulder to swat at flies or swipe sweat dripping from my forehead, the way I saw other Khmer women do. I wore a pure gold bracelet and necklace that Ma slipped on me before our plane landed in Phnom Penh, because Khmer people only wear twenty-four-karat gold, Ma said. I was willing to do or wear whatever I needed to better camouflage myself, to be absorbed into the landscape, into the place where I was born. Ma beamed when she saw my efforts to dress and act modestly, proud of my steps to move closer to my Khmer heritage.

This time, rather than turn my face away in disgust, I held my breath and ate tiny pickled crabs, and cucumbers dipped in prahok. I plunged my spoon into every bowl of soup and stir-fry nudged my way. I ran to the bathroom after nearly every meal, my stomach revolting against the local bugs and bacteria.

"You have an American stomach," one of my cousins said to me, cackling as I grabbed my gut in agony. He suggested I go around the corner to the Italian restaurant or the burger joint and eat with the foreigners. I refused. I was in Cambodia. I wanted to be Khmer, to be a part of a culture that, up until then, I had carried as a cloak. And that cloak had stayed mostly hung in the closet.

My cousins took me to see sights around town: the National Museum, the Royal Palace, the riverfront.

At the museum, the man at the ticket booth watched as my cousins and I got out of their car. He charged my cousins five hundred riel and me two dollars.

"What?" one of my cousins said. "She's one of us."

"Yes, maybe she is Cambodian, but she is from abroad," the ticket attendant said.

When we paid and walked off, I asked my cousin, "How did he know?"

"Because of the way you walk," my cousin said.

"How do I walk?" I asked.

"Fast. Really, really fast."

I realized that in Cambodia, people ambled as if they had all the time in the world. I believed I walked fast because I was a reporter, in the habit of hustling from one place to the next, constantly driven by a deadline. But Ma corrected me.

"You've always been fast, walking, biking," Ma said. "Ever since you were little. Out of all my kids, you're the one who moves with nervous energy. You can't stay still."

The next day, we went to the statehouse to tour the royal buildings. I approached with slow, measured steps, which I had to remind myself to do because my legs kept threatening to shoot out ahead of me. At the ticket booth, I balked at the five-dollar ticket price in my best Khmer, deploying the kind of dramatic flair and exasperation I'd observed my cousins using in almost every interaction that involved an exchange of cash. I spoke only limited Khmer, but exasperation needed no words.

"That's the price for foreigners," the ticket guy said. "You only pay fifteen hundred riel." Less than fifty cents.

I smiled, knowing I had just gotten away with faking my true identity, and my cousins clasped hands over their mouths to stifle their laughter.

Nearly a decade had passed between my first return to Cambodia and now, and I had grasped onto my Khmer identity with urgent resolve. Living in Seattle, where I was accepted by my friends, had helped me accept myself. I had read every book and newspaper and magazine article I could find about Cambodia and I cooked Khmer chicken wings and hot and sour soup for Meg. But in Cambodia, no matter how hard I tried to be Khmer, I could not completely hide the fact that I was American.

In whatever ways I managed to hide who I was in the city, village life exposed the bigger rift between me and my relatives.

The landscape beyond Cambodia's urban core had changed little since I was last in the country as a teenager, but among my cousins, major milestones had been reached. Most were married. Families multiplied and moved into small stilt huts as family rice paddy plots got split to accommodate new family units.

When we arrived in Chous village for Grandpa's ceremony, our relatives came to us, just as they had several years before, surrounding our car before it came to a full stop. My aunts pinched my cheeks and I smiled and let them. My cousins approached more slowly, some with babies hooked to their hips.

Nine years ago, we were teenagers, eyeing each other with curiosity. Now they were mothers. If my family and I had never escaped our country, if we had survived the genocide as my cousins had, if I had been here living in the village alongside them, no doubt I would be married and toting babies, too.

"What about you, Put?" one of my cousins asked. "Where is your husband? Do you have children?"

"No," I said, my tone part apology, part shame. "I'm not married. I don't have kids. I'm busy working."

My Khmer was still limited and stilted, but I tried to communicate this time without Ma's help. Working at *The Seattle Times* and being asked to write stories about Seattle's Khmer community had forced me to relearn a language that buzzed in the background of my American life.

"But you must be quite old," one of my cousins said. "Are you twenty-three or twenty-four years old?"

"Twenty-five," I said, which made them grumble in unison. I was already an old lady.

How was it possible that I was twenty-five years old and still not married? I reminded them that my own mother was twenty-two years old when she got married. I reminded them that things were different in America.

"In America, some women don't marry until they're thirty or forty," I said. "Some women don't marry at all."

My cousins gasped. I might as well have been an alien who had landed in their rice paddies. They could accept that women might not get married until they are older, but they could not accept the notion that some women don't marry at all. The concept was beyond their comprehension.

Then I heard the thoughts formulating in my head: And some women are gay, like me. I felt the words jostle in my mouth, but nothing came out. I worried that the guaranteed scandal such an admission would bring might overshadow Grandpa's ceremony. So I stayed quiet.

A silence shattered by Great-Uncle San's booming voice.

"Get the mats. Get the incense sticks. Get the offerings," he said, chasing all of us to our feet and over to the pagoda.

The hour was late. The monks were coming. The time had come to settle Grandpa's spirit.

"We come from the good people," Grandpa had said before he passed away. In the weeks and months after his passing, I repeated those words in my head and wanted to believe that he would have still said so if he knew his granddaughter was gay.

☐ THAT THE GAY

I wanted to marry Meg. She was both my first girlfriend and my first love. But that summer, after coming back from Grandpa Sin's ceremony in Cambodia, I was restless again. I felt a force both mine and otherworldly, pushing me from behind. I needed to run. I didn't see it then for what it was—grief was propelling me, a pain in my heart that shot through to my legs and made it even harder to stay still. I had to keep moving.

I applied for newspaper jobs in New York, Georgia, and California. When I was offered a job at *The San Jose Mercury News* in the Bay Area that tripled my salary and doubled my vacation time, I mapped the miles between San Jose and Corvallis. By car and by plane, I was still within a day's distance of home. Meg had talked about getting a master's degree in music. Berkeley was on her radar. Without ever asking her, I accepted the job and assumed she would be overjoyed to join me. The thought of starting over together in California buoyed me up.

"I'll find us a nice apartment in Berkeley, or somewhere close," I promised Meg, with a sales pitch saturated with conviction. "I can support us while you go to school."

A month later, when she came to visit me in California and we cruised around neighborhoods I thought she might like, Meg was distant. Looking back, I could have seen the coming end, my own selfishness driving my girlfriend away. But sometimes you only see the crash when you wake in the wreckage.

In the summer, before I moved to California, Meg was my date to my sister's wedding. Even though I hadn't come out yet to Ma, I begged Meg to come to Corvallis anyway. Chan and Todd had planned to have both Khmer and American ceremonies, and I wanted Meg to see and experience the kind of wedding we might have one day. Meg protested when I suggested I introduce her to my mother as my friend. Which made me plead even more. In the end, Meg came late to the wedding, but she was there.

Ma breezed around our house on Ironwood Avenue during the Khmer ceremony, greeting guests, refilling trays of her egg rolls, and rushing a cauldron of chicken curry to the table. Between all the running around to feed more than a hundred guests at the ceremony, she sat with Pa up front, Todd's parents opposite them. I had never seen her happier. Deep down, I still wanted to make her that proud, too. But I also wanted to be happy for me. Those two desires clanged inside me.

Chan chose me and our cousin Malis as her bridesmaids. We rotated into and out of five different outfits throughout the day as I sat with my legs flanked to the side and my body cambered forward in prayer through a series of rituals.

I watched Ma smile as she clipped symbolic locks of Chan's and Todd's hair, and as she tied red string around their wrists. I felt proud of my sister and grateful for our culture. In one part of the ceremony, the bride and groom stand behind their parents as the wedding achar recites mantras that acknowledge a debt settlement, or sang khun, between the bride and groom and their parents, every wedding the highest honor to a Khmer mother and father.

I couldn't hold back my tears as I watched Chan and Todd sang khun. I felt a jarring sense of hope then, that I might one day be able to sang khun, too.

At the reception, where 350 predominantly Khmer guests streamed into a Chinese restaurant in Portland, when I tried to get Meg to dance, she declined. When I reached for her hand under the table, she pulled it away. I underestimated the cost of what I had asked her to do by coming to Chan's wedding as my friend: I was asking her to lie. Meg had been out of the closet for years before I met her. I was the jerk who was asking her to go back in. She knew, when I decided to move to California, that we were through. We broke up, over the phone, six weeks after I moved to California. One week before Valentine's Day.

Back then, I believed I was laying groundwork for a future with Meg. Now I see that for the conceit it was. For how wrong I was. I had asked the person I loved to compromise herself for me, to hide who she was because I was still in hiding. I wasn't brave enough. I knew she could find someone braver and better than me.

When Ma visited me in California that spring, I was single and finally ready to tell her I was gay. I knew I didn't want to get involved with anyone else until I could be honest with Ma. And also myself.

She flew alone into Oakland International Airport for a long weekend, to see for herself what kind of life her baby was making far from home. When she arrived at the one-bedroom apartment I'd found, one block from Oakland's Lake Merritt, she reflexively shook her head in disapproval. The unit was in a five-plex, carved out of an old Victorian house with shake shingles that had grown dark and oily over the years. Ma likes new things. New cars. New homes. New money. For her, new was a status symbol, to say to the world we had succeeded in America.

"New smells good and looks good," Ma said, frowning as we entered my front door. "No one wants something old."

I couldn't explain to Ma how I loved the character of old buildings in general and my particular apartment, with its industrial gas range and a flat grill top. I couldn't explain how I loved the shaded balcony with French doors, and the back patio off my bedroom where a screen of bleeding hearts hung along the rail. I couldn't explain these things because I knew she would not understand. This was not the kind of home aesthetics or setup she had envisioned for me. To my superstitious mother, inhabiting an old house was a dubious affair. Who knew what kind of bad energy still hung in the air? New, to Ma's way of thinking, meant zero chance that the place might be haunted with someone else's spirit.

To distract my mother from her disappointment in my choice of housing, I took her for a drive.

In San Francisco's Chinatown, she joined a buzzing scrum of old women, their heads ducked into a fruit bin on the sidewalk where they were duking it out for the best pomelos. Ma got into the fray and emerged victorious with an enormous fruit she held up with both hands like a trophy. Only later did I notice the scratches on both arms. She loved this kind of food frenzy, of fighting for the good stuff. It reminded her of Cambodia.

Back at my apartment, Ma stir-fried beef with gai lan, and she made a hearty soup with winter melon and pork meatballs. I laid out day-old copies of my newspaper on the floor and we ate on top of a story I wrote about a zoning ordinance in the suburbs that banned blinking neon signs.

As we chewed in silence, my heartbeat quickened, jogging before sprinting between my ears. Tell her now, I heard myself say in my head as I took a bite of stir-fry. But no words came out. I slurped some more soup and heard myself say again, Tell her. But still I held back. Through the rest of dinner, the pressure kept building until finally, after we finished eating and sat together on the red velvet love seat I'd bought years earlier at a garage sale, Ma asked me how long I was going to wait until I got married. I dropped into her opening:

"Ma, I'm gay," I said.

My voice shook and tears sprang into my eyes. I told myself not to cry, worried that Ma would get the wrong impression and misinterpret my tears as meaning I was ashamed of being gay.

Ma stayed silent for a few minutes, taking in the information. This was the moment that terrified me most. She could cast me aside. Or she could keep me as her daughter.

There we were, on the red love seat, pinched together. I finally let myself cry.

"It's okay, gohn," Ma said, her face full of sadness and concern. "Ma love you."

In that moment, my resolve fell away. It was the first time in my life she said she loved me. All of my hesitations and angst and fear that she would reject me dissipated. At first, I thought perhaps she misunderstood me. So I said it again, "I'm gay, and I might not get married."

She held me a little tighter.

I still wasn't certain that Ma understood what I was telling her, so I loaded us up in my Honda Civic and drove across the Oakland Bay Bridge. I plunged us into the wild and beating heart of San Francisco's gay neighborhood, the Castro district.

When I was a little girl, my parents took us kids on a field trip to Wildlife Safari in southern Oregon, where Pa drove the car slowly through an outdoor wildlife preserve. A cheetah leapt onto the hood of our car, causing Pa to slam on the brakes and the rest of us to scream in terror. We kept our windows rolled up, just as we were instructed. I pressed my cheek to the window, impatient to spot all the animals.

Driving through the Castro, Ma was the one who now pressed her own chubby cheek to the window. This was Ma's version of Wildlife Safari, the human edition. We passed women with buzz cuts and chains hooked around their hips and latched at one end to leather wallets that protruded from back pockets. We passed a queen in chunky red heels, leopard-print pants, and a sequined top, sashaying expertly down the street. When we passed two men in leather chaps, their bare butts hanging out, Ma tapped the window with a forefinger.

"Put," she said, pointing directly at the couple, "dat da gay?"

"Yes, Ma, that's the gay," I said. "Stop pointing."

I rolled my eyes. We drove on. We drove home. I drove her the next morning to the airport. When she hugged me and told me again she loved me, I thought we'd be okay. I thought she understood. I thought we'd get through this together.

I didn't know, until many years later, that I had miscalculated the moment completely.

I was single and surged into San Francisco's gay scene, reenergized after coming out to Ma. I was fully free. My friend YY took me to a lesbian Jell-O wrestling contest in the Tenderloin where someone thrust a cup of beer in my hand and I watched, a little stunned, at a room completely covered in plastic and dozens of women frolicking naked all around, trying to pin each other down. I went snowboarding with my gay friends and to poetry readings with my lesbian friends and I went home, once in a while, with a woman.

Ma called a few weeks later, on a Saturday. I could tell she had just gotten off the phone with one of her Khmer friends. She was breathless, as if she had just run a race. And in a way, this call was just that, a competition. There was urgency in the way she needed to make me aware of all the ways in which her friends' children acted with virtue and demonstrated respect to their parents. She wanted me to know all the good things other Khmer kids were doing for their parents.

"Do you remember Sophon, gohn?" Ma said.

"Of course I do. We played together when we were little whenever her parents came to our house."

She was the eldest daughter of one of my mother's closest friends. We didn't keep in touch personally, but my siblings and I followed the trajectory of our childhood Khmer friends via our mothers.

"Well, she has a lot of money. I don't know what job she has, but she makes a lot and she's taking her parents to Paris!" Ma said. Her excitement turned into contemplation. "You know, I can speak French. I always wanted to visit Paris."

I rolled my eyes but still played along.

"I have money, too, Ma. Do you want to go to Paris? I'll send you to Paris if you want to go to Paris."

"But who's going to take us? Me and your dad can't find things on our own."

"I have to work, Ma. I don't have time." I knew this was not what she wanted to hear. So I searched for another solution. "Where do you want to go if you can't go to Paris?"

There was a pause on the line and then her voice, booming.

"We'll take Vegas!"

I called Chan and begged her to take time off from work to escort our parents to Las Vegas, with a pledge to pay for everything.

"You owe me again," Chan said.

In the spring of 2001, I got a phone call from the Westward Ho Hotel on the Strip. It was the only hotel I could find that suited my parents' needs, my father too intimidated by towering hotels. But nothing about Vegas is small. The Westward Ho sprawled across a full city block but at least it only had two floors. More important, my parents' room came with free breakfast, which made it perfect in Ma's mind.

"Put!" Ma shouted into the phone, her voice pitched with excitement after getting back to the hotel following an afternoon of gambling at the MGM. "It's so fun here! There's all-you-can-eat buffet. You should have seen your dad pile on the crab legs! You should be here!"

"I'm glad you're having fun, Ma," I told her, then sat back in my old apartment in Oakland and smiled, relieved to know I had done one more thing to make my mother happy.

At work, I gravitated toward covering stories about loss: the loss of language, home, families, culture. I wrote feature stories about Latina immigrants forming language clubs to meet and socialize and speak Spanish so that they would not lose their native tongue, and I wrote a series of stories about Lula Mae Truelove, a holdout in a mobile home park that had been bought by a developer for a mixed-use retail and housing project. Lula Mae was eighty-eight years old and had only ever lived in her trailer home. When the bulldozers came, she simply would not budge. She was the biggest racist I ever met—she detested the Mexican immigrants living in her midst—but I told her story anyway because she was a survivor, and there was something inspiring about the audacity of an old woman willing to stand in the way of a bulldozer coming for her home.

I was also part of my newspaper's breaking news team. We covered floods and fires, earthquakes and plane crashes. I didn't tell Ma about any of this. I called her when I got a raise or won an award. I told her whenever I went to Chinatown and spotted durian or jackfruit—her favorite fruits. She asked if I knew what to do with fresh tamarind when I reported to her that I'd seen some in a sidewalk bin.

I did not tell her about the man who shot the love of his life before turning the gun on himself because she was old and dying and he was also old and could no longer stand to see her suffer. In my story, I called it murder-suicide because that's what the police said, but in my head, I knew better. It was the purest love.

I didn't tell her about the grieving mother in a Hayward apartment complex whose little boy had been molested and murdered by a neighbor who hid his body under a mattress, and how I hated my job that night because I wanted to bring flowers to that mother and couldn't because it would be a conflict of interest. We were not allowed to bring gifts of any sort to our sources, lest it be seen as buying or bribing our way to an interview. I hated that my job restricted me from being human.

I did not tell her that I wrote a story about a transgender youth who was brutally murdered by a group of teens she believed were her friends—a story that haunts me to this day, because hate, like love, makes people do horrible things.

Of my personal life, I barely told Ma anything at all. I didn't tell her about the terrible breakups with girlfriends, about a snowboarding accident that stole my memory for half a year, or about the mountain biking accident that sent me to the emergency room with bruised ribs.

I stuck to the good stuff and hid all the rest when Ma and I had our weekly phone chats. Not yet realizing that by filtering details in this way, by tightly controlling the information I shared, I would be an accomplice in her mythmaking when she bragged to her friends and our relatives. Or that she would use everything I told her—about my salary, my promotions, and my awards—as lacquer to cover up an increasingly obvious defect in her eyes and in the eyes of the other Khmer mothers: I was twenty-six years old and still unmarried.

So long as Ma had something to point to and say, "Look at my daughter's success!" she could save herself from the judgment of others and remain safely ensconced in her reputation as a good Cambodian mother.

I won't let anyone look down on me, she had said. And I dutifully abided.

Back in Corvallis, Ma served her final lunch on the Oregon State University campus in September of 2003, and Yay Yeim died of a sudden stroke. The house on Ironwood Avenue was filled with my grandmother's loss, causing my superstitious mother to be fearful that her mother-in-law would haunt her there. No better time, my parents believed, to start anew.

The following month, she and Pa moved out of our modest ranch home on Ironwood Avenue and into their new tract home in the Vineyards, one of multiple subdivisions in Keizer that had sprung up in an open field where blueberry bushes once stood in even rows, where a mother and her kids once bent their heads against the sun and worked.

Before my parents closed on their new home, Ma called me.

"Put, can you send us some money?" Ma asked.

It was the first time she'd made a request like that. If my parents could get an extra ten thousand dollars, they would be able to buy their new house outright and not have to take out a mortgage.

"Did you ask any of the other kids?" I asked Ma, when I called to tell her I was wiring over the funds.

"No, I only asked you," Ma said.

"Why?" I asked.

"Because I know you have the money."

But the bigger truth, she didn't say. That she knew her baby girl, the daughter whose life she saved, would not deny her mother.

◘ THE SETUP

When I worked there, *The San Jose Mercury News* was one of the best newspapers in the country. I went because of the pay and the reputation. But I also went for the opportunities. The newspaper had foreign bureaus in multiple countries, including Vietnam and China. I wanted to be posted in Asia one day.

But my editors and colleagues told me I'd have to do my time, work my way up to that kind of coveted job. I had matured in some ways as I got older, but I was still very impatient. Rather than wait for a spot on the foreign desk to open, I looked for other ways. By the fall of 2004, two opportunities flung open the door on my future.

Earlier in the spring, I had applied for an Alicia Patterson Journalism Fellowship, which provided a one-year grant to midcareer journalists to work on a story of their choice, anywhere in the world. I proposed Cambodia. My story would focus on farmers who were being forcibly evicted from their lands, often under the auspice of economic development, and sometimes by corrupt business and political officials who wanted the land for personal ventures.

I had also applied for a journalism junket to travel to Bhutan and report on the country's transition from royal rule to democracy.

I was chosen for both opportunities.

In November, after two weeks interviewing Bhutanese yak herders, monks, and farmers who eked out an existence high in the Himalayas amid gray-bearded langurs, I returned to Oakland. In December, I packed up my apartment, stacked my belongings in storage, and drove home to see my mother before moving to Phnom Penh for my fellowship.

For fifteen years, since the first time I visited Cambodia and learned about my country's grim past, I had been trying to work out a feeling I'd had as a teenager that dogged me in America. I needed to figure out what part of the guilt that comes with being an immigrant and a survivor belonged to me, and what belonged to my parents. I felt guilty for escaping the war, for having landed safely in America where my family thrived, for having an education and a career. I felt guilty for being alive, something I know at least two of my siblings, Chan and Mo, felt, too, because we talked about it after their own separate trips to Cambodia. In my heart, guilt and shame sat side by side, producing an ever-present throbbing, like a toothache that swings between angry and dull.

I assumed it was the same guilt my parents felt, that some of theirs was transferred to me. But I didn't know for sure because they never talked about it. Our family was structured around a collective silence when it came to sadness. But their actions said everything. It was in the way they routinely sent money to relatives back home, and in the way they worked tirelessly to rescue other relatives by bringing them to America. It was in their eyes, dark with dread, whenever they learned of another relative's passing.

The guilt pulsed inside me, no matter if I was in America or Cambodia. I went back to Cambodia, in part, to try and calm the chaos.

I flew out of Portland on a Saturday in early February. By then, my parents' home had become a required layover on my life's various moves and transitions. Before I went off to the next new place, I was drawn, by some invisible gravitational force, back to Ma.

I had moved fifty miles from Ma when I went to college in Eugene, and eventually 560 miles away when I moved to California for my career. Going to Cambodia was my biggest leap yet from her, an entire ocean and seventy-six hundred miles separating us. But it was strange that I was going to our homeland, the place where I would feel her presence most strongly.

Ma and Pa stayed with me in a waiting area at the security checkpoint at Portland International Airport. Ma cruised through a nearby gift shop and bought a bag of chips she nudged toward me.

"A snack for later," she said, in lieu of "I love you."

At the last moment, when I had less than an hour to get to my gate, I unzipped my winter coat and wiggled out of the sleeves.

"I won't need this in Cambodia," I said, pressing the coat into Ma's arms.

"What about when you come back?" Ma said. "Won't you need it?"

"I don't know when that's going to be, Ma," I said, which made her frown. I had promised her that I was only going to Cambodia for six months, but the truth was, my sabbatical from *The San Jose Mercury News* was for a full year, and I wanted to give myself the option of staying longer in Cambodia if I wanted to pursue other stories.

Ma was quiet at the airport, even though I had heard her talk excitedly on the phone to her friends the night before, telling them my newspaper was sending me to Cambodia to write stories. This wasn't exactly right. I had explained to her many times what a fellowship was but decided to let her believe what she wanted to believe. The point was, I was going back to Cambodia, back to our country. Not as a tourist. Not to conduct family ceremonies. This time, I was going for work. I was going for me.

When I first told my parents the news that I would be moving to Cambodia, Ma cried and asked why. I had a good job and a good life in California, she said. She wasn't convinced the country was at peace, even though she had been there twice. She couldn't disassociate Cambodia from war and chaos.

"Everything's okay there," I told Ma, even though I knew it wasn't. I was going to Cambodia specifically to write about the ways in which things were not okay, about how farmers were getting gunned down and beaten simply because they wanted to keep their homes and land. But I was vague about my work when I talked to Ma. I didn't want her to worry.

As I got up to give Ma and Pa hugs, Ma dabbed at watery eyes.

"Take care, gohn," she said. "Stay safe."

When I turned to join the security line, I heard her voice

and wasn't sure if she was talking to Pa or still saying something to me.

"There she goes again," Ma said. "She's always leaving."

On the plane, as I fussed with my headphone jack and cued up a movie, I thought about my first trip to Cambodia as a teenager, with Ma and Grandpa Sin and Yay Yeim. And then the next trip, when it was only Ma and me. Now it was only me.

I had packed a backpack full of notebooks and pens. I had a single large suitcase stuffed with blue jeans, T-shirts, and photos of my parents, siblings, nieces, and nephews—to anchor me whenever I missed home.

Both of those prior trips had sparked my wonder and kept me thinking again and again about the place where Ma's story began. I was continuing my own story, as a journalist and a daughter, making good by returning to the motherland, but I wonder now if I was continuing a part of Ma's story, too. My mother's life in Cambodia ended when she turned thirty, and mine began in Cambodia at that very same age. It was as if I was returning to the country of our birth with the life she had meant to have. Returning to the point of rupture to finish out the story she had wanted for herself.

I was nervous about living in a foreign country alone. But I thought about Ma in her early years in America. If Ma could start over in a foreign land, then I could do it, too. At least in Cambodia, I understood the language. I had relatives to lean on. I was not completely alone.

In the fifteen years that had passed since the first time I came to Cambodia as a teenager, Cambodia had changed in spades. Phnom Penh had finally gotten around to paving all the main streets in town; a few traffic lights were installed at various intersections; and a row of hip new restaurants and bars had opened on the Sisowath Quay, not only for expats and tourists, but for the country's emerging middle class. The capital's accommodations had also gotten an upgrade. Grand villas with swimming pools and cocktail bars were being built by expats in small pockets throughout the city. Exclusive resorts with prix fixe menus were popping up on the coast, in Kampong Som, where I was born.

But scratch at the surface of these new changes, and the poverty was still the same. When I moved there in 2005, an estimated 85 percent of the population still lived on less than a dollar a day. Access to health care remained an enormous challenge, with inadequately trained medical personnel at the country's sole hospital. The education system was still rigged to favor the children of the country's elite; it was widely known and accepted that those with the means bribed their way to a high school or college diploma. In Cambodia, money accelerated ascension up the country's shaky and rotted socioeconomic ladder. I thought of my father and the mounds of money he made when our family lived in Ream. It wasn't corruption, he had said, just the way things were.

I found my relatives in exactly the same predicament as when I had first met them, fifteen years prior. My aunts were still cultivating rice, and most of my female cousins who had married were working alongside their mothers in the fields.

I saw my country with new eyes. The horrors of what happened during the genocide seemed, to my teenage eyes when I first visited in 1990, confined to Tuol Sleng prison. But now, as I settled into my apartment near Tuol Sleng, the high school turned torture prison that left a dark smudge in my conscience when I was sixteen years old, I saw my country for the first time for what it was—an entire nation of the walking wounded. The whole city was haunted. I had never been anywhere so burdened by a collective grief and at the same time so charged with possibility, a place so physically beautiful and yet stained with such a grim past.

Still, I sensed the hope. People like Ming Pheaktra still didn't talk politics out in the open, but I could see that even that was starting to shift. The nation's media was robust, with dozens of Khmer-language newspapers and two English-language newspapers that routinely published investigative reports on government corruption. Even before the next garment factory was built, hundreds of young women from the provinces were already lined up for interviews, clutching their family's life savings with them in order to bribe their way into jobs that barely paid a dollar a day.

At least there were jobs, and even, for the first time in Cambodia's history, an escalator. In 2003, two years before I returned to Cambodia, the Sorya Mall was built in Phnom Penh, with both an elevator and escalator to take shoppers up and down its five floors. At the top, a pizza joint with an all-you-can-pile-into-a-bowl salad bar was packed with middle-class families and young Khmer couples on nongovernmental salaries who could afford Western food. I thought about Ma piling food onto my tray when I went to visit her at work, and I thought about the vertical nature of privilege, of towers of food accessible only to those with the means to afford it.

That single escalator in the entire country became a tourist attraction for villagers who wanted to ride the moving stairs. My own cousins and aunts erupted with glee when I took them to the mall. We rode the escalator up to the top and took the elevator back down for an entire afternoon.

Back then, in 2005, I couldn't help but feel optimistic for

the country and for its emerging democracy. Common citizens were feeling empowered to protest, from the garment factory workers who protested for better wages and working conditions to the farmers and city dwellers who picketed their forcible removal from their homes. It seemed, for the first time since the war had ended, that citizens were finding their voice and using it to speak out and speak up, unafraid of standing up for their rights.

I didn't know it yet, but I had arrived in Cambodia just as foreigners and Khmers alike were using the word "renaissance" when they spoke of all the changes, in a precious moment in time when peace was robust, economic opportunities were increasing, and the embrace of democracy was strong.

Within a decade, all of this would crumble. Prime Minister Hun Sen, himself a former Khmer Rouge leader, would take Cambodia resolutely down the path of a one-party, authoritarian state by applying pressure on the judiciary to end the only viable opposition party. Opposition party leaders would be arrested, as well as journalists who wrote or aired stories critical of the government. I began to wonder if I was safe reporting my stories about landless farmers; I kept my U.S. passport close and knew if I ever felt too nervous, I could always return to America.

I rented a newly built two-bedroom apartment above a Khmer family on an unpaved road in Phnom Penh's Boeung Keng Kang III neighborhood. I knew Ma would approve, because it was so new the paint on the walls and the concrete on the patio were still drying, and also because the Khmer landlord lived just below me. Ma liked knowing I wouldn't be so alone.

I navigated on my own around Phnom Penh and the rest of the country, forcing myself to speak as much Khmer as I could. I thought about taking a Khmer language course but then decided I would be too embarrassed to sit with white foreigners trying to learn my own language. So I called Ma and Pa each week with a list of words I had heard spoken, and they talked me through the meanings. In this way, I rebuilt the language that had left my tongue in America. Ma delighted in these phone calls, amazed at all the "big words" I was learning. Back home in Keizer, she bragged to her friends. Word by word, I was moving closer to the culture that, up until then, I had experienced only through my mother's food, her folktales, and the Buddhist rituals I watched my parents perform.

But no amount of effort to speak our language concealed my identity. To the motorcycle taxi drivers, to the waitstaff at the corner noodle shop, to the sellers and the hawkers at the market, I was a foreigner, or what they called Khmer bor-da-deh, Cambodian from abroad.

As I traveled across Cambodia to interview farmers about illegal land grabs by business tycoons and corrupt government leaders, I called Ma. From Ratanakiri province in the northeastern part of the country, where the Khmer Rouge first began their revolt thirty-five years earlier, to Battambang, the province of luminescent rice paddies that Ma's favorite Khmer singers crooned about on the radio, to Kampong Som province, where I was born and where my family had last lived before the war.

Ma listened to all of my adventures amazed, her response always the same: "I want to go there!"

"Oh, Ratanakiri, where the indigenous are," Ma said, when

I told her how I interviewed tribespeople who were being tricked out of their lands by local developers. "Their Khmer is cut with other dialects. And they have big piercings in their ears. They say the wild boar meat is so good there. I've always wanted to go there."

In August, I flew back to Oregon in time for Ma's birthday. My parents' friends and my aunties, uncles, and cousins crowded around me in the backyard, where Khmer chicken was on the grill and Ma emerged from the kitchen with an enormous wok of stir-fried rice stick noodles.

"Your mom says you can speak Khmer fluently now," one of my mother's friends said, looking up at me smiling.

"Yes, I'm still learning," I replied politely, in Khmer.

Then one of my aunties sidled up next to me.

"Put, when are you getting married?" she asked, ribbing me in my side. "I want to go dance at your wedding!"

"Not yet," I said. "I'm still working."

My uncle alighted on me, beer in hand.

"My famous niece!" he shouted. "Are you going to take down the prime minister with all your stories?"

"No," I said, politely bowing my head.

My mother's friends directed their daughters to me, hoping I might help find them lucrative jobs in Cambodia. My father's friends cornered me, wanting to talk politics.

It was stressful to answer so many questions and bat away some of my mother's lies. No, I did not have a driver; I only hired one as needed. No, I did not send thousands of dollars to my parents; I merely had my earnings wired to them for safekeeping. And no, I did not buy my parents a house; I had given them only a small amount of money to help out.

I rolled my eyes at the time. But looking back, Ma trussed a myth so tight around me, I would find it harder and harder to break free. When you cannot wrap your daughter in the finest silks, you wrap her in your most elaborate stories.

After the last guests left my parents' house, giving Ma final birthday hugs, I flipped through the pages of the Chinese zodiac calendar on my parents' living room wall and counted: another five months before my yearlong sabbatical from *The San Jose Mercury News* ended and I was due to return to the newsroom. I didn't want to spend those final months idling away in Oregon. So I booked another flight to Phnom Penh, this time taking Ma with me. She wanted to see where I lived, and she wanted to visit her family again.

When we arrived in Phnom Penh, Ma was on a mission to locate more relatives and friends she had heard survived the war. The person who was the best navigator was Ming Pheaktra, but we didn't know where she lived. Ma had an address scrawled on a small scrap of paper that she handed to a cyclo driver a few days after we got to Phnom Penh.

The driver looked at the house and street number, then looked at Ma, raising his brows.

"Are you sure?" the driver said, waving the piece of paper in the air.

"Yes, uncle, please take us there."

He pedaled a block and then stopped at the corner to let us off. We looked quizzically at him.

"Are *you* sure?" Ma asked.

The driver nodded and pointed at a house facing an open sewer, with a blue metal gate, intended to keep sewer rats and thieves out. Ming Pheaktra saw us before we saw her and raced to gather us up in her hugs.

For the next couple of weeks, we saw Ming Pheaktra every day. She escorted us on a trip to Ma's village and to explore Angkor Wat. Ma invited my aunt Om Oeurn, Ma's older sister, to stay with us so Ma could catch up on her life, and Ming Pheaktra helped locate other relatives and friends Ma wanted to reconnect with.

One morning, as we ate chocolate croissants I had picked up from the French bakery near the riverside, Ma announced her best friend was coming to visit.

"Can you please not wear shorts, gohn, please," Ma begged, as she drank coffee with cream and sugar and chomped on her croissant. "This is my best friend. I want you to look proper."

I didn't know what all the fuss was about.

"What do you want me to wear, then?" I asked.

"Just wear something nice. Pants and a nice shirt," she said, gathering croissant crumbs on the table with the palm of her hand and guiding them onto a plate.

I put on blue jeans and a T-shirt and considered myself properly dressed.

This was the same friend who had accompanied Ma to the hospital in 1974, plying her with a pâté sandwich before my mother gave birth to me.

The week before Ma's best friend came to visit, Ming Pheaktra had hired a driver to take us to a local market in Phnom Penh where Ma had heard her friend was selling bananas. Ma found her stall and began bargaining so ruthlessly, her friend looked up to see who was undercutting her. When she saw my mother, after being separated for thirty years, she leapt across her inventory and landed in my mother's arms, both women crying out with joy.

Now this very friend was visiting, with her son, who happened to be thirty years old, like me. Ming Pheaktra arrived, too. Ma dispatched me to the kitchen.

"Bring tea and cookies for our guests, gohn," Ma said, waving me off with her hand.

I boiled water and pinched loose-leaf jasmine tea into cups that I arranged on a tray with fruit and Pepperidge Farm cookies I had found at the foreigners' supermarket. Ma's friend sat stiffly next to her son and I took a seat next to Ming Pheaktra, on one of the massive teak chairs the landlord's family had ordered for my apartment when I asked for furniture.

Ma loved the sheer bulk of the chairs, how they gleamed, and the blue tile wainscoting that lined the walls, Khmer aesthetics I found tacky but tolerable. I was relieved I had found an apartment that seemed to please my mother. She had called her friends back home in Oregon and bragged.

"Sahat nah!" I overheard her croon into the phone. So beautiful! "Put's house has teak doors; the wood is thick as thighs."

The teak chair was the most uncomfortable chair I'd ever sat on, so deep I sat cross-legged, my bare feet peeking out from under my knees. Ming Pheaktra tapped my leg and made a "tssst" sound with her teeth.

"Don't sit like that," Ming Pheaktra said under her breath. "It's not polite."

So I uncrossed my legs and sat up. I listened to Ma and her best friend make small talk, the conversation inevitably looping back to her son and to me. He was a soccer coach and spoke some English, so we exchanged a few words in English while our mothers grinned and nodded.

When they finally left a few hours later, Ma eased back into her chair.

"What did you think of him?" Ma asked as I put away their cups and washed the food tray.

"Think of who?" I asked.

"Of my best friend's son," Ma said. "He's a very nice young

man. His mother is my best friend. She was there when you were born."

Ming Pheaktra chimed in.

"He speaks English, Put," she said. "That's so nice. That makes things easy."

I thought of Ma's attempt to get me to meet her other friend's son eight years prior, when I lived in Seattle. But between then and now, I had come out to her as gay. Did she not believe me back then?

"Ma, I don't need help meeting people," I said. "I'm not interested in marrying your best friend's son. I'll find someone on my own to marry."

Even though I had told her I was gay, she still held out hope that I would meet a man, preferably Khmer, and get married. I was in Cambodia, after all, full of Khmer men, scant on the gays. Sin and Sope had already gotten married by then, and each of my three oldest siblings had had their first babies. Between the time I came out to Ma and the time I left for Cambodia, I didn't bring home any boyfriends for my parents to meet because I didn't have any. A couple of times, I brought girlfriends to Keizer, but Ma didn't take any of them seriously, telling my aunts I had brought a friend home.

I wasn't dating anyone when Ma visited me in Phnom Penh, and she was starting to worry.

"Look at your sisters and your brother," Ma said. "They're all married and having kids. You need to follow their example."

She said this even though we both knew they had all fallen short of her expectations, each one having married a white American.

"Everyone is different, Ma," I said. "I'll find someone. And if I don't, that will be okay, too."

When I said this, Ma sighed, tossing her head back as if she had been slapped.

"Then don't cry to anyone when you're old and lonely," Ma said. "Everyone is moving forward with their lives."

When Ma flew home a few days later, I lay in bed thinking of what had just happened, and realized why Ming Pheaktra had suddenly appeared when Ma's best friend and her son did. Ming Pheaktra was a deal maker. I had watched her in the markets bartering for bargains. It was clear Ma had recruited Ming Pheaktra to help her persuade me to consider marrying the soccer coach.

I thought about what Ma said, about everyone else progressing in their lives. Did she think my life was somehow stalled? I knew plenty of people even older than I was who were not married, and who were living happy lives. I didn't necessarily aspire to that, but I also wasn't worried the way Ma was. I had a career to continue.

Later that fall, as I prepared to return to *The San Jose Mercury News*, a worry nestled in a nook in my mind. I had watched from abroad as the newspaper industry declined, losing readers to online news sources. I worried I would be returning to a newsroom short on staff, and scrambling to adapt to an increasingly compressed news cycle. I wondered if I even had a job left.

While the newspaper industry back home in the U.S. was struggling, media development in Cambodia was thriving. The push for democracy by donor countries, particularly the U.S., meant a parallel push for a free and independent press. I was there just as the momentum for a pluralistic media was peaking.

In the fall of 2005, I opened my inbox to find a forwarded

email from a journalist friend in Bangkok. It was September 20, one week before I was slated to pack my bags and return permanently to the United States.

An organization called Internews was seeking a professional with a media background to oversee a new journalism training program in Phnom Penh for Khmer reporters. I read the job description and immediately knew the job was tailor-made for me.

But I was also homesick. And one of *The San Jose Mercury News'* top editors had promised to help move my career toward a coveted job in the state capital covering politics. I had every reason to go home. But then, three days later, after seeing the job posting for Internews, another email arrived in my inbox, announcing that *The Mercury News* was offering buyouts. If too few people raised their hands for buyouts, layoffs would follow. My friends emailed me, and I felt their mounting panic between the lines.

I had a chance to prevent at least one layoff. I emailed the paper's human resources director and told her to put my name down for a buyout. Then I emailed the contact person at Internews to apply for the journalism training job. By then, Cambodia had me in its thrall.

When I went back to Oregon to tell Ma I had quit my job at the newspaper, and had taken a full-time position with an international nonprofit media development organization, all she heard was the word "Internews." She thought it meant I would be on TV.

"Inter, like international?" she asked. "My daughter is going to be like Christiane Amanpour! I love Christiane Amanpour!"

"No, Ma, not like that," I said. "It's an organization in Washington, D.C., and we work with journalists to help them do their jobs better and safer."

"Okay, gohn," she said. "Just tell me what channel you'll be on. Me and your dad will watch."

I heard her trilling on the phone with her friends.

"Mmm-hmm, maybe on CNN . . . watch for her," Ma said. "My daughter is famous!"

Beyond choosing to mishear me, I also knew my mother was telling lies. Whenever I went home, she would start dialing numbers like a telethon, contacting her friends to tell them I was back for a visit. These friends rushed over to get a glimpse of me, to ask me about Cambodia, to tell me they would like to visit me. My aunts and cousins came, too.

One of my aunts cornered me in Ma's living room.

"Put, you must be living so good in Phnom Penh, making a quarter million dollars," she said. "What are you going to do with all that money?"

I corrected my aunt, and when she left, I confronted my mother.

"Why are you telling lies?" I asked Ma. "I don't make a quarter million dollars, not even close."

"The number doesn't matter," Ma said, waving a hand at me as if to brush my annoyance away. "The point is, you make more money than the other Khmer kids in Oregon."

I told Ma to stop lying because it put me in an awkward spot, correcting the facts about my life. But I knew it was useless. In her mind, she was telling her version of the truth, and stretching it to fit a certain narrative wasn't hurting anyone. Except it was hurting me, the person who had to live up to the lies.

I rolled my eyes and let it all go, and scarfed down as much of my mother's food as I could possibly handle in the two weeks before I was scheduled to fly out. I didn't know how long it would be this time before I came back to her, back to Oregon and her kitchen, back to her warmth that had become my anchor in the world. So I soaked it all up, let her be proud of me and tell her friends to watch for me on TV.

I flew back to Phnom Penh with a new sense of purpose and passion. When I was sixteen years old and learned about the journalists who were tortured to death at Tuol Sleng prison, I had made a promise to myself to somehow honor their lives.

Now I would be working to train the country's next generation of journalists to shine a light on our country's darkened
corners, to expose corruption and injustice and examine the
lasting societal impacts of both.

I had arrived in Cambodia that first time as a student
journalist for my high school newspaper, not knowing what
questions I needed to ask.

Now, as a professional journalist, I viewed my country with
new eyes and a deeper curiosity. I wanted to learn everything
I could about Cambodia, about my people and our history,
about my parents' past.

Ming Pheaktra helped me move into a three-story house
in the Boeng Keng Kang I neighborhood, less than ten
blocks from where Great-Uncle San lived and popular among
expatriates.

The house was far too big for one person, but I signed
a yearlong lease anyway; my new job came with a housing
stipend, and my expatriate friends had advised me to use it
all because none of it was transferable to other expenses. I
bought a sectional sofa, lamps, lounge chairs, and lights, and
filled the kitchen with pots and pans and pretty plates I found
at the local market. I thought about our house on Ironwood
Avenue, how my parents had worked and saved to buy new
furniture. How my life was unfolding, inverted to theirs.

Ma arrived to visit me one month after I had moved into
what Ming Pheaktra called the "big house." My housekeeper
from my previous apartment, six months pregnant, had taken
a leave. I didn't want another housekeeper, but when Ma arrived, she insisted I needed one.

"You're going to be busy working," Ma said. "Why do
you want to spend your time cleaning the floor and doing the
laundry when you can pay someone?"

"Because I can do these things myself," I said. "And it just feels weird, to have someone else clean for me."

Even at my old apartment across town, I'd felt uncomfortable knowing someone else was picking up after me.

"I used to clean for other people," Ma said solemnly, a reminder that was unnecessary because for all of my life, since the first time I saw it as a little girl, the image of her wrestling an industrial-sized vacuum out of the closet on night shift stayed with me. "That's how I got money. How do you think me and your dad could buy a house and buy food for our children?"

She saw my face soften to her argument, and she moved to seal the deal.

"You can hire one of your cousins," Ma said exuberantly. "You have a lot of cousins who will want to be your housekeeper. It's better than what they do now, sitting for twelve hours sewing zippers and buttons on clothes."

I knew my female cousins were working for low wages in the factories that ringed Phnom Penh, in conditions that were unsafe. The ventilation was bad, the machines could maim, the bosses were stingy with work breaks.

"Okay, Ma," I said, my moral authority undercut by Ma's practicality. "Then you can find me someone."

Thith showed up the next day, the daughter of one of Ma's cousins from the village. Ma exulted in the task of training her how to clean the floors, wash the dishes, and cook.

The next day, a young man, short and slight, toting a hammock, a radio, and a backpack with books, showed up. He said he was reporting for work. I thought he was mistaken, that perhaps he meant to ring the doorbell of one of the other foreigners on my street, until Ma bounded to the door and smiled.

"Rah!" she said, pulling the young man into the house. "Put, this is Thith's brother. He's your new security guard."

I didn't know I needed one. Ma tried to get me to buy a car and hire a driver next, but I finally drew a line. By the looks of it, with my security guard shorter and scrawnier than me, I wasn't sure who would be protecting whom if an intruder ever came into my house.

During the day, I rode moto-taxis to Internews's riverfront office, in a sprawling complex that housed dozens of other nongovernmental organizations and Khmer businesses. My assistant, Narridh, and I conducted training sessions for the journalists in our program on sleuthing for public records to bolster investigative stories, and we practiced interviewing techniques to use with public officials to hold them accountable for how public funds were spent.

In the evenings, I went to parties hosted by other expatriates that featured live bands, catered buffets with both Western and Khmer food, and more booze than I'd seen at the best bars in town. Once, at a party hosted by the U.S. ambassador, there was even a chocolate fountain with tiers of plump imported strawberries. I had seen strawberries at the fresh market and asked the sellers where they came from.

"They ship them in from America," one market vendor told me.

I stood for a long time in front of the chocolate fountain, with its dome of perfect strawberries, just staring.

On the weekends, when there was time, Ming Pheaktra would take me on the back of her motorbike and off we'd go. To the markets and the parks, to the noodle shops she swore were the best.

At home, outside my gate where Rah sat on a plastic chair, always a book hiding his face, I came to tell time by the passing of the street vendors. In the morning, at exactly 6:00 a.m., the bread guy who shouted "Pain! Pain! Pain! Pain!" in French rode his bike past my block, balancing an enormous wicker basket of bread on the back. There was the "Eht-chaay!" woman collecting plastic for recycling, the grilled-egg vendor, and the cobbler. Everyone had a hustle. I thought about Ma cutting her chives in the garden, selling them for twenty-five cents a bunch at the international market in Corvallis. "Doh doh, bing porng," she had said. Drop, drop, the bucket fills. A life gets built like this, little by little. I had learned to embrace my mother's same philosophy of saving over spending.

It's when I left the big house that I was confronted with the fact of who I was. Each time hailing a moto-taxi ride, the driver would eye me with curiosity. Some would speak in English; others took a leap and spoke to me in Khmer.

"Are you Filipino?" they would ask. "Are you Thai?"

I would shake my head, no, and insist I was "gohn Khmer," a daughter of Cambodia.

Many of these drivers did not believe me, thought I was clever, trying to pass as Khmer. And those who believed me said the thing I hated to hear the most.

"You're not real Khmer. You're Khmer pordadeh." Khmer from abroad. A foreigner. A fraud.

I took these exchanges as a challenge. The first time I visited Cambodia as a teenager, I felt far from my culture. An American kid who sulked behind sunglasses. Something shifted when I turned thirty and the need to know my culture and reclaim it became unrelenting. I don't know what it is that returns us to our beginnings, that makes us pivot and face the place where we started; something about thirty gives us pause. A part of me knew I had to go backward if I wanted to keep moving forward.

If I wanted to be seen and accepted as a "real Khmer," I knew I would have to speak and act like one. I would have to do whatever I could to build up my identity. In America, I never really felt fully American. Now in Cambodia, I had a shot at belonging—to both a place and a people.

I was having lunch with Ming Pheaktra at her house one day when I asked her if it was possible for me to get a Cambodian passport. I had heard that the government was granting passports to anyone of Khmer descent. But I didn't have a birth certificate. Or a family registration card with my local *sangkat*, my home district. My only official identification was my California driver's license and my U.S. passport.

"Why do you want a Cambodian passport?" Ming Pheaktra said. "It's meaningless to you. You already hold the best passport in the world."

"Because I'm Khmer," I said, and realized the irony of my situation. While so many of my Khmer relatives and friends were desperate for American passports, I was begging Ming Pheaktra to help me get a Khmer passport.

Ever since I had arrived back in Cambodia knowing that I would live there, at least for another year, something had shifted inside of me. I was no longer a visitor, or a temporary resident. I was there to stay. As my mentality shifted, so did my attitude. I wanted to be seen as Khmer.

At the market, I learned to crouch low in a squat when examining tomatoes or a pineapple for purchase. I picked up my produce, asked the price, and immediately scoffed at the first offer, countering with half the price until the seller and I moved toward a mutually acceptable middle. I had learned this from Ming Pheaktra.

At the temples, I learned to sit *bayn pnayn*, with my legs off to the side and my upper body torqued forward, hands pressed together and head bowed, no matter how uncomfortable that was. I never learned the chants, but I learned when to give offerings to the monks, how to back away from them with my head bowed, never turning my back to the Buddha.

Each day, I passed as being Khmer if I slowed my pace when walking, if I spoke Khmer confidently when ordering food, if I held myself in a certain breezy, nonchalant way. I could make people believe that I was Khmer and not Khmer American, and on those days, I felt victorious, as if I was being seen for who I was, even though another part of me was still in hiding.

To my friends in the expatriate community, I came out as gay. To my family in Cambodia, I kept this hidden, worried that if I told the truth, it would only invite scandal and rejection by my Khmer relatives whom I had come to love.

Then there were other moments that would drag me back to the reality of being a foreigner in my own country. Every day was a constant negotiating of who and how to be. Do I act more Khmer today and less American? Do I show my American side and shed my Khmer side? At restaurants, do I order my food in Khmer or English? Depending on how I ordered, I got different service. If I was deemed to be Khmer, service slowed. I had to ask for water, utensils. If I spoke in English and was deemed to be a foreigner, the waitstaff hustled to bring out my order and hovered nearby in case I needed anything else.

It was all part of the country's hierarchical structure. In that worldview, white men—whether they were ambassadors, tourists, or pedophiles—were situated at the top. People like my relatives, who were poor and uneducated, were at the bottom. Being both Cambodian and American, I landed somewhere in the middle.

Over time, I found a way of existing that worked for me. In the markets, I used Khmer to negotiate with the sellers in order to get the local price for items I wanted. In restaurants, I spoke a mix of Khmer and English, to make it clear that I was a Khmer from abroad. I wanted the waitstaff to know I was one of them, and also a foreigner. By doing this, I was asking for a certain level of respect. At work, as Narridh and I conducted our training sessions, I spoke in English, because that was where I needed to fight the hardest for respect as the sole female in a cohort of all men.

Being Khmer meant I could pay lower prices at the market, enter places like the Angkor temples for free, and know how and what to order at restaurants. Being American meant that I could ask for and get the respect of Khmer men, stand up to authority figures like editors of newspapers, and get better service at restaurants. In Cambodia, Khmers looked down on other Khmers but looked up to foreigners, because foreigners, it stood to reason, had money, and money meant power. I exploited both sides of me to the greatest benefit.

But I wanted a passport to prove my Khmer identity, more to myself than anyone else.

"You really want one?" Ming Pheaktra said, spooning stir-fried morning glory with garlic onto my plate. "Okay, I'll arrange it."

The next week, Ming Pheaktra took me to an office crowded with Khmers applying for passports to work abroad as migrants in nearby Thailand and Malaysia. I suddenly felt conflicted being there, wanting a passport to assuage my own self-esteem while other Khmers wanted a passport for something more basic: to be able to earn a better living. In the end, my desire to be seen as fully Khmer overrode the embarrassment I felt at being privileged.

In an open foyer, long conference tables were set up side by side with an assembly line of six men sitting behind the tables who each assessed a different part of my application. We shuffled along as each official scrutinized my papers, looked up at me and Ming Pheaktra, and scrutinized again. By the end, I was led alone into a small office with a man who looked the same age as my father, with the same haircut parted off to the side, wearing a tan government-issued outfit similar to my father's navy uniform. I quickly learned that this was the man who would determine whether I would get a passport.

"Name," he said severely, without looking up.

"KhanPutsata," I said meekly, providing my official first name.

"Birthplace," he said, still not looking up.

"I was born in Kampong Som," I said. "My family is from Takeo."

The man didn't change his tone or the severe expression on his face as he looked at me.

"You're Khmer from abroad?" he said, when he noticed my clothes and hair, the way I sat poised on the other side of his table.

"Yes," I said. "I'm here teaching English."

Ming Pheaktra had told me to tell that lie, that I should say nothing about the work I was doing with journalists because that would invite suspicion, and if I wanted a passport, I needed to fall as far under the radar as I could.

The man pored over my documents as I sat silently, my hands clasped together in front of me, my shoulders squared, waiting. After a few minutes, he took a stamp, pressed it into an ink pad, and slammed it onto a corner of my application.

"Come back in four weeks," he said, "to collect your passport."

Four weeks later, when Ming Pheaktra took me to the same building to pick up my passport and when I held it for the first time, with the Khmer writing in front and translations in both English and French, when I opened the front flap and saw my face and name and passport number, and a comment under DISTINGUISHING MARK that read "beauty spot below the right side of mouth," I grinned. Suddenly, it was as if pieces of me that had been scattered—in the U.S.; in Ream, where my family last lived before we fled; and in Kampong Som, where I was born—all surged back into my being. I felt whole.

"I'm feeling a closer identity to this country, now that I have a Khmer passport, almost as if I am bonafide now," I wrote in my journal.

I told Ming Pheaktra that I wouldn't leave Cambodia to go very far or for very long.

"My heart is here," I said, clenching my passport.

Ming Pheaktra grinned. We went to the riverfront to celebrate.

"My niece," she announced proudly, as we clinked cold glasses of Angkor draft beer, "you are Khmer!"

Later that night, I went to an internet phone booth and called Ma to tell her. I knew she would be proud. By then, I could speak Khmer fluently. I had a Khmer passport. I was increasingly becoming less American and more Khmer, a shift Ma noticed and bragged to her friends about. The next time I went back to Keizer to visit, I heard all about it.

"There's the gohn Khmer!" one of my mom's friends shouted, practically busting my parents' front door when she rushed in to see me after Ma made her usual round of phone calls, telling her friends I was home. "Your mother says you are so capable. Maybe you can persuade my children to speak Khmer!"

The passport, the language, these were tokens I tossed to Ma, to raise her up in the eyes of her friends and family in Oregon's Cambodian community. To show them the evolution of Ma's good Cambodian daughter. If mothering was a sport Ma wanted to win, I would play my part to ensure she stayed ahead of the competition. Even if I was lying to myself and everyone else to do it.

⊡ THE GREAT DIVIDE

There are times when I look in the mirror and see my mother's face peering back at me. Her flat nose and round cheeks, her almond-shaped eyes, anchored by thick eyebrows that dance when we are laughing. We are so alike that when I met one of my great-aunts for the first time, the old woman took one look at my face and said, "I know those eyes and those lips and those cheeks. You must be Sam-Ou's daughter."

We are food-focused, Ma and me, our memories driven by the best meals we've eaten, by the sweet scent of sticky rice and mango and the punchy funk of prahok steamed on the stovetop.

But while Ma had always identified only as Khmer, never considering or calling herself American, I felt a bit of both. Where she felt fully at home in Cambodia, I often felt torn, a part of me feeling I belonged there and another part of me knowing I did not.

I searched and searched for her in Cambodia, believing the more of my mother I could find in our homeland, the more of myself I might see, the more at ease I would be in my life.

One day I asked Ming Pheaktra to take me clear across the Chroy Changva Bridge, past the village of Preak Leap, to a spit of land I had seen from the rooftop bars on Phnom Penh's Sisowath Quay. We went to the place where Ma had first lived as a bride, Chroy Changva Naval Base. The base had long ago been decommissioned and destroyed, so there was no easy way to find it. Ming Pheaktra stopped to ask locals for directions. An old man who remembered where some of the buildings had once stood hopped on his motorbike and showed us the way. When he stopped at a clearing and pointed toward the water, there was nothing to see except old asphalt, buckled and broken by time. Ruins from a lifetime ago. I got off the back of Ming Pheaktra's moto anyway, just to walk where Ma once walked, to see what she also once saw.

A few weekends later, we took a bus to Kampong Som, because I was born there and I wanted to feel and smell the breeze, to know what my first gulp of air might have felt like. I stood on a corner, looking at the spot where the hospital once stood, where Ma first thought I had died in her womb. But there was nothing much to see there, either, other than an apartment building with a cell phone shop on the ground floor. I stood there for a while anyway, breathing in the briny air.

Each time Ming Pheaktra took me somewhere, she asked the same two questions.

"Why do you want to go? What are you looking for?"

Each time, I answered in the same way.

"Ma was here. I just want to look around."

I imagined how it must have been for Ma, a village girl, newly wed, uprooted from her rural life and making a new life in the big city of Phnom Penh, in a marriage she was forced to accept, in a life she never wanted. Chroy Changva Naval Base was a buffer, keeping her contained and protected from urban influences considered improper for Khmer girls—the beer halls and bars, even the cinema, known for showing movies directed by Prince Sihanouk himself.

My life in Phnom Penh in 2005 was vastly different than my mother's life in 1967, but the more I stayed in our country, the more I felt my story start to merge with hers. Just as Ma had been the anchor for her family in Cambodia, now I found myself unwittingly taking on that role, too, doing what I could to help improve my relatives' lives.

While I lived alone in my five-bedroom house, and had a housekeeper who cleaned and ironed my clothes and cooked me three meals a day, plus a security guard to protect my home, my relatives in the village resorted to eating rice with salt when drought dried up their rice paddies and they could not afford to buy meat.

Even Ming Pheaktra was scraping by. She, her older sister, her nephew, and her two kids lived in a ramshackle one-bedroom house across from an open sewer. The kitchen consisted of a two-burner tabletop gas stove set on a tiled counter in a space half the size of a prison cell and just as claustrophobic, right next to the bathroom, with a squat toilet and a flimsy plastic door that required lifting and leaning into place for privacy. The door had no hinge.

For months, Ming Pheaktra recounted to me the latest installment in a series of mishaps related to a resident sewer rat she was at war with that crawled through the house under the cover of night searching for crumbs. It was the size of a cat and meaner than an old man with too much liquor in his blood. Ming Pheaktra showed up at my house once with a bandage on her finger, because that rat nibbled at her and her children's toes and fingertips as they slept.

Another time, she caught the rat scurrying across her floor and reached for the closest thing at hand: an electric mosquito swatter.

"I didn't catch it," she said. "But I zapped it good, two times, and oh, Put, that thing convulsed on the floor before it skittered out the door and ran back in the sewer."

The next time the rat slunk around, while Ming Pheaktra was cooking, she had a two-by-four waiting. When she looked up and saw a tail between the rafters, she pounced. Ming Pheaktra grabbed her piece of wood in one hand and reached to yank the tail with the other. When the rat dropped to the floor, she beat it bloody and finished the rodent off then and there.

This last story Ming Pheaktra told me after I'd had dinner with her and her kids. We watched with delight as Ming Pheaktra reenacted some parts of the story in the exact places where the events unfolded. I laughed so hard, tears streamed down my face.

More tears came later that night, when I got home. I thought about Ming Pheaktra battling with a sewer rat while I was in my cavernous five-bedroom house, lying in bed, gazing at the ceiling fan that turned and turned to keep me cool and comfortable while I sobbed.

I had to do something. I wanted to help my family but didn't want to hand out cash, the way Ma did. I didn't want to have that kind of relationship with my relatives. I didn't want them to see me as an ATM, the way some of them saw Ma. So I made an offer: whoever wanted an education, I'd pay in full. Food, lodging, tuition, books, clothes, and anything else they needed.

Seven of my cousins raised their hands to take the offer,

including Ming Pheaktra's two kids and her nephew. Ming Pheaktra and I helped enroll each of them in English-language classes as well as regular Khmer school. Four boys and three girls. On weekends, everyone met at Ming Pheaktra's house or mine to eat and practice English.

Six months passed, and then a year. I kept paying. Not all of my cousins were successful in school. One among them was my cousin Mao. His older brother, Seng, is the cousin my father nearly beat to death when my family first arrived in Corvallis. I felt especially eager to help Mao, motivated by the profound guilt I felt for what my father did to his older brother.

But a village boy can easily lose his way in a big city. Mao fell in with a group of delinquents and started sniffing glue. Soon, he got kicked out of school and returned to the village. I blamed myself for Mao's struggle and shortcomings, for bringing village kids to the city where I could not fully protect them. I recognized then the tenuous nature of trying to do good; sometimes it backfires and harms rather than helps.

The guilt pulsed and pulsed.

I believed I was honoring my mother by continuing what she and my father had started in America—doing all that they could to help our relatives. Ma's words often drifted back to me: "They were the ones who survived the genocide."

When I was the same age as my young cousins, Ma would tell me: "When you're older, you have to go back to Cambodia and help."

She never said how. She never really said who. She never said how much.

She never said when my debt would be paid.

I became my family's ambassador, my weekends turning

into a blur of holidays, funerals, and weddings. Ma would call me using her international calling card and ask me to go to this cousin's wedding, or that great-aunt's funeral.

"Please go pay respects, gohn," Ma said on the phone once, when she called about a funeral. "This is my mother's cousin's husband. And don't forget to give alms to the monks."

I lost track of whom I was related to and how, and just went to every family gathering because Ma asked me to. Because it was expected of me. Because I was a Cambodian daughter.

I went to the village to visit Ma's oldest sister, Om Oeurn, without being asked to go, because she was quiet and kind and I loved her. I knew Ma would have been pleased and proud to know I was trying to take care of her older sister. Ma would have wanted me to bring sweets to the old woman, to make sure she had enough to eat. She was the one exception to my personal rule of not handing out money. I gave money to her. Five hundred dollars twice a year when I saw her. She bought medicine and paid for upgrades to her stilt home, which still lacked electricity and running water. I brought chocolates and cases of instant noodles, plying her with the kinds of treats she couldn't afford. As Ma would say, I gave her older sister good things to eat "while her throat was still upright."

When I pressed the bills into her hands, crisp and green as fresh-picked palm fronds, I told her, "It's time you stopped working in the rice paddies, auntie. You're too old."

She just grinned, and I knew that by the fall, when the weather cooled and the land was plowed, she would be stooped in the fields planting her crop. I understood by watching her, and by watching Ma in America, how work becomes habit. How you lose a part of who you are without it. So even when you are old and slowed down, you keep working because that is what you know.

The pressures of being my family's torch bearer sometimes became too much, even though I had volunteered myself for the role. I wanted to make Ma proud of me, to show her that her baby girl was not only independent enough to make a life for herself, but that that same daughter was fulfilling her filial role, tending to my relatives the way my mother likely would have if she was living in Cambodia.

I hadn't realized how exhausting it was to traverse my two worlds multiple times within any given day. To hang out with my friends and sip cocktails on the riverfront and attend lavish parties, and then to visit with my relatives who scrambled to earn enough to feed their hungry children. I struggled to reconcile these disparate parts of myself, and all the while, I was still in hiding. The fact that I was gay was the quicksand in the valley between being Cambodian and being American that threatened to pull me under as I moved back and forth across the great divide.

◘ MALIS GETS MARRIED

In the spring of 2007, Ma came to visit again. She had made a habit of regularly visiting ever since I decided to stay in Cambodia. I'd finished my work with Internews and gave up my subsidized five-bedroom house for something more my style, a one-bedroom flat on the top floor of a friend's house, in a quiet neighborhood tucked behind the capital's main government campus of ministries and courthouses.

When she arrived on an especially humid day in March, the air wet and weighted, I expected to collect only Ma from the airport. But she had another traveler with her, a surprise guest, my cousin Malis. Ma hadn't told me she was bringing Malis on the trip, and I didn't immediately question why. Maybe Ma wanted Malis to know Cambodia, in the same way Ma took me to Cambodia when I was sixteen years old, so I could see where I came from. It hadn't occurred to me what other motivations Ma may have had.

The following week, Aunt Vuthy would arrive, too, and together, we would go to Chous village to conduct a ceremony honoring Grandma Nhim and Nhim's parents, the Corporal and his wife, and all the other relatives and ancestors on Ma's side of the family who had long since passed away. It was the first time Aunt Vuthy had been back to Cambodia since she left in 1983. When we arrived in the village, our relatives rushed to see her.

"My god, look how fat you are!" our relatives said, in a chorus of praise that made Aunt Vuthy blush. "America has been good to you!"

The heat was harsh that time of year. The land was brown and fallow in my mother's village. Summer season was hunger season for my relatives. In good years, if my relatives had cultivated enough rice, it bridged them to the next year, the next harvest.

But 2006 was not a good year. So in 2007, my relatives were hungrier and needier than usual.

Om Oeurn and the other farmers were suffering through an extended drought. The crops died. The villagers were distraught. We made sure to organize a larger community feast to feed everyone.

Ma paid for a long and massive tent that villagers helped erect in the middle of the rice paddies where the monks would pray. More than a hundred of our relatives sat on mats, and in the absence of Pa, who ordinarily conducted these events as the male of the household, Ma nudged me to say a few words.

I spoke in Khmer, thanking all of our relatives and the villagers for attending our ceremony. I paid respect to the monks and asked that everyone join in the prayer for our ancestors. I had seen Pa make this speech back in the U.S., at the Cambodian Buddhist temple near Portland where my parents went to pray. It surprised me to find myself now holding court as he once had, taking on a role that would have been his. A man's role, filled by his daughter. I understood the improbability of the situation. As I spoke, I glanced at Ma. She was beaming. Her daughter, the journalist, was speaking in her mother tongue.

The next day, a parade of visitors descended on my apartment in a tornado of activity. Ming Pheaktra came, followed by Ma's best friend, the same friend who had visited with her soccer coach son when I first moved to Cambodia. Ma's best friend's neighbors were also in the mix, a husband and wife who were merchants in a suburb just west of Phnom Penh. Their son had driven them in a brand-new Toyota Camry—a fact Ma made sure to point out to me. It meant this family had money, and money meant everything—power, status, and respect. I watched as Ma spoke to these new friends with an abiding deference. They owned a garment factory where some of my cousins worked. Ma invited everyone to sit down. I wasn't sure why all these people were here and just assumed they were paying Ma a friendly visit.

Malis was nowhere in sight. I tracked her down in the bathroom, where she was taking her time getting ready. I knocked several times to urge her out so other guests could use the bathroom. Each time, she responded with the same wan response.

"I know. I'm coming."

Another hour passed before she finally emerged.

As I pulled up a chair to join Ma's friends, I sat down in the middle of a conversation that had everyone giddy with excitement. There was talk of a wedding and all the preparations that would need to be made. Who was getting married? I wondered. And then, as I watched Malis sit quietly near Ma, saying nothing, I knew.

My cousin Malis was the oldest of my uncle Sovann's three daughters. When she was in middle school, her mother had walked out the door and into the arms of another Khmer man in a different state. My uncle had numbed his grief with alcohol and gambling, leaving Malis to care for her two younger sisters. I learned later via gossip among aunties that she had dropped out of high school.

Now she was here in Cambodia, about to get married.

As I navigated around all the people in my apartment, fetching more soft drinks and water, a surge of anger slipped down my spine. Ma hadn't told me she was bringing Malis with her on this trip. Now I knew why. My mother, unproductive in her attempts at matchmaking with me, was having a do-over with my young cousin.

In a previous visit to Cambodia, Ma had struck a deal with her best friend's neighbors. Their son would marry Malis. The dowry was a hefty twenty thousand dollars.

In Ma's mind, she was making money for her niece, hoping to vault Malis out of her circumstance and nudge her back on track to finish school. In my mind, Ma was about to ruin my cousin's life.

The next day, I asked Ma to leave my apartment.

"You can't keep bringing people up here to my apartment," I told Ma. "I work here. I can't work when people are coming and going like this."

But I knew as I said these words that it was not about the people. I didn't want to witness my mother tampering with my young cousin's life. I didn't know why Ma was so willing to do this, and I was angry that she was playing a dangerous game.

By that afternoon, Ma and Malis had packed their bags and moved to a hotel. In their absence, I paced my apartment, trying to calm an anxiety tugging at me.

My cousin was not well. It was known in our family that she suffered from depression and obsessive-compulsive disorder. She washed her hands dozens of times a day and spent two and sometimes three hours in the bathroom "getting ready." She rarely spoke, and when she did, she sounded more like a twelve-year-old than a young adult. She was aware of herself enough to admit to me that she had OCD. She laughed when she said it.

"I just get nervous," she said, tearing at tissues between her fingers.

No one knew for sure what struggles Malis lived with, because none of the adults around her thought to try and help her. Perhaps no one in our family wanted to admit that she had a mental illness because in our Khmer culture, to be mentally ill is to be possessed by evil spirits, to have a pall cast on the entire family. The same stigma my mother feared when we went to see a family psychologist in Corvallis is the same stigma that caused Ma and my uncle Sovann to avoid getting help for Malis.

Now she was about to become a bride.

My cousin seemed to enjoy the attention. She let her future in-laws select silk of the finest quality for her wedding sampot. She went to the market multiple times to procure jewelry and shoes. She let hairstylists fuss and flit around her, preparing her for family photos before the wedding day.

For the next three days, I banked between my apartment and Ma's hotel. Ma had found a place for herself and Malis a block from Great-Uncle San's house. When I went there, Ma was perpetually in a rush, trying to coordinate the monks, the offerings, the guest list. She buzzed around excitedly like a hummingbird, the way she did during Chan's wedding.

One afternoon, when my cousins were in the room next door watching Khmer movies, I caught Ma alone.

"Ma, Malis is not normal," I said. "She has a mental illness. I don't think this wedding is a good idea."

Ma was lying on her back, resting, the air-conditioning blowing at full blast, causing me to shiver. She wore a housedress cut from the colorful cotton cloth used to make sarongs, which I only saw her wear in Cambodia. Back in America, Ma wore sweatpants and T-shirts. She seemed more relaxed in Cambodia, even if the heat constantly bothered her.

Rather than talk about Malis, Ma diverted the discussion.

"Her father is the one with real problems," Ma said. "He's so addicted to gambling. He has lost all sense of himself. He doesn't care about raising his daughters. You should see him. He's staying at Aunt Samnang's house, thanks to her generosity."

Ma complained about how she had completely lost her brother to the casinos, gambling away his life just like Grandpa Sin had. She talked until I interrupted.

"Ma," I said, "this is not about Uncle Sovann. It's about Malis. She needs to see a counselor, not get married."

Ma looked at me, her face sallow. She knew she was cornered and didn't know how to maneuver her way back out.

"Who's going to pay for that?" Ma finally blurted out.

"I don't know. There are free counseling services at the county mental health department," I said. "You need to do something."

"You don't know anything," Ma snapped, raising herself halfway up in bed. "She's at a dead end in her life. If she gets married, that could change things for her. Maybe she won't have so many problems."

I didn't buy it. I saw my cousin's capacity and doubted marriage would save her. Marriage didn't save my mother, but I kept that thought to myself.

"How is she going to take care of a husband and kids if she can't even take care of herself?" I asked.

"That's exactly what's going to help her: having a husband," Ma said. "That's what will help her become responsible."

I couldn't believe what Ma was saying. I wondered if she really believed that the solution for mental illness was giving someone more rather than less responsibility, that all my cousin really needed was mere distraction and the busyness of being a wife to help address—or ignore—deeper personal problems.

"You're gambling with her life," I said.

And that tipped Ma over the edge. She sprang up in bed and scowled at me.

"At least Malis is getting married," Ma said, her voice stiff with impatience. "It's better than living gay like you!"

Those last words hit like a missile. Perfect aim, a shot fired right to where it hurt the most. In that instant, time stood still in a sticky silence. Seven years prior, I had come out to Ma as gay. She had said she loved me. And I had believed her. I had believed she was okay with having a gay daughter, even though we never spoke about it again.

For the first time, I saw how wrong I was.

I careened out of Ma's room and broke into a run down the stairwell to my Vespa. I rode home so fast, I nearly crashed into an SUV. When I got home, I ran up the stairs to my apartment and fumbled for my keys. On the other side of the fence, just behind my apartment, schoolchildren laughed and played. I watched the girls swing a ball around a post and wondered how many of them would one day disappoint their mothers.

Malis was married on April 7, 2007, nearly thirty-two years since my family, including Malis's father, fled Cambodia. I don't know if Malis was happy or sad or confused, because I didn't go watch my relatives tie red string to her wrists. She was twenty-two years old.

When Malis was a little girl and I was sixteen years old, I bent low to give her a hug at Portland International Airport before I boarded a plane for my first trip to Cambodia. I had whispered in her ear that she would one day go to Cambodia, too. I didn't know it would be to get married. Or that Ma's attempt to help her niece would backfire and cause Malis more suffering when her marriage later imploded in America.

I wondered whether Ma's marrying off her niece in an arranged marriage had more to do with wanting to satisfy her own needs, of self-preservation as a Khmer mother because weddings are a Khmer mother's best chance to prove that she has succeeded in raising her daughters. Even as a surrogate for Malis, Ma reveled in being praised and honored, while I shriveled deeper into a dangerous shame.

PART IV

FREEDOM

◘ CROCODILE AND OXCART DRIVER

There are a lot of stories about the Crocodile in Cambodia, gohn. Who can remember them all? Go ask your pa. Ma is too old, gohn. Which one did I tell you? Oh, that's it. You know about the Crocodile and the Oxcart Driver? I will tell you again. This time, try to remember it, or maybe you can write it down, because next time you ask, I might already have forgotten it. You can't rely on me much longer.

One day, the Crocodile found himself in some trouble. He wandered out of the lagoon and now he was stranded. He was hot and suffering on the dry land and wondered if he was ever going to get back to the water, or if he was going to die of heat. But then, he saw in the distance that the Oxcart Driver was coming. He screamed and screamed to get the Oxcart Driver's attention.

"Help me! Help me!"

"What?" the Oxcart Driver said, approaching the Crocodile. "What is this? The Crocodile is not supposed to be on land. The Crocodile is supposed to be in the water."

"Mr. Oxcart Driver, you see I am stranded here. Please help me return to the lagoon," the Crocodile said.

The Oxcart Driver, feeling very sorry for the poor Crocodile, agreed to help and carried the Crocodile to his cart. They began the journey back to the lagoon.

A surprise awaited once they reached the lagoon. Instead of crawling back into the water, when the Oxcart Driver lifted the Crocodile from his cart, the Crocodile turned and snapped his long jaw at the Oxcart Driver. A few more snaps and he swallowed the Oxcart Driver whole.

That's so scary. But this is just a story, Put. It's for teaching lessons. The Oxcart Driver had saved the Crocodile's life and the Crocodile should have been grateful, but the Crocodile betrayed his savior. The Crocodile was too hungry and selfish. This is why the old people say you have to be smarter than the Crocodile. I'm not stupid like that. I don't want to be eaten like the Oxcart Driver.

Ma and I, we were angry at each other after she came to Cambodia to marry off my cousin. Our estrangement had been bothering me, and I didn't know how to close the gulf between us, to salvage our bond. In the summer of 2007, I was back in Keizer, spinning. I had no job, having finished my contract work earlier in the spring. I was not in a relationship. I had become the thing I was most afraid of being: a disappointment in my mother's eyes.

So when an opportunity appeared in my inbox to work in Afghanistan, I pursued it. I rationalized the decision by telling myself and my friends that if I was ever going to write about my parents' experiences, I wanted to know what war was like, to be as up close to it as I could get. But there was more than that.

My friend Jan pointed out the patterns in my behavior, how I flung myself into dangerous scenarios to avoid dealing with any kind of pain percolating within me. She called me out.

"Are you trying to get yourself killed?"

"I'm not that kind of journalist," I said. "It's not about the adrenaline."

"Then what are you trying to prove?"

At the time, I had no good answer. Looking back, I see clearly what choosing to go to a war zone was all about. I was trying to prove that I was more than merely a burden on my mother, that I was worthy, that I could survive on my own.

There were other options for me. A journalism training gig in Bogotá, Colombia. Contracts with other nongovernmental organizations in Phnom Penh. Even the possibility of resuming my reporting career in the United States.

But a deep disquiet had risen in me when Ma revealed what she really thought about my being gay, a piercing shame, coupled with an emerging realization that I would never be the daughter she wanted or needed me to be. I couldn't bear it. So I did what she did when she felt cornered in 1967 after learning she would be in an arranged marriage: I ran toward war.

That summer, Ma was at the kitchen counter working through a mound of pea shoots when I came in from the backyard. I pulled a paring knife out of the drawer, took a seat on one of the barstools, and began to help her trim the stems. Ma's hands worked methodically, as if by memory, her eyes locked on the greens but her mind somewhere else. She was in a state of deep thinking or meditating, which I knew well. This was one of the reasons I loved cooking, too. I could forget about everything and focus on the food.

I didn't know how to tell Ma about Afghanistan other than to just say it, as swiftly as I could.

"There's a job," I said, the words gathering like pebbles in my throat, making me choke as I spoke. "It's working with journalists again. Same as I did in Cambodia."

Our hands kept moving, reaching for the next stem, pressing the blade down against the finger that held the stem, clipping the tip, then reaching for the next one. We were used to moving in synchronicity, our hands long-accustomed to cycling through vines in the strawberry fields.

"It's in Afghanistan."

The war in Afghanistan was on the news nearly every evening. Bombings. Kidnappings. Ambushes. The awfulness on stark display. Ma kept cutting her stems. I wasn't sure if she'd heard me, because she didn't react at all. Then slowly, I watched as her face creased into a frown. Pinched, as if she was trying to hold back tears.

We kept cutting. We kept reaching. In the rhythm of our work, we could pretend I hadn't just said I was going to a war zone. We could pretend our lives would always be like this moment, calm and safe in her kitchen.

"I brought you safely from war, gohn," Ma said. "I raised you so that your body is perfect. No scars. Now you want to go and crawl in the dirt and run from bombs?"

Ma stopped moving and dropped her knife into the pile of severed stems. She didn't look at me. She walked down the hallway, up the stairs, and straight to her bedroom, where she closed the door and locked it behind her, the kind of sudden retreat I knew well.

When I followed and reached her bedroom door, I thought about knocking. I wanted to explain myself and my decision. To tell her that the money was good. It was a short contract. It would help my career. I wanted to enumerate all the reasons why I wanted to go, practical points she would understand.

I didn't know what kind of ground I was standing on with Ma. So rather than knock on her door, I walked to my own room and started to pack. I would be leaving the next day, back to Cambodia, and eventually, on to Kabul.

When the time came, Ma and Pa saw me off at the airport as they had always done. But this time, rather than offer me advice or tell me to take care, Ma stayed silent. And when it was time for me to board my plane, I went through security and veered toward my gate without looking back.

There was a final piece of business to take care of in Cambodia before I left for Afghanistan. When I moved there in early 2005, Cambodia had been at peace for twenty-five years, yet the healing was far from over. I wondered whether it was even possible for a country and its people to entirely recover from war. An official process was starting that would lay important groundwork for Cambodia to come to terms with its dark past. The Cambodian government, along with the international community, had begun negotiating an international war crimes tribunal to bring to justice former Khmer Rouge leaders. I wanted to be in the country when the first trial started.

My former colleagues at Internews had already moved on by then. Narridh was helping to launch a program to train print and radio reporters on the technical aspects of covering the trials. The lead trainer, a French journalist and expert in war crimes tribunals, had arrived in Phnom Penh fresh from covering the Charles Taylor trial in the Special Court for Sierra Leone. I wanted to meet Pierre Bossard and maybe hitch myself to the program for a few weeks before I flew to Kabul to join a new set of colleagues there.

When Pierre and I met for dinner one night, we talked for hours about the upcoming pretrial hearing for Kaing Guek Eav, aka Duch, the former head of Tuol Sleng prison. A chill slid down my spine at the thought of seeing, separated only by a glass partition in the courtroom, the man who was responsible for the brutality I learned about when I was sixteen years old touring the prison. Pierre and I talked about what Duch's trial might mean for my country, for my people, for me. We talked until we were the last customers in the restaurant, and then we met for dinner again, a few days later, to talk more. That night, when one restaurant closed, we went to the next one, and when that one closed, we ducked into a bar. When we talked through the bartender's last call, when there was nowhere left to go, we went to my place.

In a couple of months, I would be leaving Phnom Penh, which helped me rationalize plunging so quickly into an affair with Pierre. He was leaving in three weeks to return to his work in The Hague, and then onward to France to see his family. He was the perfect fling before I dashed off to a war zone. We loved each other in the crazed, reckless way of people who have limited time.

At the airport, parting ways didn't ache the way I imagined it would. Before Pierre went, we said we'd stay in touch. We said maybe we'd meet somewhere in the middle, between France and Afghanistan. I did not hold my breath. I also did not know, watching him disappear to his gate, that Pierre had slipped into an unguarded part of my heart, the part that struggled to trust men. I did not know how deeply I had slipped into his.

Before I had a chance to grieve Pierre's absence, another unexpected romance sprang into view. I tumbled into a second love affair in as many months. This time, with a Khmer American woman, like me.

We met at a party of mutual Khmer American friends. Rachany was from Boston and worked for one of Phnom Penh's nongovernmental organizations combating sex trafficking. She had been in an arranged marriage with the son of a Khmer royal. But she had known for some time she was more interested in women.

For the first time, being with another Khmer American, I realized why Ma had wanted one of her kids to marry someone from our culture. It was easy and freeing to speak the same language, to spend time with someone who picked up on the same cultural cues and nuances as I did, who laughed at the same kind of humor. For the first time, I didn't need to teach or translate my language or culture for someone else. I didn't need to explain myself.

Love and life become a little lighter and more efficient when you don't need to expend energy bringing someone else along into your culture. When we ate our meals, Rachany stood to serve me first, judiciously picking out the best pieces of meat to put on my plate. When we spoke, she called me "Bong," because I was her elder, if only by a few years. When we took weekend trips, I didn't question when she veered to the side of the road so we could light incense at a roadside shrine and pray to the guardian spirit of the road for a safe journey. I stood next to her and lit incense, too. She sang Khmer ballads in my ear and we danced the *satavan*, our hands fluttering hip high from our sides before crossing in front of us as we stepped forward toward each other.

My heart was in overdrive. Two loves in two months. Ma had wanted me to be with a Khmer man. And in my clumsy, bungling way, I got both a man and a Khmer, just not together in the same person.

When I finally left for Afghanistan, four weeks after meeting Rachany and eight weeks after meeting Pierre, my head and heart felt crazed. I thought of Meg and David from a decade before. I thought of the choice between a man and a woman. Between my Khmer side and my American side. Between Ma and me. Between the crocodile and the tiger. I thought of how close I had gotten to Ma's vision for me, how I'd managed to just miss the mark. It was hard not to believe the ancestors were messing with me.

◻ AFGHANISTAN

What do you pack for war? You make your best guess and go. You tuck into a suitcase a pair of black combat boots, tunics tailor-made to fall above the knees, scarves large and long enough to cover your head, things you never needed to own until now. Things to make you modest in a country and culture that are not your own. You slip pictures of your family into a side pocket. You bring your camping headlamp and a few loose books.

You get there, and it doesn't take long; you find yourself running for cover.

You hear a blast that shakes the earth . . . *Kaboom!* To your left, a man clutches an open wound on his chest, slumped against the wheel well of a car on fire. To your right, a woman lies on the road, with orphaned shoes, broken glass, and chaos everywhere around her. Red heat licks at your arms and face. Every corner you turn, disaster. You freeze. The thing you are told not to do. The thing that is dangerous in war—being so afraid or in shock that you are rendered perfectly useless.

"Keep moving!" a voice instructs. "Triage! Triage! If you find no sign of life, move on."

The next few minutes become a blur. Check his pulse. Make a tourniquet for her wounds. Drag those bodies away from the blaze. You scramble from victim to victim, making dubious decisions about who gets to live and who is beyond saving. It's all guesswork, deciding who is worth saving. The thought of it makes you nauseous.

This isn't real, you repeat. Your mind understands, but your body is already hijacked, tense with things it knows, things that live deep in your bones, like danger and fear and the undertow of anguish that follows.

You were told about this day in a memo your supervisor sent out. This is Hostile Environments Awareness Training, a fake war professionally built within a real war so that you can practice how to exit alive.

As your colleagues chuckle at the chicken blood smeared on faces and spilled onto the floor, and the writhing bodies overacting in pain, you stand numb at their side. An ancient pain blooms in your body. Fight? Flight? Or freeze? Your body goes berserk, your legs twitchy, your fists clenched, your stomach churning, churning. You will have nightmares for weeks after this simulation, your body incapable of calm.

You flew into Kabul one week before, in the dead of winter, the airplane's wingtips gliding past the snow-covered Hindu Kush mountain range—a natural fortress around Kabul, rising above the buildings and homes hidden behind fortified high walls and protected by heavily armed men toting AK-47s over their shoulders. Everywhere you glance, guns. You arrived at a city on lockdown, into a country convulsing with war. The blank black of the night sky zipped open by rocket grenades.

You watch out the window, on your way to work, men rushing across dirt roads hardened by freezing temperatures, wrapped in pattu shawls, hunched against the cold. Women in burkas slinking quietly by, in between mud brick homes, dragging their children who disappear in drapes of blue fabric behind them. Where you live, ice encases the rose hips of your landlady's rosebushes like amber, and you wonder: How will they survive?

You came here to work with some of the country's top journalists in a program to help build their skills at investigating corruption within governmental institutions. You came here to understand a little bit of what your parents might have felt, running from war in Cambodia. But that was just an easy surface story you told.

You really came here to hide, letting a real war distract from the one raging inside you. You don't yet know how terrible an idea this is. You learn.

Your life here is simple. You have a room in a home you share with your friends Pauline and Bernie, in a compound set behind a tall yellow gate; your landlady, Najia, lives in a house behind you, and servants' quarters are opposite her. Najia is a granddaughter of Afghanistan's last king, Mohammed Zahir Shah, robust, with a nest of jet-black hair, and she will welcome you with the warmth of a million suns and you will feel safe and content as you dig into her feast on your first day in her country: Kabuli rice, mutton curry, lentil stew, and a slab of flatbread the size and shape of a snowshoe.

You go to bed that first night, considering the door, the window, which way to exit the fastest in case of a bombing or a raid. In the morning, you will get a text. Bomb threats are high. Your boss gives you a choice: go to the office, or work from home. You go to the office, where your Afghan colleagues are. You did not come to a war zone to stay at home. You carry your Khmer passport when you leave for work, leaving your

U.S. passport behind. You hide who you are. It is safer to be Cambodian than American. And it is one of the first times you will realize how glad you are to be both.

Back home, in your room, your thoughts drift to the journalists you worked with in Cambodia, and the ones who were murdered at Tuol Sleng prison during the genocide. You think about your mother running away from her marriage, only to get tangled up in a war. You think about the female students in your program, how you want to be like them. You want to be that brave.

But that is not what you are feeling the day you go to work and the war has arrived at your doorstep: Taliban fighters and Afghan government troops are battling in the foothills directly across the street. You watch from your second-floor office window as billows of smoke rise up from the creases in the hill, explosions rattling your windows, shaking your files to the floor like autumn leaves butterflying to your feet. The office administrator rushes into your room, her words spitting out fast as machine gunfire. *Dut, dut, dut, dut, dut.*

"What is she saying?" you ask your translator, Enayat. But he didn't hear. Or he was distracted. Or he is scared. You say it again: "What the hell is she saying?"

She said: "Two children have died in the cross fire. We should prepare to go to the bomb shelter."

The administrator paces up and down the hallway.

"Do we need to move?" Enayat will ask her. "Just tell us if we need to move."

Enayat is the calmest person you have ever met. But his voice in that moment is scored with panic. You start to panic, too.

You want instructions, to be told what to do, because your mind gets stuck in situations like this, under duress. You don't move until someone tells you to move. The explosions shake the earth and you feel them vibrate in your core. You keep typing, keep telling yourself: You have a training to conduct tomorrow. You have journalists who depend on you. You have Pauline, who will make cardamom coffee in the morning, and Bernie, a Canadian Armed Forces officer, who will protect you. You have tomorrow. You have tomorrow. You have tomorrow.

You build for yourself this kind of story with a future when you are scared because it is the only thing that makes you feel less afraid. You make a shelter of hope to hide in.

Fear is everywhere. The fear of being kidnapped in the two minutes it takes to walk from your house to the corner for flatbread. The fear of entering a building that will get blown to bits by a suicide bomber. The fear of Zia, who drives you to work each day, because someone told you about a chauffeur for international aid workers who sold out, delivering foreigners directly into the hands of the Taliban. Who can you trust in war? The mind spins and spins with fear. And fear is fertilizer for trauma. This is where your trauma grows without you knowing.

There are things that made you shudder that eventually become a part of your life, things you learn to ignore. Like the Blackhawks flying so low above your compound you could stand on the roof, reach up, and grab the landing skids, the thunder they make rattling your bones and the draft of their spinning blades pulling your own breath out of you. You stand in the courtyard and stare into the sky, watching the blades spinning, like your cousin Seng's body, feeling the rush of air. The memory hits you so hard you cry.

You ignore the dull thud of bombs blasting in the distance, interrupted by the morning call to prayers of the muezzin at the nearby mosque. You repeat these words: "It's okay. You're okay. It's okay." What stays with you is the gray of the days, the landscape in sepia tone, dull brown and fringed with dust-filtered light.

You go home each night frazzled and exhausted. You want to leave, to go home, but you don't know anymore where that is. Two months pass like this, then three. One hundred and twenty tomorrows come and go before the day comes when your students hold a farewell party for you. You think for a moment, How odd, a party in the middle of war. Life goes on amid the plunder.

Aadila Abad, one of your students, will wedge her baby into your arms to free her hands momentarily as she pulls a ring off her finger. Aadila's baby presses her tiny, moist hand to your cheek, and you will feel that little hand for years from that moment.

"Please take it, teacher, for my thank-you," she will say, as she pushes her gift onto your ring finger, even as you resist. You promise yourself that one day, you will give that ring to someone better and braver than you.

The ring is a simple turquoise stone set inside a slim silver band crowned by moissanite, and that is the thing you will fuss with at Najia's table, where she has made you a final supper: spinach dumplings, vegetable soup, and Kabuli rice. She tells you between bites, "That day ago, I see you, I know I love you. Why my heart is thinking this? I know you good lady. Like daughter."

And an emotion will catch, which you will gulp with Najia's food. You eat and eat because that is how you learned to take in love.

Outside, Najia's roses are in full bloom. Pops of pink, red, and orange in the courtyard. Your mother grew a row of roses on Ironwood Avenue, and now you understand why she loved them so much. They thrive in the harshest winters and hottest summers, in the middle of war. They are survivors.

That ring is the thing you will fidget with in line at the airport, Najia there at your side, insisting on seeing you off just as your mother did all those times before, and you are glad you let her because your suitcase, bulging with Afghan rugs, clay bowls, and hand-blown cobalt glasses—gifts for your mother—has put your check-in over the allowable weight. But Najia merely waves her hand, the flight check-in crew nods at your luggage, and you are free.

That ring is the thing you will worry until it shines as the plane rises up and up above the Hindu Kush mountain range and you are overcome with the grief of knowing you will not return to this place. You will not let Afghanistan take any more from you than what it already has: Your sense of safety. Your ability to trust and hope. You leave with a simple truth: that you can never hide from your mother.

◘ CALLING ME HOME

I went home to Phnom Penh to heal. Back in my apartment, I became nearly inert, locking myself inside with the curtains drawn for weeks. I wandered between my bedroom and my patio. I couldn't concentrate. I couldn't cry. I couldn't go out and guzzle my grief down at the corner bar. I could barely eat, and when I did, I swallowed guilt in every bite. Guilt for being so privileged that I could flash my American passport and flee to safety, even as the journalists I worked with in Kabul continued to face daily threats. Guilt for being in Phnom Penh, eating at Western restaurants and bars, while my relatives in the countryside ate rice with salt. Guilt for being alive.

I leapt for cover when a car backfired, and felt like I would suffocate in an elevator or any other small, enclosed space. I felt chaos crowd in my heart.

I thought it was another depression, until I watched a counselor scribble "PTSD" into her notebook. And then I understood. All those times I saw Ma go into her bedroom and close the door behind her as she sobbed, for what appeared no apparent reason. That time Pa slumped to his knees and pounded his chest and was rushed to the psychiatric ward. Those times, in my twenties, when I tested a belt slung over the closet rod, to see if it would hold my weight. I understood. Trauma had been accruing inside me, some passed down from Ma and Pa, and now that I was home from Afghanistan, I was weighed down by the trauma I had collected on my own.

For a time, I went back to Rachany. When I declined too many times to leave my apartment and go out with her and her friends, she finally had enough and pushed a finger into my chest.

"You've changed, Bong," she said. "We used to have fun. You're so serious all the time now. I don't know you anymore."

I didn't know me anymore, either. So I let her go.

For a longer time, I went back to Pierre. We moved into an apartment near the Olympic Stadium and began commuting every day together to a courthouse on the outskirts of Phnom Penh to cover the Khmer Rouge tribunal. We threw dinner parties and went out with friends to explore the new restaurants on the riverside. His parents came to visit us for one month and I loved them, unreservedly and immediately. I thought, Maybe. Maybe this could work.

We talked about marriage and buying a house in Portland. We talked about babies. But ultimately I let him go, too. I loved him, and saw glimpses of a future together. I could have talked myself into a particular life: a house, a husband, kids running joyous and chaotic circles around us. But that is the same thing as talking yourself into a corner. And I am afraid of tight spaces.

I never told Ma about Pierre, but she knew. The day I moved out of our apartment and into my own, Ma called. No reason, she said. Just seeing how I was doing. And I wondered then whether the pineapple had seen, only minutes before her call, the tears streaking my cheeks?

I wanted to run and hide, but I didn't know where to go this time. I called Chan. I called Mo. I kept dialing international numbers until someone answered.

"I think I have PTSD," I told Mo, as I slouched against the glass partition phone booth at the internet café near my apartment, mosquitoes feasting on my ankles.

"Put, you need to exercise. You need to go to the market and get a pair of shoes. Even if it's a knockoff kind," Mo said.

Unlike my siblings, who played tennis and basketball, I wasn't involved in school sports growing up except for a short stint on the track team; our mother constantly worried I would have an asthma attack and convinced me to quit. I rarely ran after that, except away from people.

But that weekend, I got a pair of Nikes and went with Ming Pheaktra to the riverfront. She picked me up at 5:00 a.m. and we joined the convergence of other fitness-minded Khmer men and women who did aerobics and played badminton and hacky sack. Ming Pheaktra walked. I ran a mile and collapsed, then ran another mile the next day. By the end of a month, I could run a few miles. I ran in front of the Royal Palace, where Cambodia's king resided, up the Sisowath Quay, where the latest expats lounged on rattan chairs soaking up the view of the Mekong River, and around Wat Phnom, a hill crowned with a pagoda where tourists took turns riding a worn and overworked elephant. By the following summer, I was ready to run my first marathon.

After New Year's, with 2009 well underway, I started feeling better, going out more, mostly with Ming Pheaktra. We ate noodle soup in the mornings after exercising and I cruised with Ming Pheaktra and her kids up and down the riverfront, stopping to eat corn on the cob or unripe mango slices dipped in chili salt. When I found my center again, I took contract work with UNICEF to overhaul the organization's Cambodia-specific website—a job that would keep me in Cambodia for at least another year. I liked the simplicity of how my life in Phnom Penh had evolved. I thought maybe I would stay in Cambodia; maybe there was no reason to return to America.

A few months after my breakup with Pierre, Ming Pheaktra sensed my sadness, and urged me to try and work things out with him. But it wasn't so much sadness as it was a feeling that I had lost my way. I didn't tell her this. I told her mostly lies. I told her that we were different people, Pierre and I. He spent money while I saved. He loved fancy restaurants while I preferred holes-in-the-wall. I talked and talked, enumerating our differences rather than mentioning all the ways we were compatible. The truth was, I didn't want to be with a man and I wasn't brave enough to tell her, or him. Or myself.

A few weeks later, as we cooled our throats with bottles of Angkor beer on a rooftop bar and picked at salted peanuts with chopsticks, Ming Pheaktra cornered me.

"Niece," she said, sifting through the peanuts in search of slivers of savory fried garlic, "are you going to live forever single? It's time for you to get married."

I heard my mother's voice, an annoying echo from half a world away, being channeled through Ming Pheaktra.

"The years go by quickly," she said. "Don't wait too long. Don't be too picky or you'll grow old with no family around you."

Ming Pheaktra was on a tear to get me to marry someone. And Ma made one more attempt, too, recruiting Ming

Pheaktra to try and set me up with the son of her best friend in Phnom Penh. I called Ma to tell her to quit her shenanigans. It was as if I had never come out to her as gay. Or she was in denial about who I really was. It hadn't occurred to me that I might have been in denial, too.

In the meantime, to learn what was the matter with me, why it was taking me so long to find a match, Ming Pheaktra took me to a fortune-teller.

The middle-aged woman sat cross-legged on the floor on the other side of a small table set in a dark, sparsely furnished apartment, her face hidden behind a screen of incense smoke curling into the air around her. She ran coarse fingers over my palms and then looked up at Ming Pheaktra.

"Your niece is like a horse," she said solemnly, her fingers following my lifeline. "She kicks from behind anyone who dares to love her."

I glanced at Ming Pheaktra, who was looking gravely and importantly at the fortune-teller, who looked up at me, a triangle of glimpses cloaked in swirls of smoke. Then the fortune-teller dropped her gaze back to my palm.

"Don't worry," she announced confidently, "your niece will eventually find a husband and have two children."

Ming Pheaktra smiled then, and let out a slow, measured exhale, eating up every last word from the fortune-teller. I rolled my eyes, hoping Ming Pheaktra wouldn't see.

"Do you believe her?" Ming Pheaktra asked me as we left the fortune-teller's den and headed back to my house.

"No," I said. "Not a word."

Looking back, maybe the fortune-teller was a little bit right. The part about the horse, that was true. How many lovers had I kicked to the curb by then?

Several weeks later, after finishing work on my laptop

at home, I dropped into bed, lulled into a fitful sleep by the "wamp . . . wamp . . . wamp" of the ceiling fan, which stayed on, day and night, the only dependable weapon to fight the heavy heat and humidity that hovers year-round in Cambodia.

As usual, my neighborhood that night was full of sounds and voices—couples fighting, karaoke shrilling, dogs barking—a constant cacophony that unfurled reliably every night between the tall and tight rows of apartment buildings, a setup for resonant sound. It seemed the only period of peace came in the small hours, in the gloaming between midnight and dawn, when I slept.

When the nightstand suddenly started vibrating, just past 2:00 a.m., I jolted awake and glanced over to see my cell phone, screen light flashing and hopping toward free fall. It vibrated all the way to the edge of my nightstand. I fumbled for it in the darkness.

"Hello," I mumbled.

There was no reply yet, but a long string of numbers illuminated on the screen. An international call. It could only be my parents. They were the only ones who went to the Asian market in Salem and bought prepaid phone cards to call me.

"Put," I heard Ma's voice, barely audible, distant in a way that I sensed had nothing to do with the connection.

"Yes, why are you calling so late, Ma?" I asked. She knew the fourteen-hour time difference.

"Your pa," she said, and no sooner did these two words leave her lips than she broke into an awful sob.

"Pa what?" I asked urgently.

I yanked myself up in bed, sitting ramrod straight. A cat shrieked outside and crashed onto a tin roof.

"Your pa," Ma said again, before breaking into an even louder cry into the phone.

"What, Ma? Ma, stop crying. Pa what? What happened?" I asked, angry that she was crying and could not say the thing she needed to say, and then ashamed for being mad at her.

But she wouldn't stop crying, and I knew. He was dead, or was dying, and I was seventy-six hundred miles away in Cambodia—the place where we were born, the country we abandoned together.

If she had never called, I might have never gone back home. He and I, we had never seen eye to eye. I still hadn't forgiven my father for all the things he did to her, to my cousin, to me. I didn't hate him, I just didn't have it in me to forgive him. So when his heart gave out and she wasn't sure if he'd make it on the other side of quadruple bypass surgery, I went home because my mother needed me, and after all our fighting, I still wanted to be needed by her.

Chan was the first to arrive at the hospital. During our father's surgery, she clutched a telephone to her ear in the visitor's room, listening to a nurse's regular updates.

I imagined the surgeon working to slit my father in half, revealing his heart. I wondered what it looked like. What does the heart of a man who fought in a war that haunted him and then came to America and fought with his family look like? I wondered, as he was lying there in the operating room, whether it was even still beating.

He made it through surgery, and Chan, knowing I was on my way from Cambodia, took the train back to Seattle to be with her family, passing the baton to me to take care of our parents.

Meanwhile, Ma and I drew a cautious truce, unspoken but understood. I would be there that summer of 2010 in Keizer to help her. And as soon as Pa felt better, I would be gone.

When I was not in Keizer interrogating my parents

about the past, I went on dates with women and with men in Portland. I was restless and reckless with love. I shocked and angered my gay friends when I dated a male firefighter and shocked and disturbed my straight friends when I dated a woman who was eight months pregnant. I didn't care. I was more confused about myself than I had ever been.

So in 2013, when Pa was fully recovered, I made my next exit. When I opened my email to find an intriguing opportunity in Thailand to work with journalists across Asia who were struggling to secure freedom of expression, I did the thing I was very good at. I packed up my house, put it up for rent, then called Ma to tell her I was leaving.

☐ FREEDOM OF EXPRESSION

I shared a four-bedroom house in an all-Thai neighborhood in Chiang Mai—in a quiet cul-de-sac near the vibrant city life of the main road, where a parlor offering three-dollar massages was pinched amid a row of noodle shops. The scent of cloves and star anise and hot chili hovered in the air, attracting customers day and night. I went to the nearest local market, and my heart burst open to see all the fresh vegetables and foods: papayas and mangoes, banana bud and Asian eggplant. In another section of the market, old ladies sitting atop tiled counters pounded green papaya with tomatoes, pickled rice-paddy crabs, and chilis with a controlled haste in enormous clay mortars and pestles. I took home a sixty-cent bag of papaya salad and ate it with my hands.

The market smelled of sweetness and funk—the same smells as in Cambodia. The same smells as in Ma's kitchen. I breathed it all in and smiled. Shop owners spoke Thai to me as if I were one of them. "Same same," I said, pointing to my skin and theirs, "but different. I'm Cambodian." They smiled back, "Ah, Cambodia," they said, and continued speaking to me in Thai anyway. Something about the transaction felt familiar. To be taken in like that in Thailand felt good, the closest thing I'd felt to belonging. I didn't stand out so much in Thailand, the way I did in America. The way I did in Cambodia. Everybody asking "Where are you from?" In Chiang Mai, I could mix easily among the people and hide in the vertical topography of that mountain town.

I flew to Bangkok during the week for meetings and to conduct training sessions with the researchers I had hired to help me assess the decline of freedom of expression across Asia. Our job was to draft a report that donors could use as leverage and rationale for funding for projects intended to reverse the trend of a constricted and restricted press.

I threw myself headlong into the project, just as I had done in Cambodia and Afghanistan. I believed in the mission of what we were doing. I believed that it had the potential to make a difference. Journalists are meant to go where the darkness is. I understood this from my experiences in Cambodia. I wanted to help them do their job without getting killed.

I lived with my friends Rachel and Stephen, whom I'd met when I was in Cambodia and who also had jobs that allowed them to live anyplace they wanted in Asia. We had all chosen Chiang Mai because of all the outdoor adventures available to us. We hiked and backpacked, rock-climbed and road-biked. Mostly, we hung out in town frequenting our favorite Thai restaurants and searching out the latest pub where we could get cold drafts for less than the price of a latte back home in America.

In Thailand, I had all the benefits of living in Cambodia without the weight of history, without having to face the fact of my privilege versus the poverty of my family. It was a safe distance from Oregon and a big enough distance from Ma that I didn't have to answer her questions about when I was going to get married. I wasn't thinking of dating anyone in Thailand, and had accepted an increasingly plausible scenario: I might never marry at all.

In Thailand, I was also free of the cultural constraints of Cambodia, where I felt all the pressures of being a good Khmer woman and daughter. No one was watching me. The pineapple was just too far, and her eyes were starting to go bad.

So I stretched. Surprised myself. I went out with friends and got so drunk I dirty-danced across a bar top at 2:00 a.m. I ate pot cookies, because Rachel had made two kinds and I forgot which ones were for our friends' kids and which ones were for the adults. In my drug-induced delirium, I went on-stage with my friends at an outdoor concert in Chiang Mai to dance with a Thai rock star whose face I would later see plastered all over the subways and on billboards in Bangkok. I skinny-dipped with my friends Lauren and Lindy in a river when we felt confident no one was looking. At the end of the night, I still slept alone. But it was a good, deep sleep. I felt like I could breathe.

I kept my communication with Ma to a minimum. I didn't want the pressure, the questions about marriage. I didn't want to keep disappointing her. I was living in a manner I knew she would find inappropriate, one that I knew would spark her cruelest criticisms. She would tell me how my behaviors were bringing shame on the family, how she raised me to be better. She would make me start to regret everything.

Thailand gave me a soft landing spot after Cambodia, after Afghanistan, and after confronting my own privilege and mortality. Nothing was expected of me, and I expected very little of myself. The things I carried, the guilt and the shame, these things seemed to vanish in the nooks and grooves of that mountain town. I was happy enough.

At the end of January 2014, I sent for Ma and Pa. For the previous three months, Ma had been angling for a trip.

"What's it like there, Put?" Ma asked, calling me on her international phone card. "I've always wanted to see Chiang Mai."

I wanted them to visit, diverting them from the other trip they were considering: returning to Cambodia. They had always used their vacation time to go to Cambodia, but being bombarded by relatives asking for money, medicine, and arranged marriages was not very relaxing.

I met them at the airport in Bangkok, where we boarded a flight together to Chiang Mai, the three of us. Just as it was all those years ago in my youth: me, Ma, and Pa in too-close quarters. At our house in Chiang Mai, Ma and Pa made it their mission to bless our house as well as me, Rachel, and Stephen. Whenever Ma and Pa traveled anywhere, they indulged their habit to *dote touk*, or light incense and pray to the gods—for good weather, good health, safe travels, good fortune—whatever calamities or inadequacies they felt needed the attention of a higher order.

At our neighborhood market, Ma used hand and body gestures to bargain down the price of a whole boiled chicken. They bought oranges, bananas, and Chinese moon cakes. Ma wanted to light incense so that I would find prosperity and happiness in Thailand. I never heard her say it out loud, but I know Ma prayed for something else: for me to find a husband.

I know because the next morning, when Ma and Pa woke early to have coffee and fruit in the kitchen, Ma cornered my roommate while I slept in the next room. Stephen was on his way out to an Ultimate Frisbee tournament, and had stopped in the kitchen to get snacks and water when Ma waved him into an empty chair at the table, inviting him to sit down and have toast. To talk.

"Stephen," Ma said, "you are good big brother to Put. She need good man for her. Maybe you help Put find good man, like you?"

She had a twinkle in her eye. She didn't know him well, but knew he was kind and a good husband to Rachel. Ma loved him. Stephen smiled politely as he rooted around the cabinets for a water bottle.

"I think Put will find someone very good," he said, and before Ma could make any more pleas, he dashed out the door.

Three months after Ma and Pa visited me, I was back in Oregon on my own vacation. I dragged my luggage off the airplane with a fatigue that had, just that year, started setting in. I was thirty-nine years old. When you spend your life running away, you run out of breath, eventually.

Cousin Pi picked me up. I didn't want to be back in America. I was still single and with no prospects for a partner. I worried Ma would smell my shame, so I stayed away. I went to Keizer long enough to collect my snowboard and helmet from Ma and Pa's garage and then billeted myself at my friend Koto's house in Portland, intending to take advantage of the fresh powder on the slopes of Mount Hood.

Most days, I snowboarded the entire day, from 10:00 a.m. to closing time at 4:00 p.m. I went alone except a time or two when I persuaded Pi or another friend to join me.

Each time the ski lift delivered me to the top of the mountain, I felt a particular quiet engulf me, there where even the air feels different when it hits the lungs. Pure, like nothing in the world has ever touched it. I never knew I needed that kind of calm and solitude until I was finally in it. I often stopped at the top before each run just to listen and learn again what a safe kind of silence sounds like. I inhaled deeply at the sound of birds rather than bombs and felt for the first time in a long time a stillness enter my heart. Everything around me was white and soft and luminescent. It hadn't occurred to me until then that silence could hold joy just as much as it could hold pain.

But my lack of restraint caught up with me. It was my last day on the slope. In a few days, I would be flying back to Bangkok. That day, I tried to squeeze in every last run I could before the light drained out of the day.

I came down the final run on too-tired legs and hit a patch of ice. I flew and landed perfectly wrong. Now I was staring at the sky, assessing whether I could still feel my legs and arms. I wiggled my fingers and toes, moved one arm and then the other. When I realized I could move, and looked up to see the chairlifts pass by empty, one after the next, when I knew I was alone and there would be no one to save me, I unstrapped my board and limp-walked the rest of the run down.

The next day, I was so sore I stepped sideways out of the guest bedroom at Koto's house and into the kitchen to have breakfast. When I told her what had happened, she tried not to judge, but her eyes betrayed her thoughts.

"Maybe you should see a doctor and delay your trip," Koto said.

"Can't," I said. "I've got too much to do with the journalists."

"But you can't even walk."

"I know," I said. "I just gotta power through."

"Isn't that how you got injured?" Koto asked.

I stared into my cup of coffee and stayed silent.

She had a plan.

"Why don't we go to the Korean spa in Tacoma before we go to Seattle?" Koto said. "You could get a massage. You have a seventeen-hour flight. I'm just worried about you."

I am not a spa person, but that day, I became one.

That afternoon, as we drove north on Interstate 5, I counted eight red-tailed hawks as I sat halfway reclined in the passenger seat of Koto's car, staring at the sky. I told her about the journalists I worked with and the loaded travel schedule I faced in the coming months.

"I just remembered, I invited my friend April to join us," Koto said, interrupting my rambling. "I hope it's okay."

April. I had met her two years earlier, at the famous house party Koto and April cohosted annually for Día de los Muertos that more than once attracted a hundred friends.

Koto had forgotten we had already met. But I hadn't. I was dating someone when I first met her, but no, I never forgot her.

I remember during the party, April wore a black lace dress and skeleton face paint. She was maneuvering through a crush of costumed guests with a pan of cheese enchiladas when Koto introduced us. Even behind the makeup, I saw glimpses of a beautiful face and honey-colored eyes that lit her way through the dark room.

Now I had a chance to see her again.

We crossed the Oregon state line and entered Washington,

and as we got closer to the spa in Tacoma, I got bolder with my admissions.

"You know, I remember her from your Day of the Dead party," I said, as Koto half listened, half watched the sky for birds.

"Mmm-hmm, mmm-hmm," she said.

"Well, I've had a crush on her for two years!"

"Really?" Koto said.

"Really."

"Well, I don't know if she's single," Koto said. "I mean, I can find out."

"You don't need to find out. I'm about to get on an international flight," I said, then grinned. "But can I flirt with her?"

We spent four hours together at the spa, naked. The entire time, I tried to avert my eyes from April as we dipped into and out of various heated pools. She was gorgeous. I stole glances at her whenever her back was turned, when she got up for a salt scrub and when she went to rinse off in the shower. When we sat too close together in one of the hot tubs, when I could not stand another minute next to this beautiful woman, I scrabbled out, limp-walked to the cold pool, and plunged straight in to shock myself back to common sense. Hoping to cure my crush.

We spent another two hours at a Mexican restaurant in Seattle. April talked about her family. I talked about my work. Koto and another friend, Yuki, were content to just sit and eat and listen.

In twenty-four hours, I'd be at the airport checking in for a red-eye back to Asia. That night, I tossed and turned trying to sleep, thinking of April.

In the morning, my phone pinged with an email. It was Koto, suggesting that April could take me to the airport and copying April in the email. I felt a surge travel through me. I tried to submerge the feeling. I was leaving town. What was the point? I did not know that Koto had told April about our conversation in the car.

I replied that my sister lived twenty minutes north of Seattle, well out of April's way. But April wrote back and insisted she would be happy to give me a ride to the airport. Chan encouraged me to take the offer so she wouldn't have to drive me. I made a move: I agreed to a ride to the airport if she agreed to let me buy her a drink. At 5:00 p.m., she was standing at Chan and Todd's front door. April hoisted my enormous suitcase into the trunk of her new Dodge Dart coupe and zipped back down Interstate 5 toward Seattle.

We drove to Capitol Hill, where we slipped into a quiet bar to talk, and I thought about the last time I was on Capitol Hill, twenty years prior, when I sat awkwardly on a barstool scanning the patrons at the lesbian bar for a future wife. Now I was here again, on what was feeling like a date, my mind swimming circles in the thrill of it.

April was a year older than I was and worked for Boeing's engineers union. Like me, she had been in relationships with both men and women. And like me, she wasn't hung up on the gender of who she was involved with. She fell in love with the person.

"Ditto," I said, and we clinked glasses.

Four hours felt like four minutes, and we managed to cover career, family, heartbreak, and happiness. April glanced at her phone just then.

"So what time did you say you needed to be there?" she asked.

"What time is it?" I asked in response.

Quarter of eleven. My flight was in an hour. Seattle-Tacoma International Airport was still fifteen miles away.

As April sped down Interstate 5 toward the airport, I fought an old instinct to play the whole thing down, to keep my expectations in check. I was crazy to think that any kind of relationship was possible. In less than a day, a whole ocean would be between us.

At the airport, April pulled up in front of the Korean Air kiosk. I fussed for my sweatshirt in my backpack and checked my pockets for my passport and ticket, glancing everywhere in the car except at her.

"Can I kiss you?" she asked.

I stopped my nervous fussing long enough to let her.

In that single kiss, I felt the next forty years of my life. A feeling pulsed inside of me, soft and round, the calm of knowing you have just crossed paths with your future.

On the plane, I tried to prepare notes for my meetings in Bangkok. But my mind migrated to April. She loved her family and culture and spent her evenings and weekends marching with picket signs or rallying for any imaginable cause. She was half-white and half-Mexican and knew what it felt like to live between two worlds. She wouldn't leave my mind.

For three months while I crisscrossed Asia for work, I thought of her. Rather than lean away from the long shot we had of starting a relationship, I leaned into the challenge of getting to know this woman across the miles. Something about April felt different. I didn't experience the same kind of stress and insecurities of trying to figure out whether we could be a couple or not, whether she liked me as much as I liked her, as I had with other relationships. I just wanted to keep knowing her.

I sent postcards from Vietnam, Laos, and the Philippines. I fired off emails wherever I could get secure Wi-Fi. I surprised her with flowers delivered to her work, wine to her hotel when she traveled, and chocolate truffles on her birthday. As far as I was concerned, she was my single shot at happiness. I was all in.

April, in return, sent a package to Chiang Mai with my favorite coffee, homemade cookies, and a mix CD with songs she liked. We spoke on Skype and FaceTime and sent text messages in between, to stay connected in real time. Those flashes of conversation, they fed me.

As summer neared, my housemates were growing tired of their lovelorn roommate.

"Go see her," Rachel said, as we sat together in our kitchen, munching on sticky rice as the humid Chiang Mai air pushed through the slatted blinds. "You can always come back here if things don't work out. You'll never know until you are there with her."

At the end of June, I packed my bags, and instead of going to Keizer, where I had planned to take a short break and visit Ma and Pa, I switched my plane ticket to Seattle.

We fell into each other's lives seamlessly. For two weeks, we barely left April's apartment. When we emerged, I met some of her friends and she met a few of mine. We had picnics and potlucks and a backyard barbecue, where I cooked my mother's Khmer chicken.

For weeks, I let all my phone calls go direct to voice mail. When I finally got around to listening, I heard Ma's voice.

"Put, where are you?" Ma said, her voice coursing with concern. "Are you coming home?"

I'm already here, I thought.

For the first time, being with a romantic partner began to feel like a shelter.

By July, we decided to be exclusive. By fall, I was back in Bangkok. By spring 2015, roughly a year after we'd met, I began making the transition from my jet-setting life to a serene neighborhood in a crook of land on the eastern shore of Lake Union in Seattle, where a cool breeze kicked up into our open window and seaplanes splash-landed in an open lane beyond the sailboats. It was there I would finally learn how to be at peace within myself, where a foreign feeling came over me: for the first time, I wanted to stay.

▣ GAY TAX

I'd barely unpacked my last bags when Ma called in the summer of 2015. She wanted to know what I was doing with my life. Where I was working. Where I was living. I was forty-one years old.

When I told her the truth, that I had moved in with April, her voice tightened.

"This is not normal," Ma said. "Woman cannot be with woman."

I slunk deeper into the sofa when she said this. All my life, I had felt different. Ma herself had told me so many times. I had asthma. I played too hard in the schoolyard. I wore pants while my sisters wore dresses. But then I thought of gay marriage becoming legal. I thought of my gay friends who were starting families. I straightened up in the sofa, sat a little taller.

"This is America," I told Ma. "Anyone can be with anyone."

"You have to think about our culture, Put," Ma said. "You have to think about our family. What am I supposed to tell all the Khmer families?"

"Tell them the truth, Ma," I said.

No more myths. No more fictions.

The weight of who I am fell off me in that instant. If Ma was ashamed of having a gay daughter, she would have to carry that on her own. For forty years, I had tried to be the best daughter I could be. I had tried to honor both a daughter's debt and duty. I had tried to be worthy of her rescue. I decided the next forty years of my life would be for me.

Whenever Ma had her back against the wall, she tried to bribe her way to a solution. So when we came to an impasse, she had one more ace up her sleeve. She knew I didn't have a car, because when I moved to Thailand, I'd agreed to let her sell my old Honda Civic. Before that, it had been sitting, abandoned, in my parents' driveway, the monthly insurance payments draining from my bank account. Now that I was back in America, Ma hoped that I might need a set of wheels.

When I had told her months earlier that I rode the bus, she gasped. Buses and bikes, those were for poor people. Her children rode in cars. I don't know what made her feel more ashamed: having a gay daughter or a bus-riding daughter.

Her call came one afternoon as I stood stretching on our postcard-sized patch of lawn watching tourist boats cruise by on Lake Union. I saw her name on the caller ID, and suspicion was the first feeling that flared.

"Why are you calling me?" I asked. We were in fighting mode. There were no pleasantries.

"I'm calling because I want you to have a car," Ma said. "We'll sell you our car."

She paused for a beat before adding: "But you can have the Camry for free. If you stop being gay, you don't have to pay."

I laughed out loud.

"What if I'm still gay?" I asked.

"Then you have to pay five thousand dollars."

When I hung up the phone, I shook my head and couldn't believe the timing of Ma's offer. April and I were about to be without a car. Her Dodge Dart, barely two years old, had broken down so many times that it was declared a lemon, forcing the dealership to take it back. Dodge reimbursed April for two years' worth of mileage, sending a check in the mail for a substantial sum: $5,578.76. The ancestors were messing with me once more.

The next week, April and I drove in a loaner car from the Dodge dealership to Keizer with a check for five thousand dollars. For a moment, an old impulse drew me to shuffle through my wallet for my bank card and driver's license as I mapped a route to the nearest bank. I thought about withdrawing five thousand dollars in new hundred-dollar bills, presenting Ma bricks of crispy cash, knowing it would make her happy. But I stopped myself. April and I had opened a joint bank account by then, and had checks with both of our names printed in the top corner. I wanted Ma to see that we were buying the Camry together, as a couple. It was a small thing, a check versus cash. But this felt like an important line to hold.

The first time Ma and April met, in the summer of 2014, I had introduced April by name only as we piled our plates with burgers and Ma's marinated pork ribs in Chan and Todd's backyard—a birthday barbecue for my nephew. April presented to Ma a bottle of Hennessy, the liquor of choice for Khmers, which Ma accepted with a smile and then hid in her purse.

The second time Ma and April met, two months later, April had arrived in Keizer after driving more than three hours from Seattle to join my parents' annual summer barbecue. She brought a box of mangoes that she delivered directly into Ma's hands as Ma thanked her and guided her to the backyard, directly to the egg rolls and noodles.

Now, in the summer of 2015, Ma and April were meeting for a third time. And Ma understood she was my girlfriend, having confronted me by phone about the wrongness, in her eyes, of same-sex relationships. We didn't bother to stop for sweets to bring to Ma and Pa; I was still too angry at Ma for trying to bribe me with a free car if I stopped being gay.

On the drive to Keizer, I'd made a plan.

"In and out," I told April. "We're just going to drop off the check and pick up the car and then leave. It's going to be quick."

"Okay, babe," April said, "if that's what you want to do."

I hoped to keep our contact with Ma to a minimum, knowing how unhappy she was about my choice of a partner. Knowing how capable my mother was of manipulation.

When we arrived in the Vineyards, Pa was in the garage checking the fluid levels of the Camry.

"Ma's inside," he said, nodding toward the door.

When we walked in, Ma was in the kitchen, gathering sticky rice into a bowl.

"I just make it," Ma said. "You like some?"

"Sure!" April said. "It smells really good!"

We ate in silence for a few minutes, then Pa poked his head through the door.

"Put, come outside so I can show you where the oil goes, and how to check the tire pressure," he said.

I hesitated, uncertain of whether I should leave Ma and April alone. I glanced at April, and she gave me a look that said, It's okay. Go ahead.

I was gone for less than ten minutes. When I went back

inside to the kitchen, I felt a prickly tension in the air and caught both April and Ma wiping their eyes. Ma's back was turned to me and April's eyes were cast down toward the floor.

"What's going on?" I said, to no one and both of them.

April stayed quiet and Ma did, too.

Anger bloomed hot at the back of my neck. Whatever had passed between them, my mother had left my girlfriend in tears.

"Let's go," I said, turning to April. "We're leaving."

Back at home in Seattle, I was incensed.

"What happened at my parents' house?" I asked April, as we settled back into our apartment. "What did my mother say to you?"

"When you left, she told me, 'April, I liked you from the first time I met you. But Put is the crazy one,'" April said, tearing up again. "It made me sad she was saying this about you."

"And . . ." I said.

"And she said that in the Khmer culture, a woman cannot be with another woman. She asked if I could just be friends with you until she's gone, and when she's gone, we can do whatever we want."

"I'm not going to pretend anymore who I am," I said, defiant. "It was hard enough coming out of the closet. I won't let her put me back in."

As April recounted her conversation with Ma, my fury mounted. Ma must have felt ashamed and guilty, because she called Chan to confess, telling her about the conversation, and coming clean about how April ended up crying. Chan lashed back at Ma, she told me, condemning our mother for causing my girlfriend to cry. And in the upheaval, all our lives swirled and churned.

In Ma's attempt to persuade April to give our relationship a public façade of friendship, she was more concerned about her own reputation than the happiness of her daughter—a selfish motivation I had grown up with, but now, now that I had finally met someone who filled my life with joy, now Ma's selfishness stung. I vowed to never speak to her again.

That winter, after I had avoided communicating with Ma, she called to summon me home. I saw her name pop up on my caller ID and I refused to answer, forcing her to leave a voice mail message.

"You should go," April said, when I told her the contents of Ma's message.

"There's no point. What would we talk about? I can't change her mind about me," I told April. "She doesn't want a gay daughter. I refuse to change who I am to fit her vision of me."

"Just think about it," April said. "You don't have to decide now."

April did not criticize Ma, and I didn't need her to: I knew she was on my side. She offered to go with me to Keizer. She offered to have her parents talk to Ma and Pa. She held me as I cried. When I finally decided to go home, April made a tin of holiday cookies that she carefully packaged and tied with red holiday string.

I didn't know why Ma was asking me to visit, but I wanted to believe in her best intentions. I held out hope that this visit would be a chance for us to reconcile. Maybe my siblings had convinced Ma that it was okay to have a gay daughter. Maybe she was calling me home to tell me in person she would support me. Or maybe she just missed me. Even after all the fighting, I was still hanging on to hope.

◨ ESCAPE

I counted the exits. One. Two. Three.

Exit 1: The sliding glass door off the kitchen that leads out into the backyard. The fence is locked and requires a key to open. One could easily jump over the fence and be free.

Exit 2: The garage door. One button would start the machinery and the door would open, in folds, all the way up its rails, and reveal the sloped driveway.

Exit 3: The front door. It was the most direct route, I could beeline right to it.

Afghanistan taught me this: to enter a room and quickly identify all the exits, all the ways out to safety and freedom. Now I was in Keizer, sitting on a barstool in the kitchen because all three exits were in view from there. If I went too deeply into my parents' home, into, say, the family room, where Ma spent much of her time in her recliner, I would be trapped. Exiting would be awkward, harder. I told myself not to go there.

It was my first visit alone since our battle began, when Ma made it clear to me she was unhappy about my choice of romantic partner.

I pulled into the driveway at 11:00 a.m., and when I punched in the garage door code to let myself in, my parents' Lexus SUV was gone. I thought they had both left, but when I turned the knob and opened the door a crack, a waft of roasted chicken and rice rushed out. I paused for a heartbeat and inhaled that warmth, only then realizing how much I had missed her, how much I had missed home. Ma was in the kitchen chopping chicken. She pressed a quarter section into a bowl of steaming-hot jasmine rice and added soy sauce.

"Chicken is just out of the oven," she said. "Get a bowl."

So I did.

I sat on a barstool with my food, and after cutting cabbage and cucumbers and setting them in a bowl in front of me, Ma sat down on the only other barstool, next to me. We caught each other up on relatives, her declining health, my struggle in finding a job. It went like this for a few hours. Pa was at Walmart shopping for Christmas cards. We kept talking.

Then Ma moved to the family room, easing herself into her recliner.

"What do you want for Christmas?" she asked. "Money? Clothes?"

I didn't hesitate in my reply, the words taking a life of their own after they left my lips.

"I want you to be happy for me," I said.

"I want you to find a man to marry, Put," she said, her voice scratchy with emotion. "Ma and Pa are getting old. We want you to get married. You're Khmer. You have to follow the culture. This is not possible in our culture, woman and woman."

"You should be happy for me that I'm happy," I said, my voice cold as stone. "You're the mother. You should want me to be happy."

Pa came home then, inadvertently walking straight into the tension, and by doing so, giving us an easy out. We retreated then, each of us going to our rooms.

I spent the next several hours fussing on my laptop, writing Christmas cards, going through a thick stack of junk mail. At 6:00 p.m., I started packing up my car to go, intending to crash at Cousin Pi's place in Portland, before driving back to Seattle.

That's when Ma staged her ambush. When I went back inside to say goodbye, Ma called for me.

"Come here, gohn," she said, and for a minute, I fooled myself into believing it would be a tender moment, a reconciliation after months of fighting.

I went to her and she pulled me into a hug, pulling herself forward on the recliner in the process. She held me tightly and began sobbing, her head pressed into my chest.

"Ma wants you to have a job, and find a husband, gohn," she said, and soon, she was wailing. "We are too old. I want to tie red strings around your wrist before I die."

"I want you to be happy for me," I said again.

I let Ma hold me for a few seconds, then peeled her arms away from me. I don't know if I said it or only thought it, but the feeling was very clear: "Let me go."

"Ma doesn't want to lose you. You are my baby girl," she said, and sobbed even harder, her whole body quaking.

But that baby was grown up. That baby had become the person she was meant to be. I wanted to tell Ma this, that for a long time, I had believed she and I were so close that we were fused together. I did not know I could exist separate from her, that I could have dreams of my own rather than live out the dreams she had for me.

Ma kept crying. I was trapped. I didn't know if I should

let her hold me still or if I should leave. My instincts said to flee. I fumbled for a mint on the coffee table. I unwrapped it and headed to the kitchen to throw away the wrapper as Ma continued to sob.

I kept stalling and didn't know why.

"Well, they're just friends right now," Pa said to Ma.

I don't know if he said this to calm her down, or if he said it because he wanted to believe it. It was hard to count him as an ally because trusting him has always been a challenge. But he said it. And at that, I walked out, taking Exit 2.

I felt ashamed for abandoning Ma as she was sobbing, but I couldn't stay. I knew she had cried too many times over my decision to be with April, and the more I saw her pain, the more my own actions broke me. I was tearing us apart. Ma and I both accused each other of breaking the other's heart. But I couldn't be the person to comfort her then as she cried. There was nothing I could have said, other than agreeing to marry a man, that would have stopped her tears.

I would no longer bend myself to be someone other than who I was. I was, for the first time, truly happy in a relationship. Emotionally, I was better than I had ever been. I wasn't willing to give that up.

As I drove north out of their subdivision, past the same farm fields I had come to know by heart, I felt a pounding between my ears. That pounding traveled down in my body, like a shot, piercing that place in my heart where I had stockpiled pride, confidence, and self-acceptance, to buffer against a perennial depression that always managed to sling me straight to the edge. The realization I had was so clear I cried: I had lived my life a slave to sang khun, but I could never repay my mother.

There is a moment when you realize you are not the same person as your mother, and yet the things she taught you, the imprint she left, remains. I no longer had Ma's food to go home to because I no longer could go home.

So, back in Seattle, when I finally stopped crying, I went to the kitchen and started cooking and didn't stop for days and then weeks. Ma's mantra repeated in my head as I chopped, diced, and stirred: "Always have a hot meal ready for your husband." I substituted the word "wife" for "husband" and forged ahead. If I could no longer go home to eat Ma's food, I would make it for myself and the woman I loved.

I salt-roasted whole salmon and branzino; I filleted mackerel, then pan-fried it with ginger and soy sauce. I fried sunfish and tilapia and pounded *nuc mam* in a mortar and pestle to go with it, the way Ma used to do. I made rice every single day.

When April had her fill, when she could consume no more rice and finally told me so, I transitioned to the other things Ma had taught me to make—meat loaf and spaghetti, lasagna and roasted chicken with scalloped potatoes. I fell into a frenzy to feed April, to fill us both up because another corner of me had emptied out.

▣ OVERBOARD

I don't know who lobbed the first shot that started the war—me or Ma—but we had stopped talking to each other completely and slid into our own separate wells of grief by the spring of 2016. There were side skirmishes, between Ma and my siblings, when my siblings tried to stand up for me. It only inflamed Ma more that she could not convince my sisters and brother to join her in whatever sleeve of shame she chose to wear. We had both drawn a line, and neither of us was willing to budge from it. She never asked me to end my relationship with April, but I know she wanted me to. I never tried to change her views on my being in a same-sex relationship, but I wanted to.

I knew that in the silence that had grown between us, I was losing her. For days, I moped around the house. Ma said she would never be happy for me so long as I was gay, and she meant it. In the following weeks and months after my winter trip to Keizer, she called and cried to my aunties around Portland, who called me to complain that I was breaking my mother's heart.

My aunt Pech supported me privately, wanted me to be who I was, but publicly, to keep the peace with her sister-in-law—her elder—she admonished me. I understood.

"What have I done wrong?" I asked Aunt Pech. "I'm not in jail. I'm not a drug addict. I've been a good daughter."

"I know," Aunt Pech said. "I love you like my own daughter. You know this. But your mom, she called me crying . . ."

My aunt Samnang called me more than once to express her outrage, screaming into my voice mail.

"Put, call your aunt back, okay? What you are doing is wrong!"

My heart sank listening to her words.

Ma called my siblings and cried, but they struck an even tone, refusing to take sides while at the same time assuring our mother that I was the same daughter, the same person, no matter whom I married.

She stopped calling me. Instead I got voice mails from my father, who became her proxy, calling me once my siblings started refusing to act as go-betweens, transmitting information between two warring sides.

Just as a part of my heart was closing down to protect myself against Ma, another part was opening up to April.

In my twenties and thirties, as I cycled through one relationship after the next, I had regularly polled my friends who were married or in stable, long-term relationships about meeting their mates, hoping for clues I could follow to find my future spouse.

"How do you know when you've found the one?" I asked.

One of my friends said that for her, there are many "ones," but the one who stays, that is a matter of timing. Another friend said that relationships are more about the baggage we each bring and the capacity of each person to alternately carry a little extra for the other.

All of that was true, but my favorite was a simple answer my friend Charles offered: "The love just comes easy. It's not complicated."

I never knew what that meant until I met April.

There are many moments that add up and become the reason you want to stay, the reason why you want to spend the rest of your life with someone. There was the time when April encouraged me to sign up for a creative writing class in Seattle so I could switch from being a journalist and telling other people's stories to being a memoirist so I could start telling some of my own. I didn't have the money for the class, so she paid. I didn't have a car, so she drove me. When I didn't have the guts to tunnel for old emotions and turn them into prose, she told me: "You're the bravest person I know." I kept writing.

There was the time when she contracted meningitis while I was traveling for work. When I burst into the emergency room and saw her, pale and barely lucid, the ground beneath my feet gave out, and in that gash in the earth, my heart fell through. When I went back outside to fill the meter, I slumped to the curb and cried. I could not imagine a single day of my life without her.

And then there was a time in the outback of Australia, camping, when we got uncomfortably low on food. It was our last night in the Blue Mountains and the rain poured. We were far from any store. We had three things left in our camp supply: a tomato, dried pasta, and a can of sardines, items we had thrown into the food box at the last minute, "just in case." We boiled all three together, stirred, and called it dinner.

Sardines had been a lifeline on the boat that brought my family to America. Sardines kept us going in the berry fields of Corvallis. "Sardines," Ma liked to say, "that's survival food." My girlfriend gobbled up that survival food on the darkest night of our trip with the cheeriest smile on her face.

That was it for me. The moment when I knew.

In the summer of 2016, when April and I attended a friend's wedding in California, I pulled a ring out of my back pocket before heading to the reception. It was silver with a turquoise stone set in the middle—the ring that Aadila Abad had given me on the last day of class in Kabul. My hands trembled as I held it before April. Her honey-colored eyes flooded with light and tears when I took her hand and pushed Aadila's ring onto her finger. She said "Yes!" quickly, and I asked a second time to make sure.

"I'm sure," she said.

We texted our close friends and family. April told her parents and sisters and her niece. I wrote emails to my sisters and best friends. I felt a rush of pride and accomplishment. Soon, I would have a wife.

I had crisscrossed the globe searching for home, or the closest approximation to it. I believed for many years that Corvallis was home because that's where I grew up. When I went to Cambodia, I began to view that as my home because I was born there.

Only later, when I met April, and felt an immediate and steady calm in my heart, did I begin to see that home was not a place for me. Home was a person. Home was her.

I told everyone about the engagement except the person I wanted to tell the most. Up until our big battle, Ma was the person I called first whenever I had big news. She was the one who knew when I won a regional writing award in high school and the one I called when I landed my first job after college. She was the first to know when I got a promotion to go work in California. At every juncture of my life, Ma was there to cheer me on.

Now her reaction was something I feared.

I didn't know how to tell her the news, the thing I knew she never wanted to hear, that her daughter, her baby girl, the one she had such high hopes for, was marrying a woman.

So I kept my distance.

By summer, April and I had bought a home in a small town south of Seattle that hugs the Puget Sound on one side and teases a view of Mount Rainier on the other. I had lived near the airport in Portland, and now I would live near the airport in Seattle. Being so close to airplanes as they took off and landed comforted me, reminded me I could always be transported to some other place than where I was currently. We were close enough to the water to feel the sea breeze kick up through the trees, just as Ma did when she lived in Phnom Penh after getting married.

The day the home inspector came, I got a call from the editor of the Modern Love column at *The New York Times*. I had written a story about the struggle between Ma and me, submitted it after prompting from Chan and April, and promptly forgot about it. Four months later, the editor was calling to ask if he could publish it. April pulled me into a kiss and said it was a sign.

After we got engaged, April asked me when I was going to tell my parents. I said I had to feel ready. I stalled. For a month. And then six. A whole year passed. But now we had our own home. Soon, we would make a down payment on caterers, an event space, and hotel rooms for our wedding guests. It was finally time to tell Ma.

I pulled into Keizer four days before Halloween, in Cousin Pi's pickup truck, prepared to load up some remaining boxes of old files and random art that I had left in my parents' garage. Pumpkins lined the front patios of homes up and down my parents' street. Ma and Pa didn't have decorations but they gave out candy, because that's what was expected of them.

I stayed for two nights, long enough to eat Ma's *loc lak* beef, tender cubes of stir-fried beef arranged atop a bed of fresh vegetables. She piled extra lettuce and tomatoes on my plate, the way I've always liked it, and gave me double the amount of lemon-pepper dipping sauce. It had been more than a year since our angry phone calls. We didn't speak a word when I reappeared in her kitchen. She fed me. And I ate. Some roles are hard to break.

I stalled, just as I had twenty years earlier when I came out to Ma in my apartment in Oakland. I was looking for a way in, an opening to tell my parents I was engaged. But nothing came. I thought maybe I would leave Keizer and take my announcement with me. Maybe I wasn't brave enough.

The morning I prepared to leave, I sat on a stool in Ma's kitchen. I decided I would tell them then, on my way out the door, because bombs get dropped like that, in haste, so there's time to run from revenge.

I put on socks as I sat on the barstool. Pa was washing the dishes, watching out the kitchen window in a post-meal trance, when I broke his reverie.

"April and I are getting married," I said, my voice thin and my volume low.

"Who?" Pa said.

"April," I said, a little louder this time. "April and me."

He paused, keeping his gaze straight ahead out the window where Ma's persimmon tree sagged with the weight of its fruit and was starting to get overtaken by the King fig tree I had ordered in 2014 for her birthday. She sent me a picture the day it got delivered, disappointed by the scrawny little stick perfectly bare without a single leaf poking pitifully out from a pot of dirt; another little thing she would nurture until it grew.

"Why do you have to get married?"

I knew if I said the truth, that I was in love with April, that I was happy and wanted to spend the rest of my life with her, it would not be something he could hear. So I said nothing of love, of the fact that I was the happiest I had ever been, because that was not a language he spoke. Instead, I told him this.

"I'll have benefits. Health insurance, joint taxes, other benefits of being married," I said, and then my throat seized and the words got locked out. That was all I managed to say before I choked on my own tears.

"So, if you guys could come," I finally managed, more suggesting than asking.

He kept looking straight ahead, refusing to face me.

"I'll have to talk to Ma."

Ma was upstairs, getting ready to take a shower. Twenty years ago, we were sitting on the love seat in my apartment in Oakland, where she was holding me and telling me she loved me after I had come out to her as gay. I had never bothered to tell Pa, assuming Ma would tell him eventually.

Now it was Pa who I gave the news to first. That I was engaged. That there would be a wedding, for which RSVPs were already pouring in from across the country and the globe.

I left then, thinking it was good enough that at least one

of them knew. But I left in such a rush, I forgot my cell phone. When I went back inside the house, he was waiting.

"You need to go upstairs and tell your mother so she doesn't say you never told her," Pa said. He hadn't told her yet.

I hated him once more. And then hated myself more. We were both cowards. Neither of us wanted to tell Ma.

I glanced upstairs. I knew I needed to take those steps up to her, but my legs would not move until a voice within me said: "You owe it to her to tell her in person. That's what you came here for."

I moved slowly, step by excruciating step, as if bricks were tied to my ankles. I went first to the room where I was staying, just off to the right of Ma and Pa's room, and collected my cell phone. Ma saw me, so I stepped across the threshold and entered their bedroom.

"You're going, gohn?" she asked, as she reached for a towel. "Okay, drive safe in that truck."

She moved in to give me a hug. I put my arm around her back, too afraid to hold on, thinking that I might not let go, and if I didn't let go, I might change my mind about marrying April.

What do you do when you cannot go in the water or come up on land?

"We're getting married," I finally heard myself say, a whisper of a statement that I thought would be lost upon leaving my lips. I felt a pause push against my courage before I finished my sentence: "Me and April."

In that beat between, I felt us fall through the widening crack of our bond, into some dark abyss where we could no longer see.

Ma began to cry and instantly angled away from me, letting her arm fall from around my shoulder where it had been.

"I can't come," Ma said. "Ma minh doh banh dei."

"If you guys don't go, you'll be the only ones not there. Everyone else is going," I said. By everyone, I meant my siblings and their families and even my sister's in-laws from Nebraska. Of my other relatives, I had invited only Aunt Pech, who made it clear that if Ma was not going, she was not going, either.

Ma's sobbing turned into full-on wailing, worse than the year before, when I was there at Christmas.

I quickly fled her room, and stopped myself at the top of the stairs. I could not take another step forward, and I could not take a step back. Ma was in the bathroom, wailing so hard I felt a shudder inside of me. She mumbled through her sobs.

"I gave birth to you, not knowing which direction your life was going to take. And now, you've made it so difficult," she said.

She blew her nose, hard, straight into her bath towel. I worried she might collapse. I worried I was killing her with heartbreak. As my knees began to buckle, it was all I could do to hold myself up.

I was standing on the Afghan rug I had brought back from Kabul eight years before this moment. In the hallway was a mandala from Nepal that illustrated the cycle of life. All around the house were statues big and small of Buddha and Ganesh from Cambodia, India, and Bangladesh. The lengths I had traveled were all around Ma and Pa's house. The evidence of my fleeing.

Finally, finally I had met someone and planned to stay. But Ma could not see things my way.

"How did I raise you so that you turned out so different from everyone else?" Ma said. Was she talking to herself? Or did she know I was there, on the other side of her bedroom door, hesitating at the top of the stairs? "How did this happen?"

In that moment, I understood. My being gay was not about me, but about her. She saw it as a flaw in her parenting, that somehow it was an epic failure on her part that I turned out gay. I thought of that newspaper story I'd written so long ago as an intern at my hometown newspaper, where Cliff Kenagy also blamed himself for having a gay daughter.

I was worse than the Khmer kids who'd ended up in jail or doing drugs; those were behaviors that could be corrected. But being gay was something she could not change about me. Something I could not change about myself.

I understood now why my gayness carried so much weight. I was the single flaw in the beautiful fiction of a family Ma spun for the Khmer community. She had raised my siblings and me so that we would not have any blemishes, anything at all that would indicate she and Pa were bad parents who let their children fall or fail. Our family's reputation was now tarnished by the simple fact of who I am.

Grief washed over me. For that little first grader who fell and skinned her nose. For the teenager who kept running away from home. For the college student who wanted to slit her wrists and the twenty-one-year-old who slung a belt over the closet rod but was too ashamed, in the end, to kill herself. For the thirty-four-year-old who went to Afghanistan and suffered a gash in her heart where hope had leaked out. I had accumulated these scars when she wasn't watching me. I was gay, and this was a part of our story that could not be erased.

I sometimes wonder how different my life might have been if I'd had the room to be who I was from the start, if I had lived in a time of LGBTQ+ clubs at school and raised within a family fluent in the vocabulary and culture of acceptance.

What if I could have told her about the unexplainable and scary feelings I had for Amber McMichaels? And for my camp counselor in the fifth grade? And for my best friend in high school? How different might things have been if I hadn't had to hide? Would it have given Ma more time to adjust to the idea of me being gay, so that by the time I was grown up and ready to marry a woman, the years would have absorbed some of the shock and lessened some of the shame?

There is shame in making your mother cry, shame in knowing you have disappointed the woman who raised you. Shame spins and spins on a random loop inside my head, circling, waiting for its next chance to strike. The weight of my own existence bore down on me then. I gripped the banister, felt my feet tipping me forward. Her rejection felt like the most brutal pain I'd felt. I fled down the stairs and into Pi's truck, fast and far away from her.

If we had had a chance to talk without the drama and blaming, I would have told Ma it was not her fault; nothing in the way that she raised me had made me who I am. I did not become gay in America. America just gave me the freedom to be who I am.

I knew in that moment, standing at the top of the stairs, unable to take a step forward toward the future and unable to go backward to console Ma, trapped between that little baby on the boat and the woman she became, that I might never enter my parents' home again. That the abandonment I had been afraid of my whole life was finally happening. Forty years after saving me, the hope we both clung to capsized. Ma had cast me overboard.

In the months before our wedding, my siblings separately made several attempts to smooth things between Ma and me. They became champions for April and me, which made me love them even more. I could handle it if Ma and Pa opted out of going to our wedding. Could even handle the hurtful things Ma said to me. But when she tried to divide us kids, I was furious.

We were a team—me, Sin, Sope, Chan, Mo, and Pi. When we were growing up, we ate dinner every night together (even though we sometimes fought over the last drumstick or slice of beef) and we worked side by side in the berry fields every summer. When one of us was targeted by bullies, the others came to the rescue. Our closeness was born out of being the only ones in Corvallis who shared the same singular experience of escaping war, all of us having emerged on the other end still standing. I could handle it if I lost Ma's love but not that of my siblings.

In the spring, when April started planting a garden in the backyard, Sin and her family flew to Seattle to visit us. Tickets were cheap, she told me. The timing was right. The kids were out for spring break. She called Ma before she got on her plane in Nebraska.

"If you want to see your grandkids, you can come to Seattle," Sin told Ma.

For months leading up to our wedding, my siblings and their families were on a campaign to get Ma to change her mind. Sin's visit was a fig leaf. She hoped to lure Ma to Seattle so we could talk as a family, so Ma and I could maybe reconcile. But Ma could smell a trap before it was even laid. She outright refused to come.

"If my grandkids love their grandmother and want to see her, they can come to Keizer," Ma told my sister, then hung up.

The campaign to get my parents to come to our wedding was launched on multiple fronts. My old housemate and friend from Chiang Mai, Stephen, suggested he and our friend Jonathan go to Keizer to talk to Ma, because Ma adored both of them for the simple fact that they loved her Khmer food.

"She can't say no to us," Stephen said when he called me to tell me the plan. "She likes us."

"She's not listening to anyone right now," I told him.

Kim, my best friend from college, and Koto, who occasionally visited my parents over the years without me, hatched a plan to go to Keizer under the auspice of having dinner with my folks, and then slip into the conversation that our wedding was going to be a gigantic celebration with family and friends from all over the globe and they shouldn't miss the party. My friend and mentor Nhu, a retired journalist my parents' age whom Ma liked and respected, threatened to fly into Portland from her home in Berkeley and go "to talk some sense into your ma!" Nhu practically shouted into the phone.

"No, Nhu," I said. "It won't work. She's too stubborn."

So was I. And that was the trouble with us.

"She'll either decide to come or not come," I told April, as we sipped whiskey cocktails in a speakeasy in Port Townsend one night in the spring of 2017, on a reconnaissance mission to find activities to recommend to our wedding guests a few short months away. "No one can make her come. Plus, I don't want her to be there if she's going to be unhappy about it."

The RSVPs piled up in our mailbox and I watched for the twined cursive of my father's handwriting on every return envelope. For a moment, I let myself believe that perhaps Ma and Pa would come to our wedding, if for no other reason than to save face. Sin's in-laws, whom my parents were close to, and who felt like family to me, too, were making the trek from Nebraska. It would be shameful for Ma and Pa to be absent.

April and I booked a hotel room for my parents that offered a full refund if canceled with thirty days' notice. I kept my hope alive that Ma would change her mind, but convinced myself I would be okay if she was a no-show. We would be surrounded by 160 of our closest family and friends. I reminded myself to focus on who would be there, not who wouldn't.

Of all of the times Ma was there for me, for graduations and multiple moves, from Spokane to Seattle and California to Cambodia, there was no other time that I wanted or needed her more than on my wedding day. I wanted her egg rolls and noodles and to see her in her traditional Khmer sampot. It was the most important day of my life. I wanted her to see all our friends and family, both straight and gay couples, with and without kids, who were there to support us. I wanted her to see that my life was perfectly normal. A daughter needs her mother on her wedding day.

Thirty days before our wedding, I started calling around,

to Sope, Sin, Chan, Mo, and Pi. I wanted to see whether they thought Ma and Pa were coming. I watched the mail every day for their RSVP. It didn't come. I told myself, Maybe I missed it, maybe it's somewhere lost among the credit card offers and weekly supermarket flyers. Maybe they don't have a stamp. Maybe they'll still come.

Sin said Ma and Pa were not coming. Sope said he was hopeful because he had talked to them recently and Pa had said he wanted to go. Chan and Mo both reminded me that Ma tended to make decisions at the last minute, so I shouldn't rule anything out. I finally canceled the hotel room we had reserved for my parents, in time to get our money back.

"Just focus on what you need to do," Sin said to me on the phone one afternoon. I had called her, a final check-in to see if she had spoken to Ma and Pa, and couldn't contain my tears. "Don't worry about what Ma and Pa do. Just do what you need to be happy."

⬚ HAPPIEST AND SADDEST DAY

We were married on a Saturday in July, when the clouds threatened rain but tacked at the final moment and parted, like curtains, to bring us a spectacular burst of sunshine. Exactly one year before, my story about Ma and me had been published in *The New York Times*. Our wedding was now the sequel.

In our rented bungalow at Fort Worden—a two-story unit with a white picket fence that had once housed colonels serving in the U.S. Army in the northwest tip of Washington State—Michelle, April's older sister, and Koto and Cassie, her best friends, tag-teamed to help April get ready while I insisted on getting ready alone in the guest bedroom down the hall. I saw my dress in a new light—the first dress that ever made me happy, preserved in a plastic sleeve and hanging on the door.

Seeing it now, I was surprised at my own choice—a sleeveless silk gown lacking embroidery or embellishment. A little too plain, our seamstress had said. At the last minute, the seamstress had cut a strip of lace from the long train of April's dress and sewn it to the bottom of mine—a border trim that tied our two dresses together. I knew it was there, but likely few would notice that slight touch of grace unless they knew to look. It felt like a small, private thing of beauty between us.

When I pulled my dress down from its hanger, unzipped it, stepped in, and pulled it up, the dress stopped at my hips. I wiggled and pulled. It didn't move another inch. I immediately regretted my carelessness in the weeks before our wedding. At the second-to-last fitting, our seamstress had wagged a finger at me.

"No more doughnuts," she said. I grinned and agreed and knew by the weekend I'd be in line at Top Pot ordering a Double Trouble—a chocolate cake doughnut with chocolate glaze. I had denied myself my favorite treat to be able to run the Seattle Marathon with April one month before our wedding. When we crossed the finish line and collected our medals, I fell back into my old happy habit of doughnuts on the weekends.

I called out to April, my voice sharp with panic.

"I can't fit, babe!" I yelled, leaning my head out the door.

I heard silence, some shuffling, then giggles erupting from down the hallway; a voice shot back:

"Call your friends!"

I hadn't put anyone on notice to help me, confident I could get dressed on my own. But suddenly, I was on the phone frantically pressing numbers. I called Mo, who said she was finishing the sticky rice for our dessert table. She'd be over as soon as she was done. I called Rachel, and then tried Chan. No luck. I called Kim. Nothing. Most of our family and friends were out hiking, kayaking, or noodling around town, doing the very things we had urged them to do.

Finally, I reached two friends, Vanessa and Ara, and they both came quickly to our cabin along with Mo. In the end, it took three strong women, a synchronized tug from behind, and a squeeze from both sides as I held my breath to get me in, ordered, and zipped up. We pumped our fists, gave high-fives all around, and smiled, victorious. I was so tightly sealed into my dress, I felt like the vacuum-sealed sirloins we bought in bulk on our weekend grocery runs. A sudden worry gripped me: Would I even be able to eat dinner?

Mo curled my hair with the kind of controlled haste my sisters and I had picked up from watching Ma in the kitchen, and Ara helped apply eyeliner and blush—a rare time when I wore makeup. I can't remember any other time besides the times I was a bridesmaid, for Chan, Sin, and one of our cousins, when my cheeks got a dusting of rouge.

Cassie moved in a nonstop whir of activity, corralling the wedding party, making sure our bouquets were ready, drawing up signs directing guests where to park. She stomped upstairs and called for us to come down. It was time. Guests were arriving. Judge Elaine Kato, who traveled from Seattle, would be here soon.

As I took my first steps in my dress out of the room and into the hallway, Mo stopped me in my tracks at the top of the stairs.

"What about jewelry?" she said. "Necklace? Earrings?"

"Um, I don't have any," I said.

She rolled her eyes.

"How could you not have any jewelry?" Mo said. "It's your wedding day."

I shrugged.

"We need something to complete this picture," she said, glancing around at Vanessa and Ara, who glanced up and down at themselves.

"I got nothing," Vanessa said. Ara shook her head, too.

Just then, my sister-in-law Heidi came upstairs to sneak a peek at the brides. At the same moment, four pairs of eyes bore down on a thin gold chain with a quarter-carat diamond on her wrist.

"What? Why is everyone looking at me?" Heidi said. "What's going on? What do you need?"

"We need *that*," Mo said, pointing to Heidi's bracelet.

"What? This?" Heidi asked, fingering the delicate chain around her wrist.

"We just need to borrow it, just for the ceremony, then we'll give it back," Mo promised.

"Oh, this. Oh, no. This was an anniversary present from your brother, our fifth anniversary. This is very expensive . . ." Heidi's voiced trailed off. She glanced at me, jewelry-less, and glanced back down at her wrist, and in an instant, she unclasped it and pushed it over my right wrist.

"It's perfect," Mo said, and the ladies rushed me down the stairs.

I had tried all day long not to think of Ma, knowing it would cause a certain chaos in me. But there it was, in a mundane exchange between my sister-in-law and me. Just as Ma's aunt had taken a wristwatch off her wrist and put it on Ma's wrist on her wedding day, my sister-in-law had loaned me a sparkly thing so that I would not be so bare, too. Ma's presence echoing in ordinary moments. I felt a stampede of emotions but choked them down and made my way downstairs and into my future in hot-pink high heels and a secondhand wedding gown.

We were married by the sea at the Northwest Maritime Center in Port Townsend. April and I both have a connection to water and boats. She had spent her early career on the ocean, studying whales—the very mammals that sparked terror in my family on a ship in the middle of the sea in 1975—and she now spends her spare time sailing the Puget Sound, where she finds calm and where the order of the world makes the most sense to her.

I began my life on water, fleeing Cambodia with my family on an overcrowded navy vessel. I view the water not with a sense of calm but with a mix of emotions—fear and awe for its dangers, and gratitude for its deliverance of my family and me to safety.

There on the edge of the water, we were joined by our family and closest friends, two seats saved across the aisle from April's family, empty.

As I stood facing our family, our backs turned to the sea, I pulled my eyes away from Judge Kato and April only once to scan the crowd. When Ma's face wasn't there, I turned back and kept my eyes on my bride.

After her service, the judge did something she told us she had never done before. She took the tiniest pair of scissors I had ever seen and handed them to April, who was instructed to clip a lock of my hair before the scissors got pressed into my hands and I did the same to April. Judge Kato took our locks of hair and placed them in a small bag.

Then, she handed us each a length of red string. We were instructed to tie them around each other's waists. The judge had tried to make the moment meaningful, a reflection of my Khmer culture, by including two of the most important ceremonies in Khmer weddings. Except with a deviation. I didn't know whether this was Judge Kato's modified version of the ritual, or whether she simply misread my *New York Times* article, which I sent her in advance of our wedding, in which

I mentioned red string being tied around the *wrists* of the bride and groom for good luck. I never asked. I do not need to know.

After exchanging our vows in front of a long pier, we moved along with our guests to stand at the center of a compass rose made of bricks inlaid in the courtyard. North, south, east, west. In the past, I might have struggled to orient myself and asked myself, Which way home from here? But now I knew.

Wherever April is, I am home.

The joy of this truth didn't stop the tears, as April and I hugged our guests. There was another truth pulling hard at me, simple and clear, that came out as a whisper into Nhu's ears.

"I wish she was here," I told Nhu, and then collapsed into tears.

"I know," Nhu said, holding me, hugging me, as any mother would. "I know."

It was the happiest day of my life, and one of the saddest, too. Two things could be true at once.

◻ QUITTING TIME

When I was two or three years old, too little to tell which strawberries to pluck from the vine and which ones to leave alone to fully ripen, back when I was useless to my family as a worker, Ma carried me to the fields. We would walk together as a family to a central stack of empty plastic crates on wooden pallets set in a clearing in the field. As my father and siblings took as many crates as they could handle—six for Pa, and four each for my siblings—Ma took two. They banged against her thigh, light and bulky. Pa, Sin, Sope, and Chan would trudge to their rows, drop to their knees, and start picking. Ma and I, we would keep going, Ma slogging through thick fog and uneven earth to deliver me to the end of her row.

She would toss the crates to the ground, knowing she would have to return to the stack of empties to get more, and slowly lower me down, then flip the crates over and arrange them side by side, stomping them in the mud with the weight of her body to hold them in place. She'd peel off her coat, then tuck it neatly onto the conjoined crates. I would stand, watching and waiting.

"Sleep, gohn," she would say sweetly to me, motioning for

me to come and lie down on the nest she had made. "When you wake up, Ma will be here."

The moisture of that early-morning Willamette Valley air as it entered my nose chilled me. I swear I can still feel it, all these years later. It doesn't take much to remember that particular kind of cold that rattles the bones. And yet there she was, all those mornings of my youth, without her coat. Wasn't she cold? I wondered.

Just as quickly as the thought entered my head, she would be gone. I would watch as she shuffled back down to the other end of the field, trying not to trip on clods of rototilled dirt the same size as her own shoe. She'd glance back once or twice and if she saw me with my eyes still open, she would call out once more: "Go to sleep, gohn. Ma will be there soon."

Alone on my crate bed, my fingers collected dew as I ran them along the edges of the crate, up to the corners where triangular notches allowed them to get stacked neatly into place, like my brother's Legos. I felt each corner of the crate above my head and then reached my toes to touch each corner below, because it somehow comforted me to know I was marooned on that crate in the middle of a vast field. Sometimes it just feels safe to be in a box. So long as I stayed there, Ma knew where to find me. I fell asleep inhaling my mother's musk embedded in the cotton fibers of her coat, the tang of her sweat mixed in with the deep, sweet scent of summer in the strawberry fields.

Now that all these years have passed, I think about believing in the kinds of invisible forces that link us to each other. I think about how Rachel and Stephen trained their dog, Finn, to sit, to stay. They showed me once. They would hold a treat in one hand, hidden in a clenched fist. Rachel would tell Finn, "Stay. *Stay*," and then walk five paces back or disappear altogether, leaving Finn to wag his tail, searching for any sign of his owner. The dog must trust that the owner will be back. There's a reward for waiting. So he stays. Relying on a trust born out of repetition, which becomes habit, which turns into a kind of faith.

And so I stayed. I learned to trust Ma, learned to trust the distance between us whenever she backed away. I learned to have faith that even though she was not right by my side, even though she was beyond my line of sight and I was beyond hers, she would come back to me. The way I always returned to her. She would work her way toward me, at whatever plodding pace. I would not be alone for long.

As I write the final words in this story, I calculate the distance between us in terms of time. Eight years ago, she and Pa came to visit me in Chiang Mai, and while I slept, Ma spoke in hushed tones to my roommate, recruiting his help in securing a husband for me. Seven years ago, I moved to Seattle to be with April, disrupting the delicate bond and balance between Ma and me. Six years ago, she told me she would never be happy so long as I was gay. Five years ago, I wrote about the invincibility of hope between us in this nation's largest newspaper, and two and a half million readers were suddenly privy to our very private struggle. Four years ago, as Sope walked me down the aisle to marry my best friend, we tried not to notice the two empty seats on our family's side of the aisle.

In the span of five years, sadness and blame built between Ma and me. I have sometimes felt as if I might drown in the swell of emotions. Anger. Resentment. Regret. Compassion. Guilt. Shame. Loyalty. Love. A residue remains, as sticky and enduring as berry stains.

While my life was expanding with new friends and a new wife, my parents' lives began constricting. I collected bits and pieces of news from my siblings, who spoke to and visited our parents regularly. For a while, they stopped hosting parties at their house, when they could no longer explain me away. They began to turn inward, to hide from the same world they believed would judge them as bad parents for having a gay child.

But it's clear to me now that my shift away from Ma was in motion long ago, happening so slowly that we barely felt it until the crack was already upon us. I started to peel away when I boarded that plane at age thirty and returned to Cambodia. And I became my own person that moment that Ma confronted me about being gay as she prepared my young cousin from America—rather than me—for an arranged marriage in Cambodia. That was the moment we lost faith in each other, and only now do I see with clear eyes the truth of my circumstance. A part of me needed to die so that the rest of me could live.

It has been several years since the weekly phone chats with Ma ended abruptly. These days, she calls Sin and Chan and Mo. She sees Sope, who lives the closest to our parents, every other week. When there is big news, Pa calls. He left a voice message once, in the fall of 2017, his tone even, just giving the facts. Ma was in the hospital. Chest pains. Maybe a heart attack, they didn't yet know. I was in New York to speak on a panel about the Khmer Rouge tribunal. As she was clutching her heart in the emergency room in Salem, I was doubled over in pain in my hotel room in Times Square. A few days later, back in Seattle, my doctor diagnosed an ulcer.

So here we are now, Ma and me, our grief wearing us down from the inside.

I want to believe that from the rubble of our ruined relationship, we can find hope again. So I keep trying. After my wedding, I went to see Ma and Pa alone. Brought baguettes and a pear tart.

And then I went again, in December. This time with my wife. We brought a tray of fruits that April wrapped in cellophane with a crisp new hundred-dollar bill inside. We stayed for three hours and just talked.

The following summer, Ma welcomed April and her niece to join our annual backyard family gathering, even as I hemmed and hawed, worried Ma might ignore them or say something mean. She didn't.

And then, when the party was over, when the ice in the cooler had melted, leaving Coronas floating in tepid water, and the aroma of Ma's chicken curry had lifted away with the evening breeze, when the aunties had packed food to go in containers they carried from home and were starting in on long goodbyes, Ma gave a quick but warm hug to April and her niece. I didn't see it happen, but April told me later. Her arms stayed open after she let them go, for a beat of a moment. I'd like to think she held them open for me.

I have tried out anger, resentment, disappointment. None of it works. I go back to the same flush of feelings when Ma first told me how she ran away rather than get married. I go back to grace. And how circumstances so easily constrain us. She was hemmed in by a culture, a place, and a particular moment in time that set the path she was fated to follow. She could not break free of her birthright, not even in America. I was born into that same country and culture, but I was raised in America, where girls have the same chance as boys to go to school, to have a career, to chart their own way. I could have both. I could claim the Khmer and American cultures as my own and know this was the truth. I might never be a good Cambodian daughter, but I tried my best to be a great Cambodian American daughter.

I hold no grudges against Ma. We each of us wanted what we could not have. She wanted me to be the good Cambodian daughter who marries a Khmer man and continues our family's culture and lineage—a bridge safely connecting past and present. I wanted her to be the kind of mother who would accept me and fight for me no matter who I married, no matter who I am.

She had envisioned a different life for herself, not the same hard life her mother had that came with a harsh husband. Not the marriage suffused with suffering and strife that she endured. We both wanted to live on our own terms. We each reached for freedom.

She retreated.

I held on for my life.

I believe Ma still loves me, because how can a mother stop loving her baby? But we still circle each other when we see each other, like wounded animals too stubborn to stop fighting, even though there's no more point. One of these days, we'll get tired enough to stop. The anger and hurt will fade, like the light always did in those endless fields and we knew it was quitting time.

There was a party, two and a half years after April and I were married. There was cake and decorations and family and friends who had flown in from out of town. Fresh flowers in a vase. Familiar faces quietly catching up over beer and wine. But this was different. No teary toasts and playful roasts for a new beginning. This was a celebration of an ending.

My father-in-law, James Frank Rebollo, was dying.

We had known for the previous five years that my father-in-law's condition, myelodysplastic syndrome (MDS), a bone marrow disease where the body fails to produce enough red blood cells, was incurable. We knew there were things that might prolong his life—chemotherapy, blood transfusions, experimental drugs. And they helped, for a little while. But there is only one way MDS ends; it mutates into an irreversibly lethal leukemia.

That was the situation in the fall of 2019.

We stocked up on the best root beer and vanilla ice cream for floats, and chocolate éclairs from the same French bakery in Northeast Portland my parents loved. April's cousin Christina made traditional Mexican capirotada, the bread pudding

Jimmy's mother baked when he was a boy. He took a bite and closed his eyes, the sweetest smile spreading across his face.

"Let your elders eat while their throats are still upright," Ma had always said, and we obliged every last day of my father-in-law's life. Whatever he wanted, he would have.

In the weeks and months before his passing, as hospice staff arrived with end-of-life accoutrements—an adjustable hospital bed and table, an array of medications, a walker, then a wheelchair, and, eventually, a bedside commode—Jimmy wondered out loud what was the point of a funeral when he wouldn't be around to enjoy seeing everyone. Wouldn't that be a waste?

"I can't hear what people have to say about me if I'm already dead," he said, canting his head as his face opened into a wide grin.

Practical and comical, two of his endearing traits. And compassionate. It was important for him to say goodbye, in person, to the people he cared about.

We invited Jimmy's former colleagues and the nurses who cared for him during years of blood transfusions and chemotherapy. Family and friends flew in from Texas, Connecticut, and California, and drove from locales across Oregon and Washington. Weddings and deaths inevitably propel people toward each other.

Glancing at the guest list, I saw that it would be a mini-reunion of loved ones from our wedding. When my parents' names came up, I hesitated.

"They didn't come to our wedding," I told April. "I don't have much hope they'll come to your dad's party."

In the years since our marriage, I had occasionally shared with April my deep sorrow that my parents and my in-laws had not yet met, owing to my parents' stubbornness.

"I can forgive Ma for not coming to our wedding, but if your father dies without my parents ever meeting him, I won't forgive that," I told April, and only her.

April sent an email to Ma, asking her to come. The very next day, my cell phone rang.

"Put," Ma said, "how is April's father? We got April's email. Your dad and I want to go, but we don't know how to get to the restaurant."

I couldn't believe what I was hearing. After all the fighting, the silence, the accusations and recriminations, my parents were going to meet my in-laws. In this horrible ending, there was also a new beginning.

Chan was planning on driving down from Seattle for the party and offered to take our parents. We gathered at Jimmy's favorite Mexican restaurant in Portland, more than a hundred guests trickling and then pouring in. As I greeted guests, I kept one eye on the door, watching for Ma.

I didn't notice at first, but there was a fuss in the foyer, April racing toward it. Two short elderly folks, slowly making their way in.

Jimmy noticed, too, and soon made his way to my parents. And just like that, hugs, smiles, laughter. Half the restaurant, those who attended our wedding, sobbing.

I slunk behind the bar and cried, too.

If I go back to the beginning, my memory of the first time I met Jimmy is crystal clear. I understood right away the reason April loved him so much. His warmth, his big-heartedness, his easygoing nature, qualities he had passed on to April, too.

Soon, we were watching football games, going to car shows, and traveling to Canada, and Hawaii, then one cool fall day at a bar in downtown Portland, crying into our beers.

It was 2015, and my heart was racing so fast, I worried it would burst from its cage.

"I'd like to marry your daughter," I said.

Jimmy looked into our basket of chicken wings, and for a moment, I was afraid. I wanted to take those words back, until he took a napkin, wiped a slick of Tabasco from his fingers, and spoke.

"I think that's a great idea," he said, smiling, and we both dissolved into tears.

He was the first to give me his blessings to marry April. I would be the first—one month after his party—to press an ear to his chest, listening-praying-begging for a beat that would not come. I summoned April and my mother-in-law to Jimmy's side. We cried and cried and cried.

I texted Ma, the first person I used to call whenever I had good news. Now the first person I contacted with news that shattered my heart. No more reason to hide.

"He is gone."

She texted me back, three words I'd waited so long to hear, words that would begin to close the gulf between us: "Ma sorry, gohn."

Ma and Pa's wedding, April 20, 1967

Put and April's wedding, July 15, 2017
(Kim Oanh Nguyen)

◻ ACKNOWLEDGMENTS

Sometimes all you need is someone to believe in you to succeed. I have been lucky to have many such someones. I am enormously grateful to Daphne Durham for seeing the story that needed to be told before I could, for having full faith in this project, and for gently prodding me to keep excavating, multiple levels deeper, despite my resistance, to hit my narrative bedrock. And a huge thank-you to Lydia Zoells, whose eagle eyes helped this book evolve into something I am indeed very proud of.

Thank you to my agent, Stephanie Cabot, for seeing the diamond in the rough and for your unwavering commitment to get the right people at the right time to see it, too.

Na Kim, your beautiful, evocative cover design was exactly on point. Few art illustrations make me cry the way yours did.

I want to thank Ma and Pa, for their courage to plunge into the past on my behalf, for all the sacrifices they made for me, for their first and finest act of saving me. And to my Oregon aunties—Pech Pich, Samnang Koh, and Vuthy Koh—for filling in the blanks of their and our families' stories. And to my Cambodia aunties—Ming Pheaktra and Om Oeurn—whose love and support guided me through many a dark day in Cambodia. Thank you.

I'm forever grateful to my siblings—Sinaro Reang Skold, Sophea Reang, Motthida Chin, Chanira Reang Sperry, and Piseth Pich—for inspiring me every day to be a better version of myself. And to my nieces and nephews, you are the ten reasons I write every day: Kallyana, Peyton, Lydia, Tyler, Evan, Chase, Carolyn, Olivia, Max, and Addison.

For their keen insights on early drafts of this book, I'd like to thank Chanira Reang Sperry, Loung Ung, Rachel Haig, Janine Kovac, Debby Dahl Edwardson, Katrina Carrasco, and Nhu Miller. I could not have asked for a better pit crew!

I also could not have completed this project without the support of Daniel Jones, at *The New York Times*, who published the essay that started all this, and Meas Chan Kresna, who steered more than three hundred Khmers to safety, all those years ago. YY Lee, Kim Nguyen, Tyrone Beason, Elliott Almond, Dermot Randles, Charles Ward, Emelyn Rodriguez, Judith and Glenn Mason, Stephen Sonderman, David and Patricia Kutzmann, Jan Johnson, Kim Vo, the Millers (Tom, Nhu, Nathalie, and Gabby), Matthew Cuenca-Daigle and Jeff Daigle, Alberta Weinberg, Wendy Call, and the gang of indomitable warrior writers in the Flying Flounders: your encouragement was a lifeline. Thank you.

I am so grateful to the Hedgebrook (a special shout-out to the chefs who fed me!), Mineral School, and Kimmel Harding Nelson residencies, as well as the Seattle Public Library Writers' Room, for providing crucial space for me to work with the words; and to the Alicia Patterson Journalism Fellowship committee, the Jack Straw Writers Program, the Washington State Artist Trust, and the VONA writer's workshop, for helping me find my voice.

My eternal gratitude goes to Loung Ung, who insisted from the day we met on a dust-blown road in Phnom Penh that I tell my story, whose unwavering enthusiasm for this book, inspiration, humor, wit, and wise words fed me. I finally finished, girl!

And April. This book exists because of your abiding love, encouragement, and support. You are my heart, my home, my cheerleader-in-chief.

In memory of my ancestors and grandparents: Grandma Nhim and Grandpa Khann, whose lives predate me but whose legacies live on within me; Grandpa Sin and Grandma Yeim, who left whole lives behind in Cambodia in order to reach freedom; and my relatives, along with an estimated two million other Cambodians, whose lives were senselessly taken when the world looked away.